Black Women Abolitionists

BLACK WOMEN ABOLITIONISTS

A Study in Activism, 1828–1860

Shirley J. Yee

The University of Tennessee Press / Knoxville

Manufactured in the United States of
America.
First Edition.

The paper in this book meets the minimum requirements of
the American National Standard for Permanence of Paper for
Printed Library Materials. ♾ The binding materials have
been chosen for strength and durability.

Library of Congress Cataloging in Publication Data

Yee, Shirley J., 1959–
Black women abolitionists : a study in activism,
1828–1860 / Shirley J. Yee. — 1st ed.
p. cm.
Includes bibliographical references and index.
ISBN 0-87049-735-9 (cloth: alk. paper)
ISBN 0-87049-736-7 (pbk.: alk. paper)
1. Women abolitionists—United States—History—19th
century. 2. Afro-American women—History—19th century.
3. Slavery—United States—Anti-slavery movements.
4. United States—Social conditions—To 1865. I. Title.
E449.Y44 1992
305.48′896073—dc20 91-24795
CIP

To Audrey W. Yee
and in memory of Donald Y. Yee

Contents

Illustrations

Acknowledgments

I wish to thank The Ohio State University for generous financial support—the Graduate Alumni Research Award, the Ruth Higgins Award, and the Women's Studies Small Research Grant—which allowed me to conduct the initial research for this project during my years in graduate school. A fellowship from the Center For Black Studies at the University of California, Santa Barbara, and a University of Washington Research Fund summer grant provided vital financial assistance for completing this book.

Cynthia Maude-Gembler, Tana McDonald, and Carol Orr of the University of Tennessee Press gave encouragement and support throughout the preparation of this manuscript. Richard Blackett devoted much time and energy to this project, and I am grateful for his critiques and suggestions.

Many research librarians provided valuable assistance in unearthing sources on black women's lives: Edna Carnegie of the Connecticut Afro-American Historical Society in New Haven, Mary Huth of the Rare Books and Special Collections at the University of Rochester Library, Phil Lapsansky of the Library Company of Philadelphia, Susan Miller of the Presbyterian Historical Society, Adrienne Shadd of the Ontario Black History Society in Toronto, and Barbara Trippel Simmons of the American Antiquarian Society in Worcester, Massachusetts. I would also like to thank the librarians and staff of the Department of Rare Books and Manuscripts, Boston Public Library; the Essex Institute, Salem, Massachusetts; Museum of Connecticut History, Hartford; the Pusey Library, Harvard University; Moorland-Spingarn Research Center, Howard University; Schlesinger Library, Radcliffe College; Mother Bethel A.M.E. Church of Philadelphia; African-American Collection, Temple University; Trevor Arnett Library, Atlanta University Center; the Historical Society of Pennsylvania; the Sterling Memorial Library, Yale University; and the Library of Congress.

Many scholars offered their insight and advice when I began this project, including John Blassingame, Anne Boylan, Merton L. Dillon, Jacqueline Jones, Nancy Hewitt, and Randolph Roth. For their critiques of portions of the manuscript, I thank Richard Blackett, Johnnella Butler, Elliott Butler-Evans, Ruth Frankenberg, Kathie Friedman Kasaba, Becky Aanerud, Arline L. Garcia, and Cedric J. Robinson. I thank Lois Helmbold for originally suggesting the topic to me and Leila J. Rupp for her enthusiasm, guidance, and scholarly insight.

Introduction

At a meeting of the Equal Rights Association in 1867, seventy-year-old Sojourner Truth, renowned black abolitionist, feminist, evangelist, and former slave, expressed apprehension about proposed legislation to grant citizenship and suffrage, now that slavery had been officially abolished, to black men but not to black women. "I feel that I have a right to have just as much as a man," Truth said. "There is a great stir about colored men getting their rights; and if colored men get their rights and not colored women theirs, the colored men will be masters over the women, and it will be just as bad as before."[1] After nearly thirty years as an activist, Truth had witnessed more than her share of injustices—to women, to blacks, and to the poor. She ardently supported political rights for black men but worried about the fate of black women if equal rights were not granted to them as well; her bold statement may have echoed the sentiments of other black women, especially of those who had spent their lives working actively in the movement for equality. Her criticism of the men of her race and the patriarchal structure of American society points to contradictions and ironies inherent in black women's participation in a struggle that, though it offered a rare opportunity for men and women of both races to work together for a common cause, also replicated the racial and sexual tensions of the larger society.

This book explores free black women's participation in the struggle to end slavery and racial oppression in the United States between 1828 and 1860, focusing on the activities of women who either were born into free black families or had acquired their freedom through manumission or escape.[2] Historians have acknowledged the activities of several outstanding individual black women abolitionists, but they have devoted little attention to the collective role of black women in the movement or to the implications of their participation for the study of abolitionist, African-American, and women's history. One of the goals of this study, therefore, is to fill in large gaps in African-American and women's history and in the enormous body of scholarship on the abolitionist crusade.

The abolitionist movement provides an opportunity for understanding further the complex ways that race and gender have simultaneously and inextricably been interwoven in black women's lives, for it represented the context in which free black women laid much groundwork for a distinct pattern of black female activism that would become important a century later in the struggle for civil rights. Central to the experiences of black female abolitionists were community-building, political organizing, and forging a network of personal and professional friendships with other activists.

Since the eighteenth century, free black women and men had worked to build viable communities, in order to survive in a society that was growing increasingly hostile to non-whites. Through individual efforts and collective participation in black benevolent and reform organizations, schools, and churches, they provided desperately needed material and spiritual support not available in the dominant society, as well as the means to maintain family, friendship, and community ties. From the process of community-building emerged the politicization of African-American activists.

Proposals to bring about a gradual end to chattel slavery had been offered periodically since 1776, but gradualism was repugnant to this "dissenting minority" of northern whites and free blacks during the thirty years before the Civil War; they demanded slavery's immediate destruction. Free blacks, in fact, had been organizing on behalf of an immediatist antislavery and anti-racist agenda for at least a generation before white abolitionist William Lloyd Garrison emerged as the leader of "radical" abolition.[3] Nevertheless, black leaders welcomed Garrison as a sincere ally who decried the slave system as inherently evil and condemned slaveholders as sinners.[4] His enthusiastic support for racial equality and the immediate end of slavery through interracial cooperation encouraged black activists and added momentum to their efforts.

But for black abolitionists, the issues of slavery and racism inevitably struck closer to home than they did for whites; most free blacks were former slaves themselves, had relatives and friends who were still enslaved, and encountered racism in their daily lives.[5] For them, abolition meant much more than simply ending the institution of slavery. Black social, political, and economic equality were integral to their agenda; such goals might be accomplished only by meeting the enemy on many fronts—challenging racial discrimination in every aspect of American society and promoting temperance, moral reform, and education in the free black community. Black abolitionists worked on a wide range of activities, cooperating with whites as much as possible, organizing all-black antislavery societies, writing, speaking, petitioning, and participating in self-help projects in their own neighborhoods. Not all black activists were of one mind, however diverse individual experiences, opinions, personalities, and interests led to participation in the movement on different levels and in different ways, reflecting a wide range of opinions concerning the priorities and goals of the movement and the best approaches toward accomplishing those goals. Such heterogeneity led as often to conflict and competition as to cooperation. The strengthening of the community, therefore, meant the creation, not of a monolithic intellectual and political entity, but of a supportive environment in which individuals and groups worked toward similar goals.

For black women abolitionists, race, sex, and class together created a complex experience within the movement. Economic circumstances, kinship and friendship ties, marriage, and education led women toward personal definitions of their goals as activists, influencing their choice of abolitionist activities and the extent to which they could devote time and money to the cause. Associations with other women, as well as with black male activists, as wives, daughters, sisters, and nieces, also helped direct their activism. Some women, especially former slaves, were motivated by their own experiences in slavery to devote their lives to the cause of freedom.

From the beginning, female participation was an important feature of abolition. Male abolitionists, like the leaders of other morally based social reform movements of the period, accepted women into a campaign that was bent on persuading slaveholders of the sinfulness of their institution. But as in other reform movements, women were expected to participate within the confines of women's "sphere," which was interpreted as limited to organizing all-female societies and raising funds to support the male leadership.

Black women's participation in the movement, however, held a dual significance. Although, like middle-class white women in antebellum society, free black women felt bound by contemporary ideals of "respectable" womanhood, for them these gender conventions underscored an irony inherent in black abolitionist goals. On the one hand, images of women as morally superior, physically delicate, and submissive to their men actually liberated black women from racist stereotypes of black female sexuality, which depicted them as physically strong and sexually promiscuous—but on the other hand, the adoption of "true womanhood" ideology in the free black community only imposed white standards of inequality. Furthermore, ideas about what constituted "ladylike" behavior reflected illusions about female respectability that were narrowly applied only to native-born, white, middle-class women.

Thus, constructing a life that truly reflected "freedom" meant adopting many of the values of white society, in part symbolized by male dominance and female subordination. This model, however racist, sexist, and classist, prevailed in American society and became an important symbol of freedom to many black men and women, who were struggling for survival and acceptance within the dominant culture. By supporting sexual roles modeled after free society, they attempted to erase memories of enslavement and to prove false the assumption of many whites that blacks were incapable of creating stable family and community structures.

In slavery, equality between the sexes had meant equal subjugation. Slave men and women shared the same legal status as chattel of their white masters; men and women both performed heavy work, and they both endured the lash. But slaveholders had justified the sexual exploitation and abuse of black women in particular by contriving images of black womanhood that stood opposite from those applying to white middle-class women, who were portrayed as delicate, morally pure, submissive to men, and asexual. The only characteristics black and white women supposedly shared was intellectual inferiority to men, but the inferiority of black women, according to defenders of slavery, was also a function of race. Such attitudes were not confined to the South; race- and class-based sexual imagery had become ingrained in the minds of whites throughout American society and were reinforced by northern literature on "true womanhood." In the urbanizing northeast, men and women of the emerging new middle class published this literature on "proper" womanhood through domestic novels, popular gift books such as *Godey's Lady Book* in Boston, and serials such as *Ladies' Magazine* in Philadelphia.[6]

A handful of northern free blacks, who had achieved economic success despite racial barriers, could sustain the sort of family relationships that also characterized wealthy and middle-class white families: fathers as patriarchs and bread-winners, sons as primary heirs, and wives and daughters as ladies of leisure. Families such as the Fortens and Shadds had established themselves as an elite group of northern blacks who provided important role models and educated their children at an early age about their responsibilities to the community as well as about abolitionist ideology. Women from these prosperous households came closest to meeting contemporary expectations of middle-class womanhood, and because they were spared working-class women's need to help support their families, these women also could devote a great deal of time to community work, including abolitionist activities.

Most free black women, however, spent most of their days and nights earning low wages as domestic servants, seamstresses, teachers, and boardinghouse operators, in addition to caring for their own families. Nonetheless, many participated in abolitionist activities whenever they could. The complete stories of their lives have gone undocumented and may be lost forever, but we know they were active in their communities because their names appear on membership lists of local antislavery societies, charitable organizations, and churches.

Black women's involvement in community activism held both racial and sexual implications. Activities such as charity work and campaigning for education, temperance, and moral reform were closely tied to women's domestic responsibilities. Many women worked collectively and individually, often through their churches, to provide everyday necessities to their black neighbors—food, clothing, money, shelter, schooling, burial services, babysitting, and health care. They also participated in the emerging temperance and moral-reform campaigns. By engaging in these projects, black women satisfied contemporary expectations of womanhood and, at the same time, worked for the welfare of their race. But many women went further: they organized antislavery societies, wrote antislavery poetry and essays, and delivered public speeches. Some of these activities walked the fine line of female "respectability."

In New England, black and white men and women established hundreds of local antislavery societies that served as auxiliaries to the regional society. After the establishment of the national American Anti-Slavery Society (AAS) in 1833, additional black, white, and racially mixed societies appeared in the Northeast, and in Ohio and Michigan.[7] At least six black auxiliaries to the AAS were formed in 1836 alone. Free black women participated actively in the organization of all-black female antislavery societies and racially mixed societies ever since a group of black women in Salem, Massachusetts, formed the first female antislavery society in February 1832.

But despite enthusiastic responses from many sympathetic whites and free blacks, racism pervaded the movement and prevented full and equal cooperation between the two races. It was well-known that not all white abolitionists advocated racial equality, and even those who did sometimes exhibited patronizing attitudes toward their black colleagues. Race prejudice created a formidable barrier between blacks and whites that manifested itself in various ways, ranging from a myopic vision of abolitionist goals to the outright exclusion of blacks from white organizations and discrimination even in racially integrated societies. Several integrated antislavery societies maintained separate seating for blacks and whites at public events, and a few white societies fought to keep blacks out altogether. Thus, declarations of "sisterhood" between free and slave women were, for the most part, antislavery rhetoric that was true only on an individual level.

Racism within organized abolition soon became a public issue, as black leaders pointed out the secondary status of blacks in the movement. By the 1840s, several disillusioned black abolitionists, led by Frederick Douglass, broke with the Garrisonians and advocated separatism from white-led abolition. Fed up with the discriminatory treatment of blacks in the movement and the failure of "moral suasion" to end slavery, black separatists promoted self-help and the creation of independent, self-reliant, free black communities. Although some black leaders, including Douglass, opted to continue the fight within the boundaries of the United States, others came to view the cause as hopeless at home and advocated voluntary emigration to Canada, South America, Mexico, and Africa. Especially after the passage of the Fugitive Slave Law in 1850, emigrationists argued that leaving the United States was the only way the black community could survive and prosper. Many black women activists rallied behind the nationalists, some supporting separation but others retaining professional and personal friendships with white colleagues at the same time that they provided verbal and financial support for black nationalist organizations and newspapers.

While abolitionists debated the issues of racism and abolitionist strategies, the subject of sexual equality also proved contentious. By the mid-1830s, abolitionists engaged in heated debates about whether women should participate in "male" activities for the sake of the cause. Members of the clergy, in particular, argued that men and women occupied special places in public reform movements and should not overstep their bounds. Even those reformers who vigorously supported women's rights believed the issue was potentially divisive and extraneous to the "real" goals of abolition and should be pursued separately.

The proposal to allow women to share an equal voice with men as voting members in the state and national antislavery societies did in fact split up the Massachusetts Anti-Slavery Society in 1839 and the AAS the following year. Dissension had been developing within antislavery ranks since the mid-1830s. A pro-Garrisonian faction believed in universal reform, women's rights, and the continuation of "moral suasion," but anti-Garrisonians perceived political action as the most practical means of ending slavery and saw all the other issues as extraneous. The "woman question," however, was the final straw: in 1840, anti-Garrisonians walked out of the AAS meeting when the pro-Garrison majority elected Abigail Kelley Foster, a white Quaker activist, as the first woman to sit on the executive committee. Foster won a narrow vote of 557 to 451, and the decision literally cut the national organization in half.

After the election, dissenting members led by Lewis Tappan formed their own organization, the American & Foreign Anti-Slavery Society, which was committed to supporting an antislavery political party and keeping women out of executive positions in the Society. Although Tappan argued that the woman question had not been the sole reason for the breakup of the AAS, it was the primary one. In a letter to Theodore Dwight Weld after the split, Tappan made clear his position on women's rights:

> When the Constitution of the A. Anti S. Soc. was formed in 1833, and the word "person" introduced, *all concerned* considered that it was to be understood as it is usually understood in our benevolent Societies. All have a right to be *members*, but the *business* to be conducted by *men*. . . . Women have equal rights with men, and

> therefore they have a right to form societies of women only. Men have the same right. *Men* formed the Amer. Anti S. Society.[8]

During the furor over sexuality equality, a number of black women as well as white women continued to engage in activities that were considered unacceptable. For black women, however, participation in public activism not only overstepped boundaries of "respectable" womanhood within free black society, but also defied expectations of deference and humility to whites. Their activities invited mixed responses from the men of their race, some of whom, like many whites, believed that women should confine their activities within women's "sphere." A number of black male leaders, however, emphasized the racial implications of black women's activism, arguing that it benefited the cause of racial advancement and challenged stereotypes of black inferiority. But even those who supported black women's participation in non-traditional activities also endorsed strict standards of female deportment, especially in interactions with the men of their race.

The desire of the black community to disprove racist representations of black women by adopting "positive" sexual stereotypes limited the extent to which many black men and women could support complete equality between the sexes, despite the encouragement of some of the most prominent black male leaders. Black feminists, unlike some white feminists, maintained a cooperative relationship with black male activists, out of a common commitment to the welfare and advancement of their race.

Racial equality had been an integral part of the black feminist agenda from the beginning. During the antebellum years, black women's abolitionist work represented the continuation of the struggle against racism and an effort to come to terms with sexism in their lives. Racism within the women's movement, however, precluded the possibility for black and white women to work together on an all-inclusive feminist agenda. As a result, black feminist abolitionists did what they had always done in the familiar face of racism and sexism—they organized on their own. In the process, they developed a distinct pattern of black female activism that served as a model for later generations.

Black women's individual and collective presence in two movements that raised the issue of equality represented the most radical possibility for social, political, and economic change in nineteenth-century America. The issues of race and gender equality that erupted in abolition and the emerging women's rights campaign essentially ignored black women's stake in both movements. In abolition, the "woman question," by presenting the goal of equality between the sexes, directly contradicted black community goals for establishing traditional sex roles. In the emerging white women's movement, the "race question" broached the issue of racial equality. Black women's participation in both movements threatened to destroy the very foundation of American society: the achievement of racial and sexual equality would have shaken a social, political, and economic structure that was based to great extent on maintaining inequality. This study, by exploring the dynamics of race and sex in the lives of black female abolitionists, traces the route by which black feminists arrived at such a critical juncture in their history as activists.

For the purposes of this study, I have limited the scope of my analysis to those black women who operated in well-known centers of antislavery agitation: the Midwest, the Northeast, and, to some extent, California and Canada. Organized abolitionist activity for most free blacks occurred within an urban context, which is not surprising, considering that sizable numbers of free blacks, ranging from the prosperous to the desperately poor, lived in such cities as Boston, Cincinnati, New York, Philadelphia, and Rochester, New York. Blacks in these cities formed churches, fraternal organizations and sisterhoods, schools, and newspapers serving black men, women, and children. Philadelphia, New York, Boston, and Cincinnati were four of the largest centers of black abolitionist activity in the urban north.[9] Although each city had its own unique characteristics, all four areas were bustling port cities by the early decades of the nineteenth century, sites of commerce as well as of growing heterogeneous and mobile populations made up of migrants from rural areas, immigrants from northern Europe, and escaped and freed slaves from the South.

Racial discrimination in the job market, however, kept the majority of free blacks poorer than the white population. In cities, the poor, white and black alike, lived in cramped alleys and lofts, where they faced disease, malnutrition, and overexposure to extreme heat and cold. Philadelphia coroner Dr. Napolean B. Leidy reported in 1848 that of his seventy-six cases of black deaths, many adult men and women were discovered dead in backyards and alleys and "in cold and exposed rooms and garretts, board shanties, five and six feet high . . . erected . . . mostly without comforts, save the bare floor." In his investigation, he found many people living in "cold, wet, and damp cellars, with naked walls, and in many instances without floors."[10]

During this period, neighborhoods were not yet completely segregated by race, as they would be by the end of the century, nor were private residences always kept separate from businesses.[11] Thus, though pockets of racial homogeneity did exist, poor whites and free blacks often lived in close proximity to one another, though not necessarily in harmony. In Boston, for example, the majority of free blacks clustered in lower Beacon Hill, while wealthy white families occupied mansions at the top of the hill. But even in the most densely populated free black neighborhoods, there resided working-class whites, many of whom were Irish immigrants.

In Philadelphia, where black households were scattered throughout the city limits, multiracial family dwellings as well as multiple- and single-family homes for blacks could be found. For instance, the lower story of one building housed a "black man, his black wife, and an Irish woman."[12] In West Philadelphia, however, observers found improved material conditions among free blacks, most of whom were classified as "common laborers," who lived in neatly kept frame houses.[13] Cedar Ward in central Philadelphia, site of the highest population concentration and the center of black activism, contained the homes of some of the leading members of the Philadelphia black community, as well as several black churches and schools.

A similar situation existed in New York City: although black households were scattered throughout the city and adjacent Brooklyn, most black residents between the 1830s and 1850s lived in one district, around the intersection of Broadway and Canal Street.[14] Between 1820 and 1865, however, racial segregation grew more pronounced, reflecting black male and female employment patterns, the desire for physical safety and security among friends and family in the face of increasing violence against blacks, and the location of segregated schools.[15]

During the 1850s and 1860s, a period of active migration, a number of free black men and women relocated to California, where they expanded their abolitionist work. In San Francisco, in particular, black female pioneers formed community self-help organizations modeled after similar female societies in the northeast.[16] In the Canadian towns of Chatham, Windsor, St. Catherine's, and Hamilton—all in Ontario—free blacks and fugitive slaves struggled to help their fledgling communities survive.

The challenges of gathering historical data on black women are well-known. As women of color, they have belonged to two groups whose experiences have, until recently, been invisible in history. Records of black women's experiences were buried or lost, except for manuscript collections of a handful of outstanding activists. Fortunately, within the past two decades, several scholars have undertaken the painstaking task of collecting documents by and about black women in the United States and Canada, which reveal much about their experiences in slavery and freedom.[17] The most recent project on black abolitionism has been the *Black Abolitionist Papers* edited by C. Peter Ripley and George Carter. This collection, as well as organizational records, black and white anti-slavery newspapers, and personal correspondence by abolitionist men and women of both races also provide important information on black women's activist work.

Finally, this work is part of a recent shift in the direction of historical scholarship on "women of color" by portraying these women as activists, rather than as passive victims of racism and sexism. As the following chapters demonstrate, black women abolitionists, by virtue of being black and female in antebellum America, confronted a particular set of tensions and ironies in their work. Whether they directly or indirectly supported the movement, cooperated with whites or primarily with other blacks, worked in groups or independently, were financially well off or struggled to make ends meet, their lives as black women reflected complex dynamics. Race, sex, and class all emerge as factors in many dimensions of their experiences: in the movement for black liberation, in society at large, and in their personal lives. For black women activists, efforts to overcome the barriers of racism and sexism in their daily lives also enabled them, individually and collectively, to forge a particular pattern of black female activism that continued long after the movement to end slavery.

1

Kinship, Friendship, and Community

Ties to family, friends, and colleagues in community organizations and institutions intertwined to create a special set of personal and professional relationships for black women who joined the abolitionist movement. Abolitionists lent each other money, exchanged gifts and advice, and provided one another with food, shelter, childcare, spiritual support, and companionship. In the process, many established friendships outside their immediate families, and some of these relationships crossed racial lines. Many women found such connections helpful and supportive, but others saw the abolitionist community as a closed circle, especially during times of conflict when one's personal affairs quickly became privy to all.

Black women abolitionists came from all walks of life; most were wage-earners who struggled to make a decent living and worked for the cause when they could; others came from prosperous families, and a few from wealthy households. Some women became well known in the abolitionist movement regardless of their economic circumstances, but most led rather unextraordinary lives.

Family fortune was, however, an important factor shaping black women's activism and leading some women to assume leadership in their communities. These women came from the few northern free black families that had amassed considerable wealth and were well-known and respected in their communities for their activism and philanthropy. The high social and financial position of their families instilled in some of the women a self-consciousness about their social responsibility both to aid the less fortunate of their race and to maintain female respectability and prescribed sex roles. Black activist and scholar W. E. B. DuBois later described these families as the "better class" of urban free blacks, who lived in "well-kept homes" in which no family members performed menial service and "the wife engaged in no occupation save that of house-wife, except in a a few cases where she had special employment at home."[1] In short, material wealth enabled these families to maintain the patriarchal family structure that symbolized progress and success in American society.

DuBois's description accurately portrayed many of the better-known black families, such as the Shadds and Fortens, whose activism flourished during the antebellum years. In both families, the male heads of household had entered skilled trades that usually excluded black men. Charlotte Forten's husband, James, had made his fortune as a sailmaker in Philadelphia after taking over the business from his former employer. By the 1830s, Forten's assets amounted to $100,000, a sizable sum during this period. The family resided in a three-story brick row house on Lombard Street. The children attended private schools, and the daughters spent their leisure time reading, visiting, participating in community benevolence and reform, and studying the "ornamental" subjects of art, music, French, and German, all symbols of financial achievement. Unlike most black women, Charlotte Forten and her daughters could devote a great deal of their lives to social causes without the daily worries of providing for their families. Mrs. Forten frequently hosted white and black abolitionist friends, who made regular visits to the Forten home to socialize and discuss the progress of the movement. With so many reform-minded friends in their midst, the Forten children—James, Jr., Robert B., Margaretta, Thomas D., Harriet D., Sarah Louise, and William D.—received an early education in social and political activism.[2]

The Forten women quickly established themselves as part of the black female leadership in Philadelphia and were original members of the biracial Philadelphia Female Anti-Slavery Society, founded in 1833. They worked regularly with other well-known free black women, including Grace and Sarah Douglass, and Sarah McCrummell, wife of James McCrummell (sometimes spelled "McCrummill"), a prosperous black barber and dentist. Sarah and Margaretta Forten wrote poetry and essays for the antislavery press, in addition to teaching school. Their sister Harriet modeled her life after their mother's by hosting abolitionist friends at her suburban home at Byberry, where she lived with her husband, Robert Purvis, and their growing family.

The Forten-Purvis marriage had allied two prominent activist families. Purvis, born in South Carolina, had inherited a fortune from his white father. By 1850, the value of his real estate totaled $35,000.[3] In Philadelphia, he became well-known as an abolitionist, business leader, and, after the Civil War, a leader in black community politics.[4] Harriet Forten Purvis supervised the comings and goings of a hectic household, for in addition to the many guests she hosted throughout the year she also cared for their eight children, whose ages in 1850 ranged from eighteen to one.[5] White abolitionist Sallie Holley once described the Purvis house as "elegant," decorated in "tasteful English style." She dubbed their home Saints' Rest, "for here all the abolitionists find that 'the wicked cease from troubling and the weary are at rest.'" Ironically, Holley likened Harriet Purvis to a southern belle, describing her as "very lady-like in manners and conversation; something of the ease and blandness of a southern lady."[6]

In nearby West Chester, the family of Mary Ann Shadd (Cary) also enjoyed the comforts of a well-to-do household, though the Shadds were not as wealthy as the Fortens. Her mother was Harriet Parnell Shadd, of whom little is known, except that she was a mulatto born in North Carolina in 1806. Mary Ann Shadd's father, Abraham Doras Shadd, born in 1801, had amassed his wealth as a shoemaker in Wilmington, Delaware, and by the 1830s had accumulated real property valued at $5,000.[7] He gained prominence by serving as a delegate to the American Anti-Slavery Society during the 1830s. Several of the thirteen Shadd children participated in abolitionist work and, after the Civil War, pursued professional careers. Mary Ann, the eldest, attended a private Quaker school and during the 1840s taught school in Wilmington, West Chester, New York City, and Norristown, Pennsylvania.[8] Following her own convictions and the example set by her parents, she became a fervent abolitionist and, during the 1850s, a controversial figure in the Canadian emigrationist movement. Throughout her career, the Shadd family was always nearby to provide encouragement. An emigrationist himself, Abraham Shadd and several family members eventually joined Mary Ann in Canada, where Abraham became the only black to win elective office in Canada West before the Civil War.[9] Mary Ann's oldest brother, Isaac D. Shadd, became a newspaper publisher and later speaker of the Mississippi legislature during Reconstruction. Another brother, Abraham W. Shadd, graduated from the Law Department at Howard University and practiced law in Mississippi and Arkansas. Her middle sister, Amelia Cisco Shadd Williamson, was a newspaper contributor, and her youngest sister, Eunice, taught school after graduating from the Normal Department at Howard.[10]

Mary Ann Shadd's sister-in-law, Amelia Freeman Shadd, who had married her brother Isaac, also taught school in the black community in Chatham, Ontario. Amelia, the daughter of educator and black activist Martin H. Freeman, was also the product of an activist family in the United States. Amelia had traveled in the circles of black abolitionist leadership since her early childhood in Pittsburgh, where her father was vice-president of Allegheny Institute and later president of Avery College. He worked closely with black emigrationists such as the Shadds and Martin Delany, a leading figure in the movement, and served as one of eight corresponding editors of the *Afric-American Repository*. According to the *Provincial Freeman*, it was Delany who had introduced Amelia Freeman to Black society in Chatham. Before she embarked on the emigrationist trail to Canada, she taught fine arts at Allegheny Institute.[11] In Canada, she and the Shadds worked to provide food, clothing, and shelter, as well as schooling, to needy blacks. Mary Ann Shadd described her sister-in-law as "an energetic Christian woman" and "known to many respectable citizens of Pittsburg." She further noted: "She is a laborer in the Sabbath School, and is zealous in her duties as a moral and religious instructor."[12]

Most black women who came from respected activist families, however, were not as well off as either the Fortens or the Shadds, though their families were prosperous compared to most blacks of the period. The Remonds, Chesters, Douglasses, and Pauls, for example, maintained a comfortable lifestyle as long as all adults in the family brought home a steady income. The women of these families found employment in the only jobs then available to women, regardless of race: teaching, running small businesses, and domestic-related work as laundresses, seamstresses, and servants. The family of Sarah Parker Remond maintained prosperity in this manner: her father, John, a West Indian immigrant who had never been a slave, engaged in a number of enterprises as a hairdresser, caterer, and merchant trader of wine and other goods in Salem, Massachusetts,[13] and her mother, Nancy Lenox Remond, also a free-born black, operated a fancy cake-making business with her daughter Susan.[14] Three other daughters, Cecelia Remond Babcock, Maritcha, and Caroline Remond Putnam, ran a Ladies Hair Work Salon, where they manufactured wigs. Their wig factory, in fact, was the largest in Massachusetts.[15] The Remonds' financial success and activism in the movement established them as important resources within abolitionist circles.

John Remond was a life member of the Massachusetts Anti-Slavery Society. Nancy, Caroline, Susan, and Sarah frequently participated in the activities of the Salem Female Anti-Slavery Society, which began as a black female organization in 1832 and was later reorganized into a racially-mixed society. Like the Forten children, the children of John and Nancy Remond received much of their abolitionist education at home, where the doors were often open to abolitionist friends, both black and white.

Charlotte Forten, daughter of Robert and Mary Virginia Woods Forten and granddaughter of James and Charlotte of Philadelphia, went to live with the family of Charles Lenox Remond in Salem in 1853, when she was sixteen, in order to attend school, for the private school she had wished to attend in Philadelphia excluded blacks. She joined the Salem Female Anti-Slavery Society in 1855 and in 1856 graduated from the racially integrated Salem Normal School and accepted a job at Epes Grammar School in Salem, a position she resigned in 1858 due to poor health. During her stay at the Remonds, she aspired to become an abolitionist lecturer.[16] While living with the Remonds she enjoyed a lifestyle typical of young, unmarried, middle-class women; she attended school, practiced the piano, visited with friends, sewed, took long evening walks, read and recited poetry, and wrote in her diary. Surrounded by activists, she also attended antislavery meetings and lectures, read the abolitionist newspapers, and discussed the latest news of the movement. Coming from a family whose ancestors had never been enslaved, Charlotte could never completely empathize with the condition of slaves,[17] but as an enthusiastic young activist she found the subject of abolitionism "so interesting" that she was inspired after reading the Bible to remember "the poor slave as bound with him."[18]

Abolitionists Jane Marie Chester and her husband George ran a successful restaurant and catering business and were well-known supporters of anti-colonizationist activities in Harrisburg, Pennsylvania. Together they established an activist household and did their best to provide education for their twelve children. George Chester worked as the only agent for the *Liberator* in Harrisburg, a dangerous endeavor in a city where colonizationist organizations flourished. Their daughter, Charlotte, became the first black teacher in Harrisburg. Their fourth child, Thomas Morris Chester, supported emigration and, amid much criticism from anti-colonizationists, saw an opportunity for the establishment of an independent free colony of expatriated African-Americans in Liberia.[19] Their mother, Jane Chester, shared responsibility with her husband for the success of the family economy, and after George's death in the 1850s she sold homemade taffy and continued the operating the restaurant and catering service, while simultaneously running a large and busy household.[20]

Like many Americans who relied upon limited resources yet enjoyed some prosperity, these families could easily fall on hard times if their small businesses failed as a result of illness, death, fire, flood, economic downturns, or other catastrophes. Black-owned businesses and institutions were also in constant danger of destruction and vandalism at the hands of anti-black rioters. Violence against the free black community, in fact, was on the rise during the antebellum period.[21] During these times, free black men and women could often turn to black institutions and organizations in their own neighborhoods for assistance. Those who joined abolitionist circles found yet another source of support, for both black and white abolitionist friends often came to the aid of their colleagues. Since white leaders as a group tended to be better off financially than most black abolitionists, they provided a great deal of assistance. The patriarchs of the free black community—James Forten, Robert Purvis, John Remond, and James McCrummell—also were called upon to help needy blacks.

Sometimes, the death of a parent permanently altered economic circumstances. For the well-known abolitionist Sarah Mapps Douglass, hard times came when her mother, Grace, died in 1842. Upon her death, the family lost a valuable source of income from the millinery shop she had operated next door to her father's bakery on Arch Street in Philadelphia. Grace Bustill Douglass had hailed from a distinguished black activist Quaker family from Burlington, New Jersey. She was the fifth of eight children born to Cyrus Bustill, a prosperous baker, and Elizabeth Morrey, the daughter of an Englishman and a Delaware Indian woman. The Bustills were active in the black communities in Philadelphia and southern New Jersey. Grace's niece, Anna Douglass Mapps, was a teacher, as was Grace A. Mapps, Anna Mapps's stepdaughter, of Little Egg Harbor, New

Jersey.[22] Grace Douglass's brother-in-law, David Mapps, husband of Anna Douglass Mapps, was a black Quaker who often hosted Friends in his home. Grace's nephews, James and Joseph Bustill, were active in the American Moral Reform Society along with many prominent black reformers.

After Grace died, her only daughter, Sarah, brought in the family's primary source of income as a teacher. Her elderly father, Robert, lived at home, and her brother, Robert, Jr., a well-known portrait painter and lithographer in Philadelphia, probably contributed to the family income.[23] White abolitionist Sarah Grimké wrote that her friend's health was fragile during this time: "Sarah's health is so precarious that her physician tells her it will be almost the certain sacrifice of life for her to continue school-keeping . . . yet their circumstances render it necessary, for her to do something for a living." Grimké's description of the family's situation also suggests that Sarah Douglass's consciousness of her own social position prevented her from taking a job as a domestic: "I know of no active employment in which she could engage except as an assistant in a family, which I fear would neither suit her disposition or inclination."[24]

The life of another well-known black abolitionist, Susan Paul, had a particularly tragic ending. The daughter of Thomas Paul, a Baptist minister and activist in Boston, she saw her financial status founder when her father died in 1831. Although a minister's salary had afforded them few material luxuries, it was a necessary part of the family economy and had provided respectable status in Boston's free black community. For ten years after his death, Susan Paul struggled to support her widowed mother and the children of her dead sister as a seamstress and a teacher of black schoolchildren. Her modest income, however, was inadequate.

Fortunately, abolitionist friends, most of whom were prominent whites, assisted the Pauls during these difficult times. Susan had apparently developed close friendships with a number of leading whites as a result of her family's antislavery work.[25] Perhaps it was this connection and her family's elevated status in the black community that led one white friend, Anne Warren Weston, to note that Paul stood apart from other blacks; according to Weston, Paul was one of two black women chosen as delegates to the 1837 Anti-Slavery Convention in New York, mainly because she was considered "a favorable specimen of the coloured race." Weston noted further that "Julia Williams [was chosen] because the coloured people regard her as one of themselves, a light in which they do not regard Susan Paul."[26]

Soon after the Reverend Paul's death, the family's economic situation deteriorated to the point where they were unable to maintain their house. Forced to move "because its ruinous condition rendered it uninhabitable in storms," Paul searched in vain for affordable housing in "the few streets where colored people are allowed to live." At one point she found a small house in a white neighborhood, but was "assured" by its inhabitants that her family "would not be allowed to remain there in comfort and safety." Thus, even Paul's intimate connection to prominent whites did not alter the reality of racism in her midst. When she finally found a house in a predominantly black neighborhood, she relied in part upon the charity of well-to-do white friends and her sympathetic black landlord to help pay the rent.

Paul's illness with consumption further limited her ability to keep the family out of irreversible poverty.[27] According to Sarah Southwick, daughter of Hannah Southwick, Paul had contracted the disease while on her way to New York aboard a steamboat with segregationist policies barring her from the "ladies cabin" and forcing her to stay on the lower deck.[28] White friends Lydia Maria Child, Hannah Southwick, and Henrietta Sargent, with whom she had worked closely in the Boston Female Anti-Slavery Society, cared for her during her long illness. Anne Warren Weston wrote of Paul's death in 1841 at the age of thirty-four: "Miss Paul died the day I came out of town. . . . Everything was done by Mrs. Southwick, Henrietta & others for her comfort. The family will now be broken up & the children taken by sundry friends."[29] Thus, even in death, Paul relied primarily on the assistance and friendship of white abolitionists.

Women who divided their time between household duties, jobs, and community activism did not always have time to participate in all abolitionist activities, regardless of their devotion to the cause. As one black woman, Harriet Hayden, found, "time and circumstances" forced her to cut short her involvement in an 1843 antislavery fair in Boston, even though she had devoted a great deal of time to its preparation. Hayden expressed her regrets in a letter to white abolitionist Maria Weston Chapman: "In the accompanying article you will find that I have made a faint and trifling response to the call. It is the hasty production of a very short period of leisure. . . . I have been spending the last week in working for the Mass. fair, I want very much to do a great deal but time & circumstances forbid."[30]

Hayden's husband, Lewis, was prominent in the Boston black community as a small businessman who catered to a mixed clientele and an activist in the Underground Railroad. An escaped slave himself, Lewis Hayden outfitted fugitive slaves from his clothing store on Cambridge Street.[31] Harriet, like many wives of businessmen, probably assisted her husband in running his store as well as caring for a large household. Within seven years after Harriet had written her hasty note to Chapman, the household had grown considerably, and her chores undoubtedly increased. The U.S. census of 1850 listed Lewis Hayden as a "trader" and reported that the household contained thirteen members: their children, Joseph, age fourteen, who worked as a clerk, probably in his father's shop; their five-year-old daughter, Elizabeth; a white domestic servant; three other "traders"; two male tailors; a cook; and two fugitive slaves who were also gaining fame in the abolitionist community, William and Ellen Craft. The Crafts had sought shelter in the Hayden home after their escape from Georgia in 1848 and reportedly were well protected by the young, armed "traders" under Hayden's employ.[32]

The Hayden home on Phillips Street was one of many private dwellings that also served as boardinghouses to a transient black population, which included single black men and women looking for employment, seamen, orphaned children, and runaway slaves like the Crafts.[33] Mary Ann Shadd Cary described the boardinghouse of her friends William and Letitia (whom she calls Mary) Still in Philadelphia as "an elegant home at moderate charges, run by "an agreeable and highly intelligent host and hostess."[34] Boardinghouses, many of which were operated by women, served as a critical link to black community life. In addition to providing a family-like setting, food, and shelter, such establishments enabled boarders to meet people, and to gather information about employment prospects, social events, and churches and associations they might wish to join.[35] Boardinghouses also provided their female proprietors with an income that was essential, particularly during hard times.

Sheltering fugitive slaves in these houses, however, was a dangerous business, for the entire household became a target for slave catchers. Proprietors and boarders alike had to remain alert at all times. Harriet Hayden's ability to protect her household from prying strangers was recalled by a friend nearly eighty years later:

> Few black men could have done what Mrs. Hayden did in those stirring times. She had all of a woman's tact, persistence and cleverness in emergencies, and was conveniently deaf, dumb, and blind when necessary and hence she was not a popular nor useful aid to U.S. marshals and Southern masters hunting their runaway slaves in Mass.[36]

Black women activists who struggled to eke out a living by themselves still managed to participate actively in a variety of community activities. Eliza Ann Dixon Day, of New York City, was the sole support for her four children after the death in 1829 of her husband, John, a sailor and sailmaker. Despite this difficult situation, Eliza Day was an active churchgoer, a member of the John Street Methodist Church, and a founding member of the A.M.E. Zion Church in New York. She also attended abolitionist meetings, which was at times a life-threatening activity: in 1833, she was among those abolitionists who had to flee the Chatham Street Chapel after an anti-abolitionist mob attacked the meeting.[37] The incident at the Chapel, one of the city's most violent anti-abolitionist attacks, signified increasing hostility to antislavery activity in the Northeast;[38] the following year, another mob went on a rampage, destroying black churches and homes and harassing abolitionists.[39]

As a single mother of four young children, living on a meager income, Eliza Day struggled to participate in an unpopular cause that could have cost her entire family their lives. Nevertheless, she created a pattern of activism in her household and by example instilled in her children the importance of continuing the movement. As was often the case in abolitionist households, children followed the pattern of activism their parents had set, and Day's youngest son, William Howard Day, credited her as a role model who helped provide the impetus for his future success as a black leader. Like other black parents, Day did her best to educate her children, using her limited funds to enroll William in a private school.[40] He also attended the New York Manumission Society school, and at the age of nine he entered Public School No. 2 in the city, where he served as librarian for the anti-colonizationist Garrison Literary Society. But perhaps the most difficult decision Day had to make on her son's behalf was to allow a white educator to adopt him and, thus, ensure his future education.[41] The experience of Eliza Ann Dixon Day illustrates the immense sacrifices some black parents made to educate their children and train them to resist racism and protest its injustices.

For many former slaves, in particular, a connection to the abolitionist movement not only facilitated their work as activists but was necessary for their safety and survival. As is evident in the lives of Harriet Tubman and Sojourner Truth, two famous ex-slave women, life after freedom was difficult and uncertain. Tubman, famous as the "Moses of her People," worked as a cook, scrubwoman, seamstress, and domestic servant in Philadelphia after escaping from slavery in Maryland. It was not until she met black activist William Still and other Philadelphia abolitionists that she found the material support and encouragement she needed to travel back into the slaveholding south and reportedly rescue seven hundred slaves, some of whom were members of her own family. Truth, born Isabella Baumfree in Ulster County, New York, obtained her freedom in 1827 at the age of thirty and moved to New York City, where, like most free black women, she worked as a domestic servant. She ended her employment in 1843, when she "caught the spirit" and went to live in a religious commune in upstate New York. Associations with abolitionists enabled both Tubman and Truth to obtain financial assistance. In a letter to her "dear friend" Wendell Phillips in 1860, Tubman kept him abreast of her financial situation before one of her trips into the South:

> My dear Friend
>
> I write to let you know that I am about to start on my mission. I shall leave on Tuesday. As you promised if I . . . would let you know in case I did not make up my $100. I will state I lack (after paying my board) *all* or $20 of that amount. I shall not take my money with me but leave it with Mr. Walcott to forward to me at Philadelphia. Whatever you do will be gratefully appreciated by
>
> Harriet Tubman[42]

Truth's letters were actually written by friends, for she never learned to read or write. During the Civil War, she was often in poor health at her home in Battle Creek, Michigan, and relied on donations to sustain her both financially and spiritually. In a letter written by a friend, Truth thanked Gerrit Smith for his help:

Harriet Tubman—ex-slave, scrubwoman, maid, and rescuer of slaves—was called the Moses of Her People.
(Library of Congress)

> Sojourner Truth sends you many thanks for your kind donations to her & your kind words which she says has lengthened her days & made her so happy words can't express it. She is now in comfortable health. . . . She says she hopes to meet you if not here [then] in her Father's home. . . . Sends love for you all.[43]

Harriet Brent Jacobs, fugitive slave and author of *Incidents in the Life of a Slave Girl* (1861), found relative safety in the hands of white and black abolitionist friends in Rochester, New York. Born Linda Brent in 1818, she was the great-granddaughter of a white slaveholder in South Carolina. She escaped at the age of twenty-seven and, with the assistance of Lydia Maria Child, published her autobiography, detailing her life as a slave and her desperate attempts to free herself and her children.[44] Apparently, prominent friends in upstate New York, including Amy Post, had persuaded Jacobs to write her autobiography.[45] Post and her husband, Isaac, had offered many black men and women friendship and refuge in their home in Rochester.

The escape of Ellen and William Craft is one of the most colorful ones on record. Ellen was the daughter of her master and her slave mother. At the age of eleven, she was given to her mistress's daughter as a wedding present and traveled with her half-sister to their new home in Macon. There she met another slave, William Craft, whom she "married."[46] Disguised as master and servant, they fled to the free states in December 1848 by train and steamer ship. William's skills as a cabinetmaker generated a little money that facilitated their escape, and Ellen's complexion was light enough for her to pass as white; some years later, while in England, she was described as "very little darker than . . . our countrywoman."[47] She dressed as a white master, while the darker William played the slave valet. The fact that Ellen had to disguise herself as a man illustrates the restrictions placed upon white women, which dictated that they should not travel alone, perhaps especially when in the company of a male slave.[48] Further, her light complexion also enabled her to circumvent restrictions placed on blacks, slave or free, regarding travel on public transportation. Because Ellen looked like a white person, she had no trouble securing comfortable train and ship accommodations.

A free black man met them at the Philadelphia train station on Christmas day. From the moment they arrived in the free states, they became involved in abolitionist activities and traveled with leaders of the movement. They accompanied William Wells Brown to Boston, where they lived for two years at the Hayden residence and attended antislavery meetings, and there, Ellen learned to be a seamstress. The Fugitive Slave Act of 1850, however, rendered the Haydens powerless to protect them, and in that year, slave catchers arrived in Boston with warrants for their arrest. To remain in Boston under the guard of the Haydens became increasingly dangerous, not only for the Crafts themselves, but also for other runaway slaves who sought shelter in Boston. Thus, with the help of white and black friends, the Crafts escaped to Nova Scotia and then to England. They met with William Wells Brown, who had moved to Britain the previous year, and toured with him, telling audiences of their slave experiences.

Ellen Craft reportedly faded from the lecture circuit after her husband gained prominence as a speaker.[49] Initially, however, she joined the antislavery lecturers on the podium. During their stay in Great Britain, William Craft's career seemed to skyrocket, and, according to one account, Ellen seemed uncomfortable with their new fame, "somewhat embarrassed by the marked attentions paid to her. . . ."[50] As their family grew, she spent more of her time at home with their five children, though she worked with her husband in business and local antislavery activities. Their endeavors to support their family included a boardinghouse, a school, and an import-export business; they also earned income through William's cabinetmaking and Ellen's seamstress work.[51] Meanwhile, William Craft worked actively in the British antislavery organizations and even travelled to Africa to spread the message of humanitarianism and social reform. With a large family to look after, Ellen's antislavery activities were confined to participation in the British and Foreign Freedman's Aid Society and fund raising in support of the school for boys established by her husband in Dahomey, West Africa. She apparently tried to deliver a public lecture in London but was denied the opportunity because of her sex.[52] In 1868, the Crafts returned to the United States, where William bought a plantation in their native state of Georgia. They separated in the 1890s for the sake of Ellen's failing health; while William remained in Georgia to operate a school he had established, Ellen moved to Charleston, South Carolina to live with her daughter and son-in-law, who was a physician. When she died in 1897, she was buried on the Georgia plantation.[53]

Widowhood presented some women with firsthand knowledge of economic difficulties. For Maria Miller Stewart (1803–1879) and Frances Ellen Watkins Harper (1825–1911), unsuccessful dealings with financial executors after their husbands' deaths awakened them to the structural and cultural barriers facing women. Their personal experiences led them to become vigorous supporters of women's rights as well as racial justice. Stewart, a writer and the first American woman known to have delivered a public speech, was orphaned at the age of five and went to work as a servant for a minister's family in Connecticut. Her three-year marriage to James Stewart ended with his death in 1829, and she subsequently was defrauded out of her small inheritance by two white men whom her husband had named as the executors of his will. This experience inspired her to deliver several public speeches to female audiences, encouraging them to obtain education and economic power. Although she continued to support women's rights and black self-help activities, Stewart's dependence on low-paying teaching positions in black schools meant she had to move frequently, to New York City, Baltimore, and Washington, D.C.

Frances Harper also found it difficult to earn a living and, at the same time, contribute to the cause of her people. Born Frances Ellen Watkins in Baltimore in 1825, she went to live with her aunt and uncle, Henrietta and William Watkins, after her parents died when she was three. In this household, she grew up in comfortable surroundings, for her uncle, in addition to working as an administrator and teacher at Watkins Academy, a school he had established in 1820, was also a preacher, shoemaker, and self-taught practitioner of medicine. Like many of the other black activist women of her generation, Frances grew up in an abolitionist household; her uncle was well-known for his staunch support of Garrison.[54] According to William Still, it was William Watkins who convinced Garrison to oppose the colonization movement and adopt instead the more radical stance that many black activists had been promoting.[55]

His niece's childhood was not unlike that of the Remond, Shadd, and Forten children. As a young girl, Frances attended her uncle's academy, where she learned academic subjects and music. Like other young women, Frances also learned the female "trade" of seamstressing and domestic work. While working for a white family as a nursemaid, she read extensively and began writing poetry, compiling her first collection of poems, *Forest Leaves*, in 1845. Her association with influential male abolitionists Garrison and Still, from whom she received praise, helped in the publication and distribution of her works. She even resided for a time with Still and his wife, Letitia, in their apartment above the antislavery office in Philadelphia, where she continued to write antislavery poems. She traveled extensively with her cousin, William Watkins, Jr., on the antislavery lecture circuit, making her way through Canada and some of the most hostile regions of the northeastern United States.[56] She sent the money she collected on her tours back to her uncle for the Underground Railroad.

Her financial troubles seem to have begun after the death of her husband, Fenton Harper. Watkins married Harper in 1860 at the age of thirty-five and settled on a farm in Ohio, which she had purchased with her own money. During her four-year marriage she apparently gave up lecturing to raise her only daughter, Mary, along with Fenton's three children from a previous marriage.[57] After the death of her husband the executor of his estate seized the farm in order to liquidate Fenton's debts, leaving his widow with nothing but a few trinkets. Harper then resumed speaking on the antislavery lecture circuit, which at least provided her with the companionship of old friends, and returned to teaching, which she now relied on to supplement her income from the sale of her poetry.

For some black women, however, marriage did provide economic security, which proved to be a positive catalyst for their activism. In the unusual case of Nancy Gardner Prince, marriage to a prominent free black man rescued her from a life of poverty and provided her with the opportunity to travel abroad, obtain an education, run a business, and participate in abolitionist activities.

Gardner grew up no stranger to poverty, in fluctuating and often dire economic circumstances. Her father, Thomas Gardner, died just three months after she was born in Newburyport, Massachusetts, in 1799. Twice married at the time of her widowhood, Nancy's mother eventually married five times. Her third marriage to a sailor, Mony Vose, produced six more children before his death in 1812, when Nancy's mother suffered an emotional breakdown from which she apparently never recovered. In her memoirs, Nancy reflected on her mother's condition: "She was young, inexperienced, with no hope in God, and without the knowledge of her Savior. Her grief, poverty, and responsibilities were too much for her; she never again was the mother that she had been before."[58]

The death of her stepfather threw the family into poverty. Thirteen-year-old Nancy and her brother gathered and sold berries to support the family. She later recalled that she and her brothers stayed with their mother "until every resource was exhausted." She left home to find work in Salem, first in the home of "a respectable colored family," and, later, with white families.[59] She was still responsible at the time for her younger siblings, caring for them and helping them find suitable jobs and homes. She convinced her sister, Silvia, whom she described as "one of my greatest trials," to leave a house of prostitution in Boston.[60]

Her fortunes turned for the better when she met Nero Prince. After their marriage in 1824, she traveled to Russia, where her husband served as a footman at the court of the czar in St. Petersburg and she opened a boardinghouse and made diapers and childrens's clothing. When she left Russia, she settled in Boston, started a seamstress service, and participated in the activities of the biracial Boston Female Anti-Slavery Society, to which she made regular donations. She also gave public lectures about her travels[61] and quickly became respected in abolitionist circles as a speaker and businesswoman. Garrison once described her as "a respectable and intelligent colored female."[62]

Black women who married prominent abolitionist men endured a common set of difficulties, especially if they were not financially well off. Like white abolitionist wives, many black wives participated in abolitionist activities, but a number of them also shouldered the sole burden of maintaining an emotionally and financially secure homelife. Moreover, wives of abolitionist men, regardless of race, often lived in their husbands' shadows, though their husbands' connections within antislavery circles helped them establish friendships with other abolitionists' wives, both black and white. Such friendships became especially valuable when their husbands were away for extended periods on antislavery business, providing material assistance and allying the sense of isolation that must have accompanied marriages to famous men.

Anna Murray Douglass, Elizabeth Brown, and Elizabeth Remond, for instance, were the sole supporters of their families while their famous husbands traveled extensively in Europe and the United States. Anna Murray Douglass, the first wife of Frederick Douglass, supported their five children as a shoebinder in New Bedford and then Lynn, Massachusetts. Born in Maryland in 1813, Anna was the eighth of twelve children and the first child in the family to be born free. As a young woman, she worked as a domestic servant in Baltimore and, unlike her future husband, had money and some possessions. After his escape in 1838, they were married in New York City by the Reverend J. W. C. Pennington, a black preacher from

Hartford, Connecticut. They settled in Massachusetts, where Anna took in laundry and cared for their home and children, and her husband engaged in low-paying, unskilled seasonal work, loading boats, shoveling coal, and sweeping chimneys.[63]

The connections they made with local abolitionists had both positive and negative results for Anna. On the one hand, they provided valuable assistance during hard times. When her husband fled to Europe after the publication of his slave narrative in 1845, Anna was left to support their family. Cousins of white abolitionist Lucretia Mott cared for the Douglasses' eldest daughter, Rosetta, in Albany, New York, while Anna struggled to earn a living and care for their other three children. According to Rosetta Douglass, her mother scrupulously avoided debt. In the meantime, Anna devoted her "spare" time to participating in the female antislavery societies in Boston and Lynn. Her participation in these activities enabled her to befriend other abolitionist women, but when Frederick returned to the United States three years later, he moved his family to Rochester, New York, where he published the *North Star* and launched his campaign for black nationalism and separatism.

Clearly, Anna felt the consequences of her husband's growing fame as an antislavery lecturer and black leader, especially when rumors circulated about his friendship with Julia Griffiths, a white woman who assisted him in the publication of his newspaper. Anna herself probably contributed little to the newspaper business, since she had never learned to read or write. Her husband's frequent absences, rumors of his relationships with other women, and isolation from old friends must have put strains on their homelife. Rosetta Douglass recalled, however, that her mother seemed to weather these difficulties well, dutifully maintaining a comfortable and hospitable home throughout their marriage. Anna Douglass reportedly was Frederick's greatest fan; when he went on trips, she made sure he had fresh, pressed linen and sometimes sent clean clothes ahead to his destination.[64]

In some ways, Elizabeth Schooner Brown's marriage to William Wells Brown was similar to the Douglasses', but the Browns had an unhappy and controversial relationship that eventually ended in a permanent separation. Like Frederick Douglass, William Brown was a former slave who married a free woman, joined the abolitionists, and gave lectures on his firsthand slave experience. Like Anna Douglass, Elizabeth Brown was left to care for their children while her husband was away. Her only connection

Anna Murray Douglass.
(Library of Congress)

with the movement, however, was through her husband. During William's absence, Elizabeth reportedly had an affair with another man. William reacted by moving the family one hundred miles away from their home near Buffalo, New York, which did not help; Elizabeth remained isolated and discontented. In 1847 she left William and their two young daughters, Clara and Josephine, and shortly thereafter he placed the girls in schools in New Bedford, Massachusetts.

In this situation, the Browns' connections to antislavery friends did not benefit Elizabeth. When she appealed to the Massachusetts Anti-Slavery Society for financial support from William, the committee appointed to investigate the matter sided with him. After the separation, his absences from home continued, and William left his daughters with black abolitionist friends, visiting when he could. Until her death in 1851, Elizabeth reportedly searched for her children.

According to William, however, Elizabeth saw her daughters at least once on a visit to Boston and New Bedford, where they boarded. In a letter to Amy Post in July 1848, he wrote that Elizabeth had arrived in Boston at the end of June, presumably to find her children: "She at first refused to see me, until persuaded by Mrs. Garrison to do so. She at last consented, and came down, and I had some two hours talk with her." Apparently, Elizabeth then left New England, "satisfied that it is of no use to follow after [me] or the children." William believed that his meeting with Elizabeth placed him in "a better position in New England," where some people had accused him of deserting his wife. Such aspersions would have damaged both his reputation in abolitionist circles and the ongoing efforts to disprove racist assumptions of black immorality.[65] The Browns' marital troubles made the newspapers: the *New York Daily Tribune* in March 1850 published Elizabeth Brown's allegations of desertion against William, but the article ended by questioning her motives: "We know none of the parties, but we suspect Elizabeth is slightly malicious."[66]

During their parents' separation, Clara and Josephine Brown attended schools in New Bedford, France, and England. When the Fugitive Slave Law forced William to remain in London longer than he had expected, he arranged to bring his daughters to London, where they later became teachers. During their school years, Clara and Josephine had often relied on their father's abolitionist friends, who sent them money for tuition and expenses, as well as gifts. In 1851, for instance, Clara Brown, then fifteen, received permission from her father to request five dollars in spending money from Wendell Phillips.[67] The young women remained close to their father and his friends, both in the United States and Great Britain, and they remained estranged from their mother. In fact, in her biography of her father, Josephine Brown never mentions her mother.[68]

Elizabeth Brown's failed marriage and unsuccessful appeal to the Massachusetts Anti-Slavery Society left her bitter and resentful toward her abolitionist acquaintances. In one letter, Elizabeth referred to them as "hypocritical friends of the opressed," who "worked against me and my desert child."[69] For Elizabeth Brown, her associations with the movement, however tangential, had resulted in a life of economic hardship, loneliness, and frustration.

Elizabeth Remond and her husband Charles Lenox Remond found themselves dependent on the assistance of Wendell Phillips for material necessities, such as clothing and rent. Charles's income was meager and sporadic, and his work as an antislavery lecturer and agent for the Massachusetts Anti-Slavery Society took him away from the family much of the time. Their financial troubles strained their marriage; Elizabeth later claimed that while Charles was at home they incurred debts, but during his absences she managed to remain solvent: "I am very happy now to think all the time Mr. Remond has been from home I never borrowed one cent & never got anything on credit so all the debts were acquired before he went away."[70]

In 1863, Elizabeth wrote to Phillips for a $100 loan the day before Charles left for Washington, D.C., to recruit black soldiers for the war; the money was needed to support the family, she said, because Charles had earned "little or nothing by his profession for nearly two years." After he returned the following year, the family was still in need, despite Elizabeth's small earnings, and she wrote to Phillips for another loan in order to buy winter clothes for the family: "It is impossible for me to earn them by labour," She explained. "I attempted last winter to work a little & the consequence has been that I am entirely overpowered with mending & making for the family." At the same time, she expressed frustration over her husband's inability to help repay the previous loan: "Mrs. Putnam gave me the receipt for the $1900 which I am very much obliged to you. . . . I feel very sorry Mr. Phillips that Charles has not allowed me to keep my *word*. I promised to refund the hundred in a few months *with Interest* but I unfortunately have not influence enough over him to get it, though he is able and has been ever since his return from Washington."[71]

The money she earned as a seamstress and Phillips' early loan apparently enabled the family to survive during Charles's absence. But four years later, the Remonds' financial troubles recurred; in a letter Elizabeth wrote to Phillips then, thanking him for a loan, she reveals not only a continual reliance upon trusted friends in the movement, but deep anxiety about the family's indebtedness: "I have been so busy & anxious about the Mortgage Money since I saw you that I could not until now thank you sincerely for your kindness. . . . I have been overwhelmed with care and anxiety over two years but I have good friends now who stood by me in my poverty & of course I shall retain them if I succeed in getting my money back. . . . I think I am very fortunate."[72]

Sometimes the roles of husbands and wives were reversed. Mary Ann Shadd's marriage to Thomas Cary, for example, though unusual by nineteenth-century standards, was, reportedly, a happy one. In this case, Mary Ann was the better-known activist in the family. She had married Cary, a barber and bathhouse proprietor, at St. Catherine's in 1856, five years after she had begun her teaching and emigrationist activities in Canada. Her marriage at the age of thirty-three, unlike the marriages of many of her contemporaries, did not lead her into a life of domestic solitude and wage-earning; instead, she continued her traveling, newspaper publishing, teaching, and activism for emigration, while her husband stayed at home tending to his businesses. Clearly, Thomas Cary controlled the family finances. When they lived apart, he sent money to Mary Ann when he could, but during the 1850s, even the prosperous hit hard times. In 1858, he wrote to his wife, instructing her to find a cheaper place to live if she could not negotiate a rent reduction: "[I] wish you to see Miss [illeg.] and have a Reduction made in the Rent of the house, and if not look out for another for I will not pay that rent any longer." Cary enclosed seven dollars with his letter and promised to send more money "as soon as I can get a hold of some."[73]

As their family grew, Mary Ann sometimes took her infants with her on her trips, accompanied by her mother and sisters. She eventually had five children: Ann ("Annie"), Thomas, Jr., John, Sarah Elizabeth, and Linton. Her husband, mother, and younger siblings, especially her sister Sarah, provided assistance that enabled Mary Ann to travel, teach, write, and continue her work on the *Provincial Freeman*.[74]

Friendships between abolitionists often went beyond economics; they counseled one another, exchanged gifts, and shared joyful times. In 1855, when Sarah Douglass was apprehensive about her upcoming marriage, at the age of forty-nine, to the Reverend William Douglass (no relation), her friend Sarah Grimké tried to reassure her: "I do not wonder you shrink from sexual intercourse, yet I suppose in married life, it is as much the natural expression of affection as the warm embrace & ardent kiss." Grimké, who never married, assured her that "Time will familiarize you with the idea."[75]

Despite economic hardships, abolitionists sometimes were able to send presents to friends. William Still once sent Mary Ann Shadd Cary a volume of Shakespeare's works as a New Year's present.[76] In 1838, Sarah Douglass expressed appreciation to Abigail Kelley Foster with a gift of a book, "in token of my ardent love . . . respect and gratitude to you, for having stood faith so nobly in deference of women and the slave. . . ."[77] Douglass also attended the wedding of Angelina Grimké and Theodore Dwight Weld in 1838; her presence at the ceremony was described by Philadelphia newspapers as evidence of amalgamation between the races.

Familiarity with abolitionist networks also helped blacks who traveled overseas to pursue their antislavery work. Sarah Parker Remond was well-connected to the abolitionist community through the activism of her parents and siblings. As an agent of the regional society, her brother Charles provided her with news of meetings and of the activities of significant persons in the movement; more significantly, he introduced her to influential New England abolitionists such as Garrison, Phillips, Maria Weston Chapman, and Samuel J. May, with whom Sarah maintained close ties even after she moved to Great Britain.

Remond had begun her speaking career in 1856 at the age of thirty, traveling throughout upper New York state with her brother and several well-known white abolitionists, including Parker Pillsbury, Samuel May, Sr., Susan B. Anthony, Stephen S. Foster, Garrison, and Phillips. In December 1858, Sarah accompanied Samuel J. May to Great Britain to participate in the antislavery lecture circuit there. When she arrived, she found companionship and assistance from British abolitionists who knew her family and friends in the United States—Maria Weston Chapman, in particular, was instrumental in connecting Remond with British activists. In 1859, Chapman advised Remond to call on "our old tried and true friends" and offered to provide her with letters of introduction, though "it will be just as well to say—'Mrs. Chapman bids me convey to you her grateful remembrances, and her wish that I may share . . . for the cause's sake, the great benefit of your friendship and counsel.' "[78] Remond also stayed at the home of William and Ellen Craft for a time. She was aware of the importance of such connections, as she once expressed to Samuel May, Jr., in a letter noting that without their "influence and money" she could "not have done the antislavery [work]."[79]

Although many black abolitionists had developed close friendships with whites, black men and women, regardless of their fame or economic circumstances, shared a common experience with racism that differentiated them from their white colleagues. Sarah Forten once explained to her friend Angelina Grimké that though her family's wealth alleviated race prejudice to some degree, because the family knew they might face discrimination if they ventured outside of Philadelphia, where they were well-known, they tried to stay close to home. When they did travel, they only entered establishments where the proprietors explicitly opened their doors to both blacks and whites. Forten considered her family's tactics important: "We meet none of these mortifications which might otherwise ensue. I would recommend to my Colored friends to follow our example and they would be spared some very painful realities."[80]

Sarah Remond recalled that her first experience with racism occurred at the age of nine, when she had attempted to enter an all-white secondary school and, though she had passed the entrance examination, school officials refused to admit her. Unlike the majority of less well-to-do free black families, the Remonds withdrew their children from an all-black school, which they considered inadequate, and relocated to Newport, Rhode Island, where Sarah and her sisters attended a private school for blacks.

Of course, most black families lacked the economic wherewithal to make such choices. Sarah Douglass noted to Grimké that she encountered race prejudice all of her life. Racism even overcame common religious convictions; according to Douglass, the Quaker meeting house on Arch Street was a frequent scene of racist incidents: "Even when a child my soul was made sad hearing five or six times during the course of one meeting that language of remonstrance to those who were willing to sit by us. 'This bench is for the black people.' And often times I wept, at other times I felt indignant."[81] Quakers at the Arch Street Meeting discouraged Sarah's mother from applying for permanent membership in the Society of Friends, despite the fact that she and her family had attended the Meeting since childhood. Sarah eventually left the meeting and joined Philadelphia's First African Presbyterian Church, which her father had helped found, but her mother chose to continue at the Quaker meeting, a decision that must have been difficult but that demonstrates her tenacity and personal commitment to the faith.[82] Evidence of her devotion to Quaker principles appears in a long letter she wrote in 1819 to the Reverend John Gloucester, first pastor of the First African Presbyterian Church, in which she emphasized the importance of a simple, austere lifestyle, devoid of extravagance.[83]

Sarah Douglass described for Grimké a racist encounter during her brief stay in New York City as a teacher. At a Quaker meeting there, she was approached by a white woman who assumed she was a domestic servant and asked her, "Doest thee go a housecleaning?"[84] Douglass, as an educated woman from a family that was prosperous and respected in her home community, found such a remark particularly cutting. The incident, reflecting the reality that most black women found employment in domestic work and the stereotype that all of them were involved in this low-paying, low-status occupation, no doubt helps to explain Sarah Grimké's speculation that her friend would probably refuse to accept a position involving domestic work, even when desperate for money.

Sarah Remond felt that racism had denied her an adequate education, despite the fact that she had attended private schools and had continued her education by reading widely on her own and attending lectures when the family returned to Salem in 1841, as she wrote to her friend Abby Kelley Foster: "Although my heart was in the work [on the lecture circuit], I felt that I was in need of a good English education. Every hour since I met you I have endeavored as far as possible to make up for this loss. And when I considered that the only reason why I did not obtain what I so much desired was because I was the possessor of an unpopular complexion, it adds to my discomfort."[85]

Remond recalled that during her lecture tour through upstate New York, she and her brother stayed at the homes of friends, to avoid "heartless and vulgar prejudice" from hotel and boarding house proprietors, which their white colleagues were powerless to prevent. These owners had welcomed the white members of the party but refused to admit the Remonds into their establishments. Mary Ann Shadd Cary reported in 1856 that during her travels through Illinois, local hotels were "afraid to take colored female travellers." Her assessment of the town of St. Charles was that "altogether the moral pulse throbs but feebly."[86]

Even their professed friends could make racist remarks at times. Anne Warren Weston once described a visit to her home by Charles and Sarah Remond. While she expressed admiration for Charles's "high breeding" and "talk of Shakespeare," she noted that "Miss R on the contrary has many of the manners & ways supposed to be peculiar to her race. She is not in the least like the pretty one we saw at the N[ew] E[ngland] Convention."[87] Thus, even the most devoted white abolitionists were not exempt from prevailing stereotypes regarding appearance and deportment, which shaped their perception of their black colleagues.

As the case of Elizabeth and William Wells Brown indicates, not all relationships between black abolitionists were supportive or even congenial. Divisions among black and white abolitionists over black separatism and such issues as the "woman question," ideology, and tactics sometimes went beyond friendly and respectful debate, descending into outright personal battles. Mary Ann Shadd's ongoing feud with black emigrationists Henry and Mary Bibb exemplified the conflict that sometimes characterized the black activist community, testing even friendships between blacks that had been rooted in personal and family ties as well as in a common devotion to the cause. Twenty-one-year-old Charlotte Forten wrote in her diary of such strain in her relationship with Sarah Remond after learning that Remond had severely criticized Forten's essays, *Glimpses*. In her entry for September 11, 1858 she noted that "Miss S. P. Remond I hear, has burst out most venemously upon my poor 'Glimpses'—accusing them of being pro-slavery, and heaven knows what all. I pity her."[88] The criticism must have stung, for during the years when Forten had been part of the Remond family, she had enjoyed Sarah's companionship as they traveled around Boston together and attended antislavery meetings, readings, and lectures.

The web of social relations within the abolitionist community was dynamic and complex, and it affected black women in various ways, depending on the nature of their association with the movement. In activist families, relatives often served as role models for young black women, and female relatives, in particular, made up a special circle of activists who provided guidance and inspiration. Black women abolitionists also served as role models and sources of inspiration to their sons. The connections that free black women formed, through either their own initiative or the influence of relatives, provided many of them with important resources for both financial and emotional support, forging a network that proved particularly valuable in light of increasing hostility from white society and the relatively poor economic condition of the free black community. Some black abolitionist men and women developed deep and lasting friendships across racial lines, and political networks among free blacks often crossed class lines for the sake of the cause. Well-to-do black women sometimes made up the leadership of the black female activist community, but poorer black women could also take leadership roles, as evidenced by the careers of Sojourner Truth, Frances E. W. Harper, Maria Stewart, and Harriet Tubman.

Economics played a crucial role. "Ladies of leisure" in prosperous households fulfilled black community goals for middle-class conventionality, but at the price of precarious economic dependency on husbands and fathers, whose fortunes might turn at any moment. Women married to activist men who were not financially well-off found themselves the primary supporters of their families; in hard times, they depended on supplemental income provided by abolitionist friends. For women in all sorts of economic circumstances, close ties within their own community as well as within the abolitionist network often proved invaluable to their comfort, intellectual inspiration, and survival.

In the cases of Sojourner Truth and Harriet Tubman, two former slaves, connections in abolitionist community actually helped them to retrieve kinship networks that had been disrupted by slavery. Even so, these two women, who maintained close friendships with abolitionists, chose to work independently of antislavery organizations, perhaps because their experience as slaves had taught them to place a high value on self-sufficiency and resilience. As the experiences of Truth, Tubman, and the Crafts suggest, ex-slaves often depended on sympathetic whites and free blacks to secure a physically safe environment, particularly after the passage of the Fugitive Slave Act.

Although ties to abolitionists provided many Black women with vital emotional and material comfort, such ties only produced an exacerbated sense of loneliness and exclusion for other women, especially those who had no connection to the movement except through their husbands. Unfortunate women like Elizabeth Brown found the tightly knit circle a hindrance rather than an advantage. Like so many wives of abolitionist leaders, she had been the sole supporter of the household while her husband was away, and she had not borne the strain well; Unlike more dutiful wives in her position, she never received financial assistance or sympathy from the abolitionist community.

Moreover, no matter how strong were the personal and professional connections between black and white abolitionists, personal experience with racism inevitably bonded black men and women abolitionists together in a way that ties to the white community never could. Class differences, however, could work against the racial bonds, as seemed to be the case with Susan Paul, who apparently forged closer ties with prominent whites than with the free black community.

Women who benefited most from involvement with the black and white abolitionist community lived in areas with relatively large populations of free blacks and white abolitionists. In an urban setting, fugitive blacks could obtain assistance, protection, and even anonymity from trustworthy free blacks and sympathetic whites. For those who lived in areas populated by few blacks, however, finding a supportive community was difficult, to say the least, and feelings of isolation probably ran high.

2

Black Women and the Cult of True Womanhood

The sexual ideology of antebellum free black society, as embodied in white ideals of "true" womanhood and manhood, made community activism a special duty of black women and a basis for their involvement in abolitionism, in addition to shaping "proper" social relations between the sexes, both within the household and in society at large. Contemporary magazines, books, and religious literature instructed women on their responsibility for upholding the four basic virtues that supposedly governed women's nature: piety, purity, domesticity, and submissiveness. Religious commitment or piety lay at the core of female virtue, requiring that women uphold religious devotion in their families to offset the material values that their husbands were expected to embrace. For young, unmarried women, their greatest strength was their purity; if they were truly virtuous, they would keep lustful men at bay, but if they lost their virginity before marriage, they would fall from virtue. Once married, they were to remain dependent on their husbands, because submission to husbands, fathers, and brothers, as perhaps the most feminine of women's qualities, provided order in a household in which males held the ultimate authority. The proper setting in which "true women" were to exercise their virtues was a domestic one, for they should never lose sight of their familial responsibilities: housekeeping, childbearing, and childrearing. Adherence to these virtues, which supposedly gave women the power and responsibility to maintain morality within the household, served as the model for constructing a female sphere of influence in public activism.[1]

In urban white society, the increasing materialism and economic uncertainty that accompanied industrialization seemed to require that women provide comfort and emotional support for their husbands and children. That such ideals also permeated the free black community during this period illustrates the pervasiveness of dominant cultural values in communities struggling to gain acceptance, but it also represented freedom for black men and women, the ability to exercise power over their own lives, and the opportunity to create their own institutions and methods of social organization.[2]

To the extent that the notion of submission and passivity might define white womanhood, it perhaps held less meaning for most black women, especially for the majority who helped support their households financially or for those who were encouraged by the men of their race to participate actively in racial "uplift" activities.[3] They were not passive victims of oppression, but active participants in efforts to help their families and communities and to secure racial equality. Even they, however, like their white counterparts, were urged, in the name of submissiveness, to keep their participation in public reform within assigned parameters.

In free black society, "true womanhood" ideals represented the antithesis of the slave experience, which had denied black men and women autonomy over their life and labor and had perpetuated racist stereotypes. Myths about black women's "character," particularly with regard to the slave experience, were part of nineteenth-century notions about sexuality. The negative images of black women resulted directly from their dual economic role as slave laborers and sexual commodities. Although as workers, they shared with black men a powerlessness in which every aspect of slave labor accrued to the master, women performed a further service as breeders for the slaveholding economy.[4] Only within the slave quarters could black men and women exert any autonomy over their lives.[5]

Antebellum ideas about women's sexuality, classifying all women as either good or evil, crossed lines of race and class but also stereotyped women based on race and class. While middle-class white women were placed on a moral pedestal and depicted as pure, physically fragile symbols of "good" womanhood, black and poor white women shared the stigma of "bad" womanhood.[6]

The image of the "bad" black woman, in particular, which has persisted into the twentieth century, portrays her as sexually promiscuous and, because of her hard work as a laborer, physically powerful. For example, a female slave was described by her mistress in much the same terms that might have been applied to a working-class white servant: "an immense strapping lass." When northern white abolitionist Ellis Gray Loring attempted to procure employment for newly freed black women, he described them as "strong and healthy."[7] His description probably befitted the type of jobs available to black women, which usually required physical stamina.

Prevailing images of black women's sexuality and strength, combined with the fact that in freedom they provided vital economic support to their families, led to stereotypes of the black family in the United States as matriarchal and, hence, pathological.[8] Many historians since the 1960s have shown that slaves struggled hard to sustain strong commitments to family and community, and some have challenged the underlying assumption of inherent pathology in families headed by women.[9]

Racist and sexist imagery of womanhood had become standard perceptions in the eyes of white society. But stereotypes of black and white women were mutually reinforcing images, not simply opposites; the assumption that black women were sensual and physically strong served to buttress the notion that white women were delicate and passionless. A white man in Kentucky once told a traveler that black women, unlike white women, were "destitute of virtue or intelligence, and were fit only to perpetuate the race, and could never be qualified for society."[10]

The sexual exploitation of slave women, however, meant more than reproducing the slave population. Although slave men and women were both subject to the absolute authority of whites and often suffered the same types of punishment, slave women also lived under the constant threat of rape by white men.[11] Sexual harassment and rape by white masters and overseers was common in slaveholding households. In interviews and in their own writings, ex-slave women often told of their powerlessness to repel the sexual advances of their white masters.[12]

The presence of racially mixed slave children on plantations forced whites to acknowledge that sexual intercourse occurred between white men and black women. To admit white men's culpability, however, would have undermined notions of white moral superiority. Thus, rather than perceiving slave women as victims of sexual abuse, whites blamed them for initiating sexual relations with white men and, as a result, portrayed black women as seducers. James Henry Hammond, governor of South Carolina, defended white womanhood in his letters on slavery by claiming that the majority of prostitutes in the South were black. He also expressed indignation at the thought that white men would willfully degrade themselves by engaging in sexual relations with black women and denied the frequency of such liaisons:

> But it is said, that the licentiousness consists in the constant intercourse between white males and colored females. One of your heavy charges against us has been, that we regard and treat these people as brutes. . . . I will not deny that some intercourse of the sort does take place. Its character and extent, however, are grossly and atrociously exaggerated. . . . I have done with this disgusting topic.[13]

Combining notions of black inferiority and sexual depravity, Hammond argued that prostitution was not degrading for blacks because as a race they had "not yet been lifted into sensibilities, the possession of which necessarily brings, with indulgence in the vice, the consciousness of degradation."[14]

Sexual relations between white men and slave women underscored the patriarchal structure of southern white society, in which white women, who needed the system in order to secure their relatively elevated social and economic status, had to endure the unfaithfulness of their husbands. In her diary, Mary Boykin Chesnut blamed the system of slavery for producing infidelity among white men and "prostitution" among slave women:

> In slavery, we live surrounded by prostitutes. . . . God forgive us, but ours is a monstrous system, a wrong and an iniquity. Like the patriarchs of old, our men live in one house with their concubines; and the mulattoes one sees in every family partly resemble the white children. Any lady is ready to tell you who is the father of all the mulatto children in everybody's household but her own. Those she seems to think, drop from the clouds. My disgust sometimes is boiling over.[15]

White women's frustrations with the racist patriarchy under which they lived often had dire consequences for slave women, particularly for female houseslaves, who lived under the constant threat of sexual imposition.[16]

The strength and complexity of negative sexual imagery about black women, however sexist, gave the idea of "true womanhood" deep significance, racial as well as sexual, for free blacks. Acceptance of these notions reflected an understandable desire to erase the stereotypes that had been developed to justify their subjugation and to attain a sense of independence. But by championing for themselves "ideal" roles and stereotypes that supposedly characterized "free" women and men, free black men and women found themselves trading one set of stereotypes for another.

The effort to recast the image of black womanhood and foster separate sex roles for men and women is reflected in the speeches and writings of free blacks of both sexes. Contemporary black newspapers, such as the *Colored American, Freedom's Journal,* the *Weekly Advocate,* and the *North Star,* served as a primary means of communication between black leaders and the community. They described the women of their race in terms usually used to represent middle-class white women. When black abolitionist Robert Banks addressed the Colored Female Dorcas Society of Buffalo, he emphasized women's ability to exert either good or evil: "Well it may be said, there is no place under the broad canopy of heaven, no condition, situation, or circumstance, into which female influence may not enter, enter for good or evil, a blessing or a curse."[18] One contributor to the *Weekly Advocate*, known only as "Philo," claimed that women were particularly suited to reform activities: "Their perceptions are quicker, their love stronger, their power of endurance and sacrifice superior, and their will, as a general thing, unchangeable."[19]

In addition, writers frequently advised black women of their domestic responsibilities and the positive influence of women's "nature" within the home. One writer noted in 1827 that a female presence comforted him when he encountered racism:

> When race prejudice had barred the door of every honorable employment against me, and slander too held up her hideous finger; when I wished that I had not been born, or that I could retire from a world of wrongs, and end my days far from the white man's scorn; the kind attention of a woman, were capable of conveying a secret charm, a silent consolation to my mind. Oh! nothing can render the

bowers of retirement so serene and comfortable, or can so sweetly soften all our woes, as a conviction that woman is not indifferent to our fate.[20]

Samuel Cornish, black Presbyterian minister and editor of *Freedom's Journal*, published several essays on women's character and proper behavior. In "Female Temper," he asserted that women, more than men, risked their respectability if they lost their tempers:

> It is particularly necessary for girls to acquire command of their temper. . . . A man, in a furious passion, is terrible to his enemies; but a woman, in a passion, is disgusting to her friends; she loses all that respect due to her sex; she has not masculine strength and courage to enforce any other kind of respect. . . . The happiness and influence of women, both as wives and mothers, and indeed, in every relation so much depends on the temper, that it ought to be most carefully cultivated.[21]

Other black leaders expressed similar sentiments. Frederick Douglass, in his newspaper, the *North Star,* warned young women to avoid coquettishness: "There is certainly something in the ordinance of human affairs, in the organization of society, which demands from the female sex the highest tone of purity and strictest observance of duties pertaining to woman's sphere."[22] Philip A. Bell, a black abolitionist who migrated from Boston to San Francisco in the 1850s, where he wrote for the *Pacific Appeal,* denounced women who failed to act like ladies: "Gallantry would induce me to notice the lady first, but when a female so far deviates from that strict line of propriety which characterizes the woman of correct principles, as to indulge in slang phrases and low personalities, she must not expect to be treated with that courtesy which is universally paid to ladies."[23] Editors of the *Colored American* even remonstrated a group of black women in New York who had participated in an attempt to rescue fugitive slaves from prosecution, urging the women's husbands to control their wives: "Everlasting shame and remorse seize upon those females that so degraded themselves yesterday. We beg their husbands to keep them at home and find some better occupation for them."[24] Despite such criticism, black women continued to use physical force in order to seek justice, as in a widely publicized incident in Boston in 1847, when a group of women bodily removed a slave catcher from a neighbor's home. Nancy Prince, who had joined in the struggle, apparently had recognized the man as a "kidnapper" and, "with the assistance of the colored women that had accompanied her, had dragged him to the door and thrust him out of the house." The crowd of mostly women and children then chased the man down the street, "their numbers constantly increasing."[25]

Although a number of black spokesmen clearly held to rather strict standards of female propriety, concern for the advancement of the race precluded complete opposition to the participation of women in business and politics. In white society, ideals of true women's "character" as tender, delicate, and morally superior translated into the supposed incapability of women to govern or run businesses. Although some black men may also have made this connection, the lives of women such as Grace Douglass, Jane Chester, Harriet Hayden, and Nancy Remond and her daughters, in the context of the goals of black abolition, contradicted the assumption that women were unsuited to such activities. The lives of black female activists illustrates that participation in public activities and displaying "ladylike" behavior, especially toward the men of their race, were not necessarily incompatible.

Sometimes, women submitted essays on the proper behavior of women, such as black educator Mary Still, who published her "Appeal to the females of the African Methodist Episcopal Church" in 1857:

> The moral or degraded condition of society depends solely upon the influence of woman, if she be virtuous, pious and industrious, her feet abiding in her own house, ruleing her family as well. Such a woman is like a tree planted by the river side, whose leaves are evergreen; she extends in her neighborhood a healthy influence, and all men calleth her blessed. But if unhappily she should be the reverse, loud, clamorous, her feet wandering from the path of virtue, neglecting to rule her family, then indeed is the demorelizing effort of a bad influence felt in all avenues of her life.[26]

Sometimes, apparently, male authors may have signed women's names to their writing, as may be the case with "Ellen," a "young woman" who wrote that she overcame her reluctance to appear in the "public press": "There is a delicacy in a young and unknown female writing for the public press, which nought but my anxiety for the elevation of my people, and the improvement of my sex, together with the importance of the subject, could induce me to overcome." "Ellen" asserted that women possessed the capability of exercising either a positive or negative influence on men, but that the proper way for women to use their influence was at "the domestic fireside"; where "she can show her power over the lords of creation—there she can shine her true glory." In the home, female influence can "mould the character of man, and direct his mind into what should be its proper channel."[27]

In an article for *Freedom's Journal* on "Female Scandal," "Maria" chastised women for gossiping and expressed her conviction that women possessed the power either to destroy or to maintain stability and happiness: "It is a shame to think that woman, who is considered the emblem of tenderness and mercy, is constantly employed in endeavoring to destroy the peace and happiness of others. No music sounds so melodious to the ears of the *scandal monger* as the story of a friend's errors. . . ."[28] The adoption of dominant views on "respectable" women, however, extended beyond comments on women's nature to the actual roles they were supposed to play in both the family and the community. As in white society, public and private schools in the black community played an important role in preparing girls and boys for the responsibilities respectable men and women were supposed to shoulder.[29]

Since the end of the War for Independence, both blacks and whites had established schools for black children and adults living in northern towns. The Revolutionary ideology of equality and freedom, as well as the declining profitability of slavery in the North, had induced many northern slaveholders to free their slaves under new state manumission laws; leading white men believed that newly freed slaves were inadequately prepared to handle freedom and in need of guidance of whites to acquire basic middle-class values: thrift, sobriety, and hard work. Manumission societies made the earliest attempts to start public schools for blacks: the New York Manumission Society established the first such school, serving black children and adults, in the 1780s. In 1787, members of the society opened the African Free School for free blacks and slave children, which adhered to goals of moral training similar to those of white schools of the period, "in hopes that by an early attention to their morals . . . [students] may be kept from vicious courses and qualified for usefulness in life"[30] Forty-three years later, the goals of the school were still to teach black children "usefulness and respectability."[31] White teachers and administrators, however good their intentions, were not devoid of racist attitudes, and during the 1830s, black parents lost confidence in one energetic white proponent of black education, Charles Andrews, white principal of the African Free School on Mulberry Street. Many parents withdrew their children from the school after Andrews allegedly reproached a young student for calling a black man a "gentleman."[32]

Some teachers in public and private schools educated black boys and girls together in the same school but others taught them separately, in single-sex schools. At least three sexually integrated schools existed in New York City by 1827. An evening school, probably under the auspices of the Manumission Society, existed for "persons of color" in the African School on Mulberry Street. A school on Roosevelt Street was established by the African Mutual Instruction Society "for the instruction of Colored Adults of both Sexes." In 1828, a B. F. Hughes established a private school "for Coloured Children of both sexes," and in 1830, a Mrs. Williams opened a school for blacks in Boston that instructed "adults and young persons of both Sexes." In Cincinnati, a Mr. Bacon opened a Colored Infant School in order "to prepare the black population for future usefulness."[33]

Some black girls and women attended schools for females. In February 1828, for example, the New York Manumission Society established an all-male African Free School on Mulberry Street and an all-female school on William Street. The following August, the trustees set up another black female school for "girls living in the upper parts of the city."[34] The desire to maintain separate schools for the sexes suggests that, in this instance, at least, white community leaders were more concerned with following the tradition of sex-segregated schools that paralleled white schools than with the convenience of allowing black girls to mix with boys in a school that already existed.

Such schools, many of which were operated by whites, sprang up in northern cities throughout the 1830s. In Boston, several white teachers opened private schools for black children. In March 1834, "two white teachers" opened a "new school for colored females"; one month later, a school "kept by a white lady" opened on Vine Street "for the instruction of Colored Females in spelling, reading, writing, and needlework, &c." A group of subscribers to *The Liberator* proposed the establishment of a "private school for colored youth" at the West Centre Street Chapel.[35]

Several male and female abolitionists encouraged abolition societies to promote the education of black women. In 1834, Samuel Cornish, who helped edit the *Colored American,* argued in the AAS's first annual report that education of black women was essential to the cause: "Every measure for the thorough and proper education of [black] females is a blow aimed directly at slavery."[36] Education for black women as well as men constituted a form of overt resistance to racist practices, for at the time that Cornish made this observation, it was still illegal to teach slaves to read and write. Lucy B. Williams, who may have been black, and white leader Samuel J. May, both of Boston, wrote to Lucretia Mott, a leading white abolitionist of Philadelphia, urging the female antislavery societies to support black female education:

> It has occurred to me that while the leading object of Female Antislavery Societies should be the same as the National Society i.e. to enlighten the public mind and awaken the public feeling—they might regard it as one of their specific purposes to encourage and assist those ladies in different parts of the country who may be devoted or willing to devote themselves to the education of colored females.[37]

The purpose of educating boys and girls differed, regardless of whether or not they learned the same subjects. In 1839, Samuel Cornish expressed typical expectations of female education: "We expect our females to be educated and refined; to possess all the attributes which constitute the lady."[38] In some schools, black girls and boys learned reading, writing, arithmetic, English grammar, and history.[39] Other schools provided girls with additional instruction in domestic skills, while boys received preparatory training for trades. At the African Free School for girls, the students were taught sewing and knitting in addition to academic subjects. For boys, formal education was intended to prepare them for their future roles as heads of households, in which they controlled the family finances, to train them as learned "gentlemen" in their own communities, and to prepare them for the few professions that did not exclude them, such as the ministry. For girls, however, "book learning" prepared them for lives as educators of their children and as interesting companions for their husbands.

A contributor to *Freedom's Journal,* signed "Matilda," submitted an essay in which she championed Black women's rights to education and argued on behalf of their efforts to use their education for more than "fathoming a dish kettle":

> The influence that we have over the male sex demands, that our minds should be instructed and improved with the principles of education and religion, in order that this influence be properly directed. Ignorant ourselves, how can we be expected to form the minds of our youth, and conduct them in the paths of knowledge?[40]

"Matilda" also revealed her own perspective on the obstacles that racism had placed in the path of black women, noting that white women clearly had an advantage over black women: "We possess not the advantages with those of our sex whose skins are not coloured like our own, but we can improve what little we have, and make our one talent produce two-fold."[41]

While any education for girls, however rudimentary, helped prepare them for their eventual role as teachers of their children, training in domestic skills prepared them for lives as efficient housewives. Black abolitionist leader Charles B. Ray expressed typical expectations of female education in the *Colored American* in 1837: "Daughters are destined to be wives and mothers—they should, therefore, be taught to know how to manage a house, and govern and instruct children. Without this knowledge, they would be lost, and as mothers destracted, their homes would be in disorder, and their children would grow up loose and without character."[42] In 1848, Frederick Douglass similarly argued that domestic training was essential to female education:

> A knowledge of domestic affairs, in all their relations, is desirable—nay, essential, to the complete education of every female. . . . A well regulated household, in every station of society, is one of woman's brightest ornaments—a source of happiness to her and to those who are dependent upon her labors of love for the attractions of home and its endearments.[43]

Samuel Cornish praised the efforts of white teacher Prudence Crandall, who had defied hostile whites in Canterbury, Connecticut, by admitting black women into her school and daring "to teach them, as if they were white—to treat them with the same delicacy and respect which an instructress is expected to extend to young ladies in good society."[44] Crandall, in 1832, had admitted a young black student, Sarah Harris, into her exclusive Female Boarding School in the small town of Canterbury, as a day student. Parents of many of the white students had demanded Harris's removal, and when Crandall refused, her white students withdrew. Crandall then announced the opening of a new school for "Young Ladies and Little Misses of Color." Her students came from New York, Providence, and Boston, as well as from Connecticut, and one of them was Elizabeth Douglass Bustill, a cousin of Sarah Douglass.[45] Whites in Canterbury harassed both Crandall and her black students. The state legislature passed a law the following year prohibiting the teaching of blacks from out of state without permission from local authorities.[46]

But despite efforts by educators of both races to provide schooling for free blacks, their accomplishments had by no means reached Cornish's expectations for black education. The ultimate failure of Crandall's attempts at racial integration, as well as the inadequate facilities generally available for black pupils, led a disheartened Cornish to express his dismay at the state of education for black women: "we fail to provide the means whereby they can acquire an education which will fit them to become wives of an enlightened mechanic, a store keeper, or a clerk."[47]

Unlike black men, black women found that whatever education they did receive served a dual purpose, preparing them not only for lives as knowledgeable and efficient wives and mothers but also providing practical training for employment. More often than middle-class white women, black women used their domestic training to earn a wage. Economic necessity in many antebellum urban black families required wives and daughters to contribute to the economic survival of the family in addition to fulfilling their domestic responsibilities.[48] Because most black men were barred from skilled labor, and thus forced to work in low-paying menial occupations, they could not live up to their prescribed role as sole provider, which prevented their wives and daughters from living as "ladies of leisure."

Young black men frequently found avenues of employment closed to them regardless of how long they had attended school or how well they had performed. Charles C. Andrews reported that even after spending several years in school, they were "doomed to encounter as much prejudice and contempt, as if he were not only destitute of that education . . . but as if he were incapable of receiving it." Even industrial education did not substantially improve their job prospects, despite cries for practical education by black leaders such as Martin Delany and Frederick Douglass during the 1840s and 1850s. Andrews reported the case of a seventeen-year-old black youth who could not secure employment in his trade as a blacksmith. After leaving the Mulberry Street school "with a respectable education, and an irreproachable character," he found he could not complete an apprenticeship, that "every place that appeared suitable to his object, was closed to him, because he was black!"[49] Limited job opportunities even for well-educated and trained black men often forced them to look far from home for work; as a result, many young black men, especially those living in port cities, looked to the sea for excitement and employment as sailors, servants, and cooks.[50] In some instances, however, black men found jobs as carpenters, masons, barbers, waiters, well-placed domestic servants, ministers, and educators.[51]

Free black women usually found employment within the proximity of their homes, primarily because of the high demand for cheap domestic labor. They earned wages in various forms of domestic-related work, perhaps most commonly as servants in the homes of white families, or else in their homes, taking in laundry and mending.[52] According to one report on the free black community in Philadelphia in 1795, most black women worked as laundresses: "The Women generally, both married and single wash clothes for a livelihood."[53] Forty-two years later, the situation had changed little: a *Statistical Inquiry* for the city in 1837 listed the following occupation as most common for 4,249 black women: washer women, needle women (dressmakers, seamstresses, tailoresses, milliners), cooks, "occupied at home," day work, and live-in servants for families. "Raggers and Boners" occupied the bottom of the list. Listed separately were occupations that were probably considered professional or skilled work, including keepers of "boarding houses and oyster houses," school mistresses, cake bakers, white washers, hucksters, confectioners, mat-makers, shopkeepers, and carpet makers.[54]

The life of ex-slave Chloe Spear (1750–1815) illustrates the heavy burdens many black women shouldered. A memoir of Spear, by a "Lady of Boston," described her life as a freedwoman:

> After returning from a hard day's work, she many a time went to washing for her customers in the night, while her husband was taking his rest—extended clothes lines across her room, and hung

> up her clothes to dry, while she retired to bed for a few hours; then arose, prepared breakfast and went out to work again, leaving her ironing to be done on her return at night. Cesar [her husband] having been accustomed to cooking, & could, on these occasions, wait upon himself and boarders, during her absence; but was quite willing that she make ready a good supper, after she came home.[55]

As Spear's experience suggests, most free black women still shouldered women's traditional domestic responsibilities in addition to earning a wage. One free black woman, for example, refused to marry at all, knowing that she would have to fulfill family responsibilities in addition to her work as a weaver. She declared that marriage "involved such a WASTE OF TIME!"[56]

Advertisements in black and white abolitionist newspapers indicate that many black women in northern cities turned their household chores into private businesses. In New York, a Mrs. Sarah Johnson of 551 Pearl Street advertised her services in *Freedom's Journal* in 1828 as a seamstress and hat mender, announcing to her "friends and the Public" that she had opened a business in "Bleaching, Pressing, and Refitting Leghorn and Straw Hats in the best manner" and in dressmaking and "Plain Sewing." In the 1840s, Nancy Prince continued the business she had begun in Russia when she announced in *The Liberator* the opening of her seamstress service, "where she will attend to dress and cloak-making, pantaloon-making, etc." Grace Douglass's hat shop on Arch Street in Philadelphia was important to the family income until her death. Such enterprises were often quite profitable, as the experiences of Grace Douglass, Nancy Prince, and the Remond women attest. Martin Delany reported in 1848 that several women operated successful seamstress businesses in Pittsburgh.[57]

Evident in some of these advertisements was consciousness about standards of propriety within the free black community, especially with respect to women who ran boardinghouses out of their own homes. Proprietors often made a point of welcoming "respectable" blacks in the community, perhaps to distinguish their establishments from houses of ill-repute. For example, in 1828 Gracy Jones of 88 South Fourth Street in Philadelphia opened a boardinghouse "for the accommodation of genteel persons of colour," and Eliza Johnson of 28 Elizabeth Street established similar accommodations, describing her boardinghouse as "healthy and pleasant." In 1835, Amelia Shad advertised in *The Liberator* the opening of her boardinghouse "for Genteel Persons of Color who may visit Philadelphia" during one of the black abolitionist conventions.[58] Both Shad and Jones clearly wanted to attract a particular group of blacks to their establishments; their appeals to "genteel" or "respectable" black patrons may reflect a sort of class consciousness within the free black community.[59]

The application of domestic duties to community needs enabled many black women to survive financially and to avoid black men's problems with job competition and overt racial hostility over employment when they sought work outside the black community. Black women's work experience differed as well, of course, from that of middle-class white women, who did not need to earn a wage, but it was similar in many respects to that of poor white women. The fact that black women and poor white women worked for a wage tends to support the idea that both class and race were strong determinants in the formation of labor patterns in the United States.[60] Black women's need to work for wages, and the limited range of work open to them during the antebellum period were clear indications to many free blacks that they had not yet attained complete freedom.

Thus, black education, though carefully modeled on the white educational system, held a different meaning for black men and women once they reached adulthood. While it effected little direct improvement in the lives of black men, it had a significant impact on the lives of black women, despite its emphasis on unachievable expectations that the lives of black women might fit the dominant white model. Unlike middle-class white women, black women discovered that even after marriage they would continue to work for wages outside the home in addition to assuming family responsibilities.

Despite the economic realities, leaders in the free black community, many of whom commanded the black press and the ministry, continued to promote contemporary images of male and female roles. Black writers who concerned themselves with women's "proper" role in society asserted that women were expected to use their presumed power to influence men's lives by maintaining morality and virtue in the home and the community. During the 1820s and 1830s, some contributors to the black newspapers suggested that women should limit their activities to those considered acceptable for "respectable" women, believing that women could best exercise their influence in the community as supporters of male activities.

One such supportive activity that, despite the economic difficulties of most free black families was nonetheless considered an important part of black female activism, was fund-raising. Raising money to assist black institutions, such as the newspapers and the churches, must have been exceedingly difficult for these women who, in addition to soliciting funds from less well-to-do blacks must have undoubtedly relied to a great extent on donations from the more prosperous free black families. In Philadelphia, for example, black entrepreneurs such as James Forten, Richard Allen, and Cyrus Bustill were important benefactors in antislavery and community organizations.[61] In 1839, Cornish printed an editorial praising the women of several female societies in New York who had pledged financial assistance to the *Colored American:*

> To our warm hearted female friends, we also appeal. You can do much. Among your friends, around the social circle, for every object which inlists your sympathies, or to which you bend your energies, you can do more than our male friends. When woman lends her influence she will succeed. . . . We remember with gratitude how nobly two female Societies once assisted us; one in Buffalo, and the Ladies Literary Society in this city—be not now lukewarm.[62]

Black men encouraged the women of their race to participate in community activism, as part of their duty as women and as blacks. One writer included a separate report on women's contribution to the community in his review of the "Progress of the Colored People of San Francisco" in 1854: "We have a large number of respectable ladies here, and their influence is felt and acknowledged."[63]

But some men may have feared an increase in women's participation in public activities, as is suggested by several newspaper editorials in the 1830s. In an address to the Colored Female Dorcas Society of Buffalo, New York, Robert Banks emphasized to the women in the audience the importance of women's power to influence the behavior and character of men as well as to bestow "peace and comfort" in the home: "It is the female influence that polishes manners and elevates the mind of men. She is the ornament of his life, the kind protector of his peace and comfort, and her heart is the home of his affection and love."[64] In November 1838, Samuel Cornish devoted "a large space" in his newspaper to comments on "female character, influence, and eloquence." In an editorial, he made it clear that women should exercise their influence within the domestic sphere and engage in activities befitting "respectable" women, which included raising money to support male leadership activities. He expressed disapproval of "some of America's virtuous and talented daughters" who pursued "masculine views and measures" instead of serving as the "help-meet" of men:

> We are anxious that woman, lovely woman, should fill the whole of her important and truly elevated sphere. Let not an iota be taken from her influence, or curtailed from her appropriate efforts. Woman was created to be the "help-meet," and not the idol or slave of man; and in everything truly virtuous and noble, she is furnished by our bountiful Creator, with all the intellectual, moral and physical requisites for her important place.[65]

At the time that Cornish wrote this editorial, much furor had erupted within the clerical community about the activities of Sarah and Angelina Grimké. The two white southern-born women, who had moved north in the 1820s as converts to Quakerism and opponents of slavery, had embarked on an antislavery lecture tour in 1836. Public speaking, however, was deemed a male activity, and women who dared to deliver speeches, especially to mixed audiences, endured criticisms from those who believed they had stepped outside their assigned sphere. The Grimkés had sustained the brunt of criticism from the clergy, as well as from one prominent social reformer and proponent of women's "sphere," Catharine Beecher.[66] These critics asserted that the sisters had violated not only the standards of female propriety, but even the biblical teachings that instructed women to "keep silent."[67] Apparently, a number of black leaders either held similar convictions or did not consider women's rights a high priority; when the American Anti-Slavery Society split in 1840, Cornish and several black delegates sided with the faction that opposed a proposal to admit women as voting members in the national organization.

As indicated by the leading role of black clergymen in the movement and the community, black churches played a vital role in the lives of their congregants. Since Carter G. Woodson's history of the black church in the United States in 1921, several scholars have written institutional histories of the various Protestant denominations in the free black community, tracing the ways in which a distinct African-American religion evolved out of the slave experience. Black men and women had organized all-black churches as a means of administering to the needs of the free black community, as well as in response to exclusion from and discrimination in white churches. In addition to serving as worship places, church buildings provided schoolrooms, facilities for social and political events, and meeting places for benevolent societies and activities. During the antebellum period, black churches were especially valuable as refuges for fugitive slaves.

Few sermons that dealt specifically with the behavior and morality of church members have been preserved; most published sermons by black preachers dealt primarily with political issues, such as colonization and abolitionism. The records of individual churches, however, reveal a great deal about topics of particular concern to church leaders, such as supervising the manners and morals of their communicants and maintaining "proper" relations between husbands and wives. The Reverend Richard Allen, pastor of Mother Bethel A.M.E. Church in Philadelphia, in conjunction with the church committee, once "disowned" a woman who refused to "submit to her husband as a dutiful wife." In black Baptist churches, leaders expressed similar concerns and expelled members for failing to maintain harmonious marriages.[68]

The black church held special significance for women. The fact that the African Methodist Episcopal Church in Philadelphia was nicknamed "Mother Bethel" symbolized the piety that was supposed to be the special domain of women. Within the church hierarchy, most black women, like white women, functioned in supporting roles, though many women sat on committees that made important decisions regarding church policy. A handful of black women even assumed the position of minster, which was otherwise a male domain.[69] The Rev. J. W. C. Pennington argued against the ordination of women as preachers, on account of their supposed inferiority, maintaining that the ministry, like the army, navy, and "all the learned professions, where mighty thought and laborious investigation are needed," was clearly a masculine calling that "the weaker sex is incapacitated for, both physically and mentally." He questioned whether "the Church, that needs the most manly strength, the most gigantic minds to execute her labors, [should] confide them to those whom nature has fitted for the easier toils of life?"[70]

Although not all black preachers took such a conservative line, prescribed "female" roles determined acceptability of church activities for many black women, as for white women. Nevertheless, churches helped them move from the home into the public sphere. Church fund-raising activities were among the most acceptable and popular projects engaging free black women, who found that through such activity they acquired organizational experience that could be adapted to antislavery and community self-help activities. Like white women, black women throughout the free states participated in fund-raising fairs for their churches to purchase and maintain church property and liquidate debts. In 1837, for example, the female members of the African Methodist Episcopal Church in New York City held a fair at which they offered for sale "a general assortment of Fancy Articles, Dry Goods, Toys, Confectionary, &c." William Cornish served as the elder in charge of the event. The black female members of the Second Baptist Church in Columbus, Ohio, held a similar fair in 1844. In Boston, the women of the First Independent Baptist Female Society, auxiliary to the First Independent Baptist Church of the People of Color, sponsored a fair in May 1845 "for the purpose of liquidating a debt incurred by repairs on the meeting-house." Many of these women apparently divided their time between church-based projects and citywide activism, for most of the members of the fair committee also belonged to the racially integrated Boston Female Anti-Slavery Society.[71]

The most powerful institutions within the free black community—the press, the schools, and the churches—provided the greatest support for a gender ideology during the antebellum period. The acceptance of contemporary notions of male and female natures and separate sex roles as a measure of free status represented an attempt to destroy the stereotypes that slavery had engendered, but at the price of precluding a complete departure from oppressive stereotypes: free blacks traded one system of oppression for another. Black leaders seeking more positive images of blacks emphasized the necessity of training girls for their future roles as efficient managers of the household with "all the attributes which constitute the lady." Leaders such as Charles B. Ray, Samuel Cornish, and Frederick Douglass, as well as less well-known members of the community, stressed the special powers of women, their "secret charm" and ability to bestow "peace and comfort" in the home.

The economic realities underscored the contradictions in "true womanhood" ideology. But these ideas, no matter how unrealistic, were transmitted so strongly through black institutions that they helped define black women's participation in racial "uplift" activities. Although black leaders did not explicitly articulate a link between sex roles and a demonstration of free status, the institutions they established reflected their desire for such a demonstration, in addition to meeting everyday needs. In the process, these "positive" images undoubtedly helped build pride and self-confidence.

On a more practical level, women provided necessary services for their black neighbors. Popular images of womanhood bestowed upon them the responsibility for maintaining morality and stability in their households and extending their benevolent "nature" into the community at large. The local church provided the structure that enabled many women to organize charity and moral reform activities for the benefit of their neighbors, many of whom were fugitive slaves. Like white women, most free black women occupied a supportive, auxiliary status in social interaction with men, but when they had to, they defied the social prescriptions of femininity by taking a militant, even physical stand against injustice. Such activism was their duty, as well as their right, as free women.

3

Working for the Welfare of Our Race

In 1852, Frances Ellen Watkins Harper summed up the goals of black abolitionists: "The condition of our people, the wants of our children, and the welfare of our race demand the aid of every helping hand."[1] The same year that she wrote this passage from her home in York, Pennsylvania, a group of "colored inhabitants" in the Canadian settlement of Chatham, Ontario, passed a resolution describing black women's role in the abolitionist movement: "We regard female sympathy in the cause of freedom and humanity, to be of the most vital importance, and that we hereby most earnestly solicit the aid and cooperation of our sisters in the elevation of our race."[2] From the beginning of the movement, such a call for self-determination on the part of the black community and for the assistance of black women had been central to abolitionism.

In 1839, black leader Lewis Woodson provided specific instructions to young black men and women:

> . . . they would find that elegant language and polished manners would give them greater currency in society . . . and that a cultivated mind is of higher consideration than dollars and cents. They would cease to haunt our church doors and the corners of our streets, offending the moral sense of all who go in and out, or that pass by, and [instead] crowd into the lecture room or library; and instead of drinking grog or smoking tobacco, they would read the newspaper.[3]

Maria Miller Stewart had argued in 1832 that improved education for blacks would eventually force whites to abandon their race prejudice and recognize the "moral and intellectual improvement" of the free black community. William Still put forth a similar argument in 1854: "One thing is certain, and that is, our own education and elevation is to be one of the main levers to overthrow the institution of slavery in the United States."[4] Woodson, Stewart, and Still all held forth the hope that "elevating" the race would eliminate the prejudice they believed was the basis of enslavement and discrimination in the United States. But for them and many others, community activism would accomplish other goals as well: it was a form of protest and encouraged blacks to organize on the basis of race and provided the community with material as well as spiritual sustenance. Black women played a central role in this aspect of abolitionist activity.

Black men and women worked together to assist their neighbors. But women's work of the sort was especially valued, on the basis of prevailing gender expectations and contemporary ideas of Christian morality.[5] As one contributor to the *Weekly Advocate* told the "Females of Color" in 1837, their participation in community activism was essential: "In any enterprise for the improvement of our people—either moral or mental, our hands would be palsied without women's influence. We ask then for the exertion of her influence. It is now needed."[6]

Churches were important avenues through which black women could participate in community benevolent and reform enterprises, providing the structure as well as necessary financial and spiritual support. In addition to reinforcing and justifying beliefs in women's potential for moral superiority and obligation to improving the condition of their community, religious doctrine also enabled them to carry out their roles as Christian women. In a larger context, black church women committed themselves to helping the materially and spiritually poor, regardless of race.[7]

Both black and white abolitionists believed that one of the basic ways to improve the free black community was through education. In a letter to black leader John B. Vashon in 1832, William Lloyd Garrison wrote of his enthusiasm for education in a patronizing yet supportive tone:

> Nothing encourages me more than to witness such unanimity, and efforts for mutual improvement, among my free colored brethren. True, they have not yet fully aroused to the importance of aiming at

> high intellectual and moral attainment; but they have accomplished much in a short time, and are evidently making rapid strides to respectability and knowledge.[8]

Education was central to the community work of many black women. Their own education had trained them to accept their domestic role in the family and in the community. A number of them worked collectively to encourage blacks to enroll in the local schools; some became teachers, and some also organized intellectual societies for their own improvement. Of course, their contemporaries expected them to conduct their educational efforts according to prevailing standards of female propriety, so when their work involved cooperation with black men they usually assumed a supportive role by forming auxiliaries to male organizations. In New York City, twelve black women met in 1838 to form an auxiliary to the men's committee "for the purpose of adopting some measures for the further encouragement of education among our people, and especially securing a more numerous and punctual attendance of colored children at the public schools." Black abolitionist and cleric Stephan Gloucester remarked that the men's committee had called upon "the cooperation and the influence of women" to ensure the attainment of their goals.[9] Another group of black women had formed the Female Education Society under the sponsorship of the Reverend Theodore Wright's Presbyterian church in New York, the purpose of which was to raise money to send poor young black men to college.[10] The women who headed the organization perceived their activities not only as a way to promote education but also as a contribution to the general welfare of the black community.[11]

To pursue their own education, many black women organized female intellectual societies, which existed independently from men's literary societies. While men's intellectual societies stressed the development of debating, reading, composition, and scientific skills, female societies encouraged members to improve their minds in order that they might fulfill their female responsibilities.[12] In 1831 a group of black women in Philadelphia formed the Female Literary Association for "the mental improvement of females." At the suggestion of Simeon Jocelyn, a leading white minister, "respectable colored females" in Philadelphia organized regular meetings at the homes of individual members, at which antislavery was regularly discussed. This group, which was formed one year before the Philadelphia Female Anti-Slavery Society, promoted not only the education of its members but antislavery, as an important component of its work. The Association literary collection included books and pamphlets on antislavery.

At their "Mental Feasts," members of the Association engaged in "moral and religious meditation, conversation, reading and speaking, sympathising over the fate of the unhappy slave, improving their own minds, &c. &c."[13] Sarah Douglass, who served as secretary, wrote to Garrison and Isaac Knapp of *The Liberator* requesting a copy of Garrison's *Thoughts on Colonization* for five dollars and presenting an update on the status of the Association: "Our association is increasing in number and usefulness."[14]

In 1832, black women in Boston organized the Afric-American Female Intelligence Society, with a preamble to its constitution that reflected the moral nature of the commitment of these "women of color" to female education:

> Whereas the subscribers, women of color, of the Commonwealth of Massachusetts, actuated by a natural feeling for the welfare of our friends, have thought fit to associate for the diffusion of knowledge, the suppression of vice and immorality, and for cherishing such virtues as will render us happy and useful to society, sensible of the gross ignorance under which we have long labored.[15]

At one "Mental Feast" in 1832, "an accomplished young colored lady" delivered an address in which she emphasized women's special responsibilities: "How important is the occasion for which we have assembled ourselves together this evening, to hold a feast, to feed our never dying-minds, to excite each other to deeds of mercy, words of peace."[16] Her comment suggests that black women viewed their own education as a way of helping each other live up to expectations of women's piety, and that intellectual gatherings such as "Mental Feasts" provided them with the opportunity to put this virtue to work by encouraging the performance of "deeds of mercy."

Leading white abolitionists gave whole-hearted support to black women who organized these societies. Benjamin Lundy, editor of the *Genius of Universal Emancipation*, praised the initiative "among our colored sisters" and wished the black women of Boston and Philadelphia "success and a long career of usefulness," adding that "our Afric-American sisters are becoming more sensible of the value of mental cultivation, and are exerting themselves to procure it."[17] Garrison commended the Philadelphia women who established the Female Literary Association and said he would refer to it when arguing against assumptions about black inferiority. In a letter to Sarah Douglass, Garrison noted that black women were important agents of socialization: "The formation of this Society is a source of unspeakable satisfaction to my mind. . . . It puts a new weapon into my hands to use against southern oppressors. . . . My hopes for the elevation of your race are mainly centered upon you and others of your sex. To you are committed, if not the destinies of the present, certainly those of the rising generation."[18]

Abraham Shadd noted in 1833 that though women led the drive to organize black intellectual societies, many of them accepted members of both sexes. One "Colored Female" observed in *The Liberator* in 1834 that the Female Minerverian Association to which she belonged was "not confined to any particular class or sex." The stated purpose of the group, however, seemed particularly geared to its female members: to "improve the mental condition of all who feel disposed to participate in the knowledge of piety," as well as "truth and justice," in the hope that, as a result of the organization's efforts, "pride and prejudice" would "ere long cease."[19]

Schoolteaching sometimes became a livelihood for black women, as well as a way to promote education, and during the thirty years before the Civil War several black women became well known as educators in their communities. Maria Miller Stewart, Sarah M. Douglass, Susan Paul, Mary Bibb, and Mary Ann Shadd Cary divided their time between teaching and participation in antislavery societies and community improvement projects. As teachers they were expected to support the ideals of black education and contemporary society by behaving like "ladies."

Black women abolitionists who conformed to expectations of female humility and participated in activities that extended but did not challenge their domestic roles received unequivocal praise from abolitionist leaders. Sarah Douglass was noted for teaching the "higher branches" of knowledge and emphasizing domestic skills in her school for young black women in Philadelphia. In the process, she trained many of the public-school teachers in Philadelphia. When Samuel Cornish, whose dissatisfaction with the general state of black education was well-known, visited Douglass's school in 1837 he estimated that more than forty women attended and he praised Douglass for selecting students "from our best families, where their morals and manners are equally subjects of care and deep interest." Whether or not Douglass's students actually came from the "best families" in the black community, Cornish's comment perhaps reflects concern for instilling the "morals and manners" befitting the higher classes. He was also pleased with the curriculum Douglass offered her female students, describing the courses as "good and solid," which "together with many of the more ornamental sciences, [are] calculated to expand the youthful mind, refine the taste, and assist in purifying the heart."[20]

In addition to her teaching and administrative responsibilities, Douglass also delivered guest lectures on a variety of subjects, many of which reflected concern for women's domestic responsibilities. Her address in 1859 to a group of women in Philadelphia on "Anatomy, Physiology and Hygiene" was especially well received. A male writer for the *Weekly Anglo-African* referred to women's family obligations in praising Douglass's presentation:

> It is very generally acknowledged, that an acquaintance with the structure and offices of the human system, is necessary to those whose especial duty it is to protect the health of the young; they who argue that such knowledge is inconsistent with the delicacy of woman's character, can never have realized that the human frame is the work of the same All-wise and Holy Being, who endowed woman with her pure and refined nature.[21]

In 1898, sixteen years after Douglass's death, a group of former abolitionists wrote a "Tribute of Respect," referring to her as "one who has long and faithfully served in the elevation and culture of a race and as a pioneer of education among her people in Philadelphia."[22]

Susan Paul's primary school for black children combined general education with religious instruction. She also organized the Garrison Junior Choir, named after the abolitionist leader, and was best known for holding annual public programs to demonstrate the talents of her students. In 1834 she organized her first "Juvenile Concert," which featured her pupils at the Primary School No. 6 in Boston. The program featured songs about the school, such as "In school we learn," and music that reflected the students' religious training, such as "Suffer little children to come unto us."[23]

Paul's efforts enjoyed the support of Boston abolitionists who advertised her concerts and sold tickets for twenty-five cents. Garrison noted in *The Liberator* in 1834 that the programs had "a powerful tendency to beget sympathy, to excite admiration, and to destroy prejudice."[24] James Loring, a white abolitionist, and James G. Barbadoes, a black abolitionist, were in charge of ticket sales at the office of *The Liberator*.

Teaching, however, proved financially unrewarding for most black women, especially for those who established private schools, and even teachers from middle-class black families struggled financially. Motivated by their desire to improve educational opportunities for blacks as well as to support their own families, they worked constantly to keep their schools open. By the 1840s, Douglass's teaching became vital to her family's survival after her mother's death. Paul's family also relied on her income as a teacher after her father died: Paul supported, in addition to her elderly mother, four nieces and nephews. Lydia Maria Child, a leading white abolitionist, once noted that Paul's job as a schoolteacher was apparently not enough to keep the family afloat, for she also worked as a seamstress in her spare time: "For several years she [Paul] has taught a primary school, the proceeds of which have supported her and a widowed mother. . . . The few hours when she is not in school are diligently employed in sewing for their support."[25]

Teachers often turned to religious organizations or antislavery societies for financial help. Sarah Douglass's affiliation with the racially integrated Philadelphia Female Anti-Slavery Society enabled her to obtain financial aid from its parent association, the Pennsylvania Abolition Society, when financial difficulties nearly forced her to close the school during the 1830s. The Philadelphia Female Anti-Slavery Society also contributed regularly to her school.

Neither Paul nor Douglass, in their careers as educators, challenged the authority of men or engaged in "unfeminine" activities. As a result, they consistently received praise and encouragement from male abolitionist leaders. Women who acted aggressively and participated in "male" activities sometimes met with scorn from male colleagues, as was the case when Mary Ann Shadd Cary made her commitment to black education and self-sufficiency a hotly disputed political issue in the free black community in Windsor, Ontario.

Mary Ann Shadd had arrived in Windsor in the winter of 1851, optimistic about the chance to teach and work with the emigrationists.

Runaway slaves and free blacks had sought refuge in Canada since the 1810s, but the passage of the Fugitive Slave Act in 1850, which made it a federal crime to assist escaped slaves, intensified the frustration that had been building for at least a decade among black abolitionists and created a heightened sense of urgency for the safety of all blacks living in the United States. Between 1850 and 1860 the black population in the Canadian provinces rose from approximately forty thousand to sixty thousand.[26]

Ex-slaves Mary and Henry Bibb, who had helped establish the Windsor settlement the year before Shadd arrived, were among many black activists who considered Garrison's policy of "moral suasion" a failure and who resented the racism and myopia of white abolitionists in the United States. Shadd had agreed with the Bibbs that education was vital to the new community, but she disagreed about the types of schools needed and the source of financial assistance to keep the schools open. Part of the conflict involved the issue of integration and separatism, but it quickly became a personal feud that would last until Henry Bibb's death in 1854.

While the Bibbs favored government-sponsored schools for blacks, Shadd favored private schools that made no color distinctions. In 1851, the Bibbs exercised their right under Canadian law to petition the government for segregated schools, a decision probably based on financial contraints as well as a desire to build an independent community. Their own experience with the hardships of running private schools probably convinced the Bibbs that their schools could sustain themselves only with government assistance.

Mary Bibb was an experienced teacher who had graduated from the Normal School in Albany, New York. Born Mary Elizabeth Miles in Boston, she taught school in Massachusetts, Philadelphia, and Cincinnati, Ohio. She met her future husband in 1847 and married him a year later. After arriving in Canada in 1850, Mary Bibb had opened a small school for fugitive slave children in her home. Within a year, increased enrollment forced her to move her students to a nearby schoolroom, and she soon encountered financial problems. In February 1851, she reported that though enrollment in both her "day school" and the Sunday school had increased, the physical condition of the schoolrooms, the Canadian weather, and the absence of adequate supplies were grim realities: "The day school in this place has increased from twelve to forty-six, notwithstanding the embarrassing circumstances under which it started, namely, a dark, ill-ventilated room, uncomfortable seats, want of desks, books and all sorts of school apparatus." She reported similar problems with a new Sunday school class: "We commenced a Sunday-school four weeks ago; present, thirty-six; there are now forty members, and much interest is manifested both by parents and children, some coming in inclement weather the distance of two or three miles. We are entirely destitute of bibles, there being four testaments in the school, one of these being minus several chapters.[27]

Within a few months, she clearly felt a financial bind. In April she reported that most of her pupils had quit school after the winter term to hire themselves out to farmers for the spring and summer. Bibb complained publicly that the parents whose children had attended that winter had failed to pay her salary, adding that she would have accepted partial payment, "but even this has not yet been given."[28] The Bibbs must have been suffering at home as a result of the non-payment of school fees, for in addition to supporting themselves, they often sheltered several fugitive slaves in their home. In 1852, Mary Bibb reported in *The Liberator* that within ten days, they had given shelter to twenty-three fugitives.[29]

During Shadd's first year in Canada, she wrote to George Whipple, secretary of the American Missionary Association, that Windsor was "by universal consent, the most destitute community of colored people." In Sandwich, a small village south of Windsor, according to Shadd, "the school . . . though a government affair, does not afford apparatus nor anything for instruction, nor support to the teacher; the very trifling sum to be paid by parents is not furnished, and they even express the inability to provide firewood."[30]

The poor condition of black public schools in Canada convinced Shadd that the Canadian government could not be counted on for help in the building of their settlements. Mary Bibb had eventually sought aid from organizations in the United States, such as the American Missionary Association, when the Canadian government had refused financial assistance to the fugitive slave communities in its provinces. Throughout the 1850s, Shadd argued that though both white and black parents paid taxes to Canadian public schools, white leaders in the boroughs used the money for good schools for the white children, while black schools remained shabby and lacking in supplies. The black inhabitants of St. Catharine, Shadd reported in 1855, were "debarred equal school privileges."[31]

The following year, she wrote in the *Provincial Freeman* that in Canadian boroughs "large and handsome school houses are erected for the children of the whites, while but a single miserable contracted wooden building is set apart for the children of the colored taxpayers of the entire town." She also pointed out that the children who attended these schools often traveled far from their homes to the nearest black school, which usually employed only one black teacher. Consequently, black children had little hope of advancing their education: "The children of this Colored School, are not promoted to the Grammar (white) School, neither are they led to hope that they might be." She expressed outrage that more prosperous black Canadians paid for private instruction, as well as paying their taxes, in order to obtain a good education for their children.[32]

The Bibbs' proposal for the construction of a "colored government school" for blacks met with strong disapproval from Shadd. Although she was a staunch emigrationist and supporter of black unity, she opposed segregated or "caste" schools. As she wrote to Whipple in 1851, "I beg you will not consider my effort here, an attempt to encourage the spirit of caste. I am utterly opposed to such a thing, under any circumstances." Shadd's opposition to black separatism, as she told Whipple, led her to break with the A.M.E. church "because of its distinctive character." In her eyes, black support for racially separated schools would only perpetuate the custom of segregation that had kept blacks subordinate for three centuries, and public "caste" schools undermined self-sufficiency among blacks. Thus, she opposed the Bibbs' petition for government aid.

Shadd even hesitated to accept a grant from the AMA to finance private schools, fearing that once black parents knew of such a donation, they would stop paying altogether. She knew the schools needed outside funding and finally accepted the grant, but when she tried to delay informing the black community, Henry Bibb publicized the AMA's donation in his newspaper. Bibb later defended his action:

> We heard her say that she was receiving 'three york shillings, from each of her pupils,' which sum was not enough to support her from about 29 children and after we learned that the above society [AMA] had granted her the sum of $125, we thought that they did well, and we even used to give publicity to the fact, for the encouragement of our people in Windsor as they were entirely ignorant of it to that time . . . and not knowing that she wished this information kept from the parents of the children, we gave publicity to it.[34]

Mary Ann Shadd was only twenty-eight years old when she emigrated to Canada, but she had quickly gained the respect of black Canadians, even of those who disliked and, perhaps, feared her. Amid the controversy with the Bibbs, who were acknowledged as the community's founding leaders, Shadd had her supporters. One observer noted that in the face of attacks by the Bibbs, Shadd "continues to enjoy the confidence of the entire Canadian population of Windsor, if we except the editors of the *Voice*, with their wives and even they respect her as much as they fear her."[35]

What had begun as a disagreement over schools, however, degenerated into a personal feud between Shadd and the Bibbs, which quickly came to the attention of the American Missionary Association. In a series of letters to Whipple, Shadd put forth her version of the events. In 1852, she wrote: "I am not at all surprised that your attention should be called to my Case, indeed the many assertions made by Mr. and Mrs. Bibb, publicly and privately, at my being 'nearly down now' with the certainty of a still more dishonorable position . . . made their dishonorable actions . . . in supplying Rev. C. C. Foote with falsehoods. . . ." According to Shadd, the Bibbs "make my residence here an impossibility too apparent." She insisted that Bibb was "a dishonest man, and as such must be known to the world."[36] She also had rather unkind words for Mary Bibb, whom she described to Whipple, in a letter probably written in the heat of the moment, as "a *profane* swearer and drug taking woman," even though her scholarly qualifications were good enough to teach school.[37] Early in the controversy, Shadd lamented to Whipple that even though the AMA had employed her to teach for only one year, she would like to teach five, "if God's willing that I live so long, but the vicinity of Henry Bibb and Wife, will ever be a hindrance to both teachers and preachers stationed here."[38] The next year, she wrote that "Henry Bibb says he could see me dead and in Hell."[39]

Shadd's opposition to the Bibbs was no secret. In 1852 she had helped publish the *Provincial Freeman*, originally founded by Samuel Ringgold Ward, which rivaled Henry Bibb's *Voice of the Fugitive*. In her newspaper Shadd objected to nearly all of the projects the Bibbs promoted among Canadian blacks, displaying a willingness to challenge male leaders that was considered unseemly for a respectable woman, as Henry Bibb himself observed in his newspaper: "Miss Shadd has said and writes many things we think will add nothing to her credit as a lady."[40] Bibb's language indicates that he may have looked upon Shadd not simply as another

The only known photograph of Mary Ann Shadd Cary—writer, lecturer, emigrationist, teacher, and lawyer.
(National Archives of Canada, c-29977)

opponent, but as a female who had overstepped her bounds of respectability. Even so, despite their disagreements, he reported in 1852 that Shadd operated "a very respectable school of colored children."

Shadd defended her position on the public-school issue to Whipple:

> I stated to the people in the first school meeting held here, that if they wanted an exclusive school I would not teach them, and he [Bibb] was aware of it . . . in another meeting . . . which was an attempt to get up a colored government school, I told them if they would desist I would teach twenty children, for three shillings per month advance, and take all children whose parents were not able [to pay].[41]

Shadd claimed that despite her offer, Mary Bibb pushed to petition for a government school: "Mrs. Bibb was present and urged them to move early in the school if they wished a government school . . . [or] their petition would not be granted. I stood alone in opposition to caste schools."[42] Shadd and her sister-in-law, Amelia Freeman Shadd, established a school in 1859 that was open to all young people, male and female; "No complexional distinctions will be made," its advertising proclaimed.[43] But despite the public pronouncements against racial segregation, evidence indicates that the school taught mostly black children, apparently because few white parents were willing to send their children to a school associated with the black community.[44]

Fluctuating attendance and poverty continued to present difficulties for Shadd in the Canadian settlements. She noted that the twenty parents in Windsor who had originally promised to pay their children's tuition had not lived up to their agreement, resulting in high absenteeism: "some who have purported to be of the twenty are not able to pay at all, and at least twenty-five children are out of school."[45] By 1859, she was forced to swallow her pride and request aid again from the AMA, in an application to Whipple that cited the school's poor condition and shortage of supplies and pointed out that "the educational facilities, of the colored people greatly need enlarging by the fostering care and sympathy of the friends of our degraded people."[46] Determined to keep the school open, Shadd left Canada for several months to gather donations from sympathizers in the United States. Turning to the AMA for financial assistance must have been especially galling for Shadd, who six years had been dismissed from the group on grounds that she was not an evangelical. Shadd was a Catholic, which she believed was the sole reason for her suspension.

Financial troubles were not the only difficulties facing the Canadian schools; measles and cholera epidemics caused a decline in attendance but, Shadd reported, had not lessened the community's interest in education. "Fever and diseases incident to children at this season affect several," she told the executive committee of the AMA in the late summer of 1852.[47] In August and September, cholera hit the village, and Shadd herself was afflicted by "a slight attack of cholera" but said the disease was "in its worst form" in Windsor. She reported that parents forced her to give her students a month's vacation: "I have not much fear for myself, but parents say they cannot risk the health of their children in the old school room."[48]

Despite political rivalries, epidemics, and economic struggles, Shadd remained a staunch supporter of emigration and self-help in the Canadian black communities, even when her efforts to promote black initiative in the settlements placed her in the center of controversy.

Education, as black leaders argued, was essential to the eventual success of the community. Economic independence for black men would enable black men and women to create separate sex roles that placed men in the workplace and women in the home. Some black women who participated in organized efforts to promote education thus sought to fulfill contemporary expectations of women's "proper" place, either by improving opportunities for young black men or by forming intellectual societies to advance their own education. Both approaches advanced the principles of female education, in which girls and young women were to be prepared for future roles as educators of their own children and interesting companions for gainfully employed husbands. But some female educators, like Mary Ann Shadd, challenged contemporary expectations of female behavior in their effort to promote black achievement and encountered heavy criticism in the process.

Throughout their careers, black women educators in both the United States and Canada, like many white teachers, faced continual financial hardship and struggled constantly to find the funds necessary to keep their schools open. As individual activists, their mode of participation in the movement for black education depended to a large extent upon their personalities and individual aspirations, as well as on their personal circumstances. In some cases, the need to bring home income from schoolteaching coincided with a commitment to community activism to motivate black female educators to keep their schools going.

Other forms of community activities, such as benevolence and moral reform, promised even less economic return but illustrated the extensiveness of black female activism. As in the case of education, benevolent and reform activities often reflected the political positions of the participants, which sometimes led to conflict as well as cooperation.

Both men and women in the free black community had formed a variety of benevolent organizations during the antebellum period, including charitable organizations, fraternal lodges, and maternal, literary, temperance, and moral reform societies, all of which enabled black men and women to provide assistance to needy members of their community. The exact number of these societies is difficult to assess, because many dissolved soon after their foundation and many of those that survived left few records. In addition, contemporary observers often disagreed over the estimated numbers of community organizations. But the existence of these societies throughout the eighteenth and nineteenth centuries, however sporadic, indicates an ongoing effort by free blacks to provide assistance to their communities.[49] The goals of these societies were varied and included aid to widows and orphans, temperance, education, crime control, and, of course, the abolition of slavery.

As in the larger free society, black men and women organized and belonged to separate male and female societies. Free black men had organized self-help societies earlier than did black women. Two black ministers in Philadelphia, Richard Allen and Absalom Jones, had formed the Free African Society in 1787, seven years after the formation of the first black benevolent organization, the African Union Society in Rhode Island. Leading black men in other cities also formed self-help societies and fraternal lodges to dispense aid to needy black men, women, and children. In Boston, black men founded the African Society in 1796, which functioned simultaneously as a benevolent and antislavery society. In 1808, a group of black men in New York City met in one of the schools for black children to form the New York African Society.[50]

For black men as for white men, fraternal lodges differed from the mutual aid organizations only in that members of lodges shared the same forms of employment. The Masons and the Odd Fellows were the oldest black fraternal orders in the United States. The black Odd Fellows organized their lodge in 1843.[51] One black leader wrote in 1857 of the importance of community service to members of fraternal lodges: "The relief of the widow and orphan is the greatest boast as well as the brightest diadem in our Masonic crown."[52]

Black women also formed a variety of self-help organizations, which represented their deep commitment to improving the condition of blacks through their own initiative and also realized the contemporary ideal by which women held special responsibility for the welfare of their race.

Historians have explored the participation of upper- and middle-class white women in community-based benevolent and moral reform activities in terms of moral stewardship, social control, women's power, and the creation of a "sisterhood" in the lives of female activities. Several such studies have concluded that white women's experiences in organized community reform and benevolence were different from those of male reformers. Although white female reformers often came from families whose men were politically and economically powerful, their involvement in reform and benevolence meant more than simply fulfilling a social responsibility to the "worthy" poor. Their reformer husbands may have been motivated mainly to control the growing urban masses, but many of the women did not see themselves as assistants in such efforts.[53] For them, participation in charitable work and reform represented an exertion of women's power based on their status as moral custodians of their households and communities. By applying prevailing ideas of women's superior morality, groups of women in local churches and reform organizations helped shape their communities by imposing stricter standards of behavior. Some historians have asserted that in the process reform women also created a sense of "sisterhood" with other women that, to a degree, transcended class, religion, and, perhaps, race.

As black women's experiences reveal, the tenacity of racism in American society severely limited the possibility of any cross-racial "sisterhood." Black women who organized societies to aid the poor, widowed, and orphaned and campaigned to stop prostitution and excessive alcohol consumption were motivated not only as women but also as blacks. They worked extensively to help needy blacks in their own neighborhoods.

Black women had been active in benevolent societies at least since January 1828, when a group of black women and men met in New York at the Manumission School on Mulberry Street to discuss plans for creating a "Fragment Society" among "Females of Colour."[54] Twenty-one black women, advised by a committee of male ministers, formed the leadership of the African Dorcas Society (ADS) when they officially formed their organization in February. The ADS constitution identified black schoolchildren as the primary recipients of relief efforts; attributing the frequent absences of children in the African Free Schools as "owing to want of suitable clothing," the central goal of the ADS was to "afford relief in clothing, hats, and shoes, as far as our means may enable us, to such chiłdren as regularly atend the schools belonging to the Manumission Society."[55]

Black women activists performed the tasks that were typical of most women during the nineteenth century. Twice each month, ADS members met in small sewing circles to make and mend clothing for "the destitute boys and girls" enrolled in the local schools.[56] One observer, known only as "A," praised the women for their activism and suggested that benevolent activities were extensions of their domestic responsibilities: "How *pleasant* and how *profitable* must it be to our females to spend their leisure evening, in clothing and making comfortable, & thus keeping in school (where they may learn wisdom and virtue) many little children, who may be otherwise running the streets at this inclement season, suffering from the want of clothing and learning nothing but wickedness!"[57]

As in other community activities, black women reformers often cooperated with black men and supported male leaders. In 1837, black men and women in Troy, New York, celebrated the fourth anniversary of the African Female Benevolent Society at their new church. The secretary of the society praised the members and their activities on behalf of improving the black community: "Sisters of benevolence, do not your hearts beat high with gratitude to God for his goodness to us? . . . We see in various forms, the improvement of our people. . . ."[58] In New York City, the women of the all-black Female Assistant Society requested that black leader Henry Highland Garnet read their annual report at a meeting in the Zion Church in 1838. At the meeting, Garnet delivered an address to the men and women in the audience in which he singled out women as central figures in benevolent activities, both as recipients and as dispensers of charity: "The charitable woman, while she sits by her quiet fireside, enjoying the bounties of a kind Providence, remembers the poor. When she hears the keen north wind whistling around her dwelling and her children draw closer and closer to her bosom, she thinks of the many mothers who are houseless and roaming in penury and want. . . ."[59]

Benevolent and reform activities of black women were well publicized in black and white abolitionist newspapers. Black female benevolent organizations existed in Boston at least as early as 1831, when the directors of the Female Benevolent and Intelligence Society, "whose members are persons of color," placed a notice of an upcoming lecture in Garrison's *Liberator*.[60] One year later, a group of black women formed the Colored Female Charitable Society in Boston. As usual, the primary objects of benevolence were widows and orphans, a responsibility that black women reformers believed was rooted in Biblical teachings. In a call for volunteers, "Hope" stated that "to visit the widow and fatherless in their afflictions, is a scriptural injunction, that ought to be obeyed."[61] In Philadelphia, black women, some of whom were members of the Philadelphia Female Anti-Slavery Society, participated in activities to aid fugitive slaves. In cooperation with men, these women formed an auxiliary committee to the Vigilance Association, in which they raised funds to clothe, shelter, and feed newly arrived runaways.

Black women's attempts to meet the needs of diverse groups of blacks in part accounts for the increase in benevolent organizations during the 1830s. Many of these organizations were affiliated with churches, as the names of the societies and their memberships suggest. According to Mary Still, the efforts of women, though not always acknowledged, were necessary to the survival of their churches: "We are sometimes told that females should have nothing to do with the business of the Church. But they have yet to learn that when female labor is withdrawen the Church must cease to exist."[62] In fact, she noted, women had a history of forming benevolent associations as part of their work in the church: "For the purpose of mutual aid, they [women] banded themselves together in society capacity, that they might be the better able to administer to each others sufferings, and to soften their own pillows. So we find the females in the early history of the Church, abounded in good works, and in acts of true benevolence."[63] Sometimes, several benevolent and reform societies functioned under the auspices of one church. The female members of St. Thomas Methodist Episcopal Church, for example, had organized at least two female "beneficial" societies: the Female Benevolent Society, formed in 1796, and the Daughters of St. Thomas, established in 1822. As of 1831, both were functioning simultaneously, though each kept its own treasury. The Daughters of Wesley, the Female Methodist Assistant Society, the Female Beneficial Philanthropic Society of Zoar, the Benevolent Daughters of Zion, and the Daughters of Noah Bethel Church, all formed between 1822 and 1828 in Pennsylvania, reflected affiliations with major religious denominations. And, in the case of the Daughters of Zion Angolan Ethiopian Society, black female religious benevolent associations proudly displayed particular ethnic affiliations as well.[64]

In 1835, a group of black women in Troy, New York, organized the United Sons and Daughters of Zion's Benevolent Society, two years after the formation of the African Female Benevolent Society. The United Sons and Daughters functioned under the direct control of the local Black Methodist Church in Troy and was designed specifically to help destitute church members.[65] The formation of this organization among black women Methodists demonstrates the importance of the church in black women's lives, for the church enabled them to form alternative organizations tailored to the needs of specific groups of blacks.

Organizations that existed simultaneously to help the local poor, however, did not necessarily operate harmoniously or in cooperation with one another. Competition, personality clashes, and conflicts over methods and goals were always a danger, as Elizabeth Wicks of the African Female Benevolent Society indicated in her anniversary speech in 1834. Also present at the celebration were members of the Female Union Society. Without mentioning anyone in particular, Wicks prayed aloud that God would intercede to prevent "discord, contention, and jealousy; and in their place rear the banner of love, unity and friendship."[66] This society also insisted on harmonious behavior among its members. Article 15 of the constitution reserved the right of the majority to expel any member who became "obnoxious."[67]

The black churches served not only as an organizational basis for community benevolent associations, but as a spiritual foundation as well. Many who participated in black female charitable societies did so out of a sense of Christian duty, as missionaries for the materially and spiritually poor, regardless of race. As one member of the African Female Benevolent Society at Troy stated in 1834: "Then shall the Indian no more adore the sun, nor think to wash away his moral pollution in the streams; but all nations shall adore one God."[68]

The increase in black emigration to Canada after passage of the Fugitive Slave Act in 1850 prompted leaders of benevolent societies in northern cities and Canada to increase efforts to aid fugitive slaves, most of whom arrived in a destitute condition. To help them secure clothing, housing, and food several charitable organizations were formed in the black Canadian settlements. Mary Bibb had expressed concern in 1851 about the effectiveness of efforts to alleviate the destitute condition of fugitive slaves in the Canadian settlement at Sandwich. She lamented that "many dollars have been expended in sending agents, clothing and food, to this Province . . . yet they are in need."[69]

Factionalism developed, however, among black organizers with respect to the most effective way to provide systematic assistance. One of the issues that pitted Shadd against the Bibbs involved the Refugee Home Society, for which the Bibbs served as local leaders in Windsor. Founded in 1851 with the financial backing of whites, the RHS collected funds and material goods and sold land it had purchased from the Canadian government to the black population. By 1855, the RHS had purchased two thousand of a proposed fifty thousand acres of land and resold one thousand to blacks. One hundred fifty Blacks had settled on the land, though not contiguously, which made development of centralized community services extremely difficult. RHS agents continued to sell land to blacks sporadically throughout the 1850s.[70] Shadd's faction opposed the RHS, calling it a "begging scheme" that undermined black initiative.

Inadequate internal resources within the Canadian black communities forced agents to solicit financial support at church and antislavery-society meetings in the United States and Canada. Such "begging" became another point of conflict between Shadd and the Bibbs, though the real issue may have been who would control the benevolent activities in the black Canadian communities. In 1861, Shadd herself was accused of begging by a group of black Canadians who opposed her activities.[71]

In January 1853, Horace Hallock, treasurer for the Refugee Home Society, referred to Shadd as a "malign influence" who was "not only a 'busy body in other men's matters,' but a notorious mischief maker to the extent of her ability—if half that I hear of her efforts in that line be true."[72] Later that month, Hallock assured a friend that despite Shadd's actions as a "mischief maker," "no serious evil to the cause of the poor homeless refugee will grow out of it."[73]

The desperate need for bare necessities in the black settlements was well publicized but despite the efforts of many black women, most fugitive slaves remained in need. Shadd charged the directors of the RHS with cheating blacks by selling the land at inflated prices and failing to return to the black community the majority of funds gained from solicitations. She continually warned the readers of her newspaper about blacks and whites posing as RHS agents to defraud contributors of food, clothing, and money. Agents did in fact keep twenty percent of what they collected as commission, and at least one agent, C. C. Foote, retained twenty-five percent.[74] Contrary to her earlier assessment, Shadd claimed that reports of "utter destitution" in the Canadian black communities were untrue, a ploy "to fill the coffers of the Refugee Home and similar institutions, from which they are not *getting* and have not derived any aid at all."[75]

Several other organizations besides the Refugee Home Society were also established in black Canadian communities, though they were probably less controversial. In 1855, black men and women formed the True Band Society of Amherstburg, C(anada) W(est) and vicinity "for the benefit of the colored people in Canada, and to invigorate the panting Fugitive, who is fleeing before the baying bloodhounds of the slaveholder." Black women also established all-female benevolent associations, such as The Victoria and the Daughters of Prince Albert, both of which boasted about forty members in 1861. These organizations assumed responsibility for caring for the poor and sick and burying the dead.[76]

Female benevolent associations, or the churches under which many of them functioned, arbitrated disputes between members, perhaps because blacks turned to such groups, rather than relying on the city judicial system, to resolve conflicts. The Daughters of Africa Society, founded in Philadelphia in 1821, gave out loans to members for rent and other necessities and donated money for the burial of a member or her relative, for aid to the sick, and for temporary help to the survivors of a deceased member. The society also served as a forum for members to air their grievances against one another, as in June 1832, when a member named Francis Sharp was notified "to come forward at the next stated meeting to answer the charge Brought against her by Hester Brown."[77] Daughters of Africa committees penalized members who had acted "disorderly and improper in the Extreame" by fining or expelling them; members Hannah Johnson, Rachel Gunsey, and Martha Pill were each fined twelve dollars for "extreme offenses to the house."[78] In August 1823, a committee expelled a woman for stealing, and the following May another was expelled for "immoral conduct."[79]

Members of church-based female benevolent associations often went before church committees, over which the pastor usually presided, to settle conflicts between members. At Mother Bethel A.M.E. Church in Philadelphia, an all-male board intervened in disputes that had arisen within the Society of the Daughters of Bethel Church. At a special meeting in November 1823, Richard Allen presiding, the committee found Abigail Jones guilty of an unnamed charge, settling the case with a promise that "each Side never to mention it again for it stir up strife."[80] At the same session, Mary Hinson answered to a charge brought by David Crosby that she had failed to follow customary procedures in caring for his sick wife and had usurped the authority of the Benevolent Society by taking matters into her own hands. Hinson claimed she had done all she could for Maria Crosby's illness and had followed correct procedures in caring for an ill member. In her testimony, she defended her actions:

> I say that sister Maria Crosby said that she was sick and thought she had the same disorder that her child died with, I thought she might die—also I [went] to a Doctress woman by her request, after this woman had given her some moth water. . . . Sometime after I [went] to sister Crosby & she told me that she knew what the stuff was that the woman gave her. I did not wish to come again. . . . I knew or heard that it was the prerogative of the Society . . . to call in a physician & git his advise which I did.[81]

The case of Crosby v. Hinson illustrates the willingness of benevolent society members to defend their society against attacks and also demonstrates the close ties some church-based female associations maintained with their church hierarchy.

Black women also operated orphanages for black children. In New York, for example, black women participated in the daily operation and development of education at the Colored Orphan Asylum, though white women had founded the orphanage and dominated its board of directors.[82] Originally established in 1834 by two white Quaker women, Anna M. Shotwell and her niece Mary Murray, the asylum served as the city's only refuge for black orphans, for blacks were not accepted by the three other orphanages in the city, which according to one male benefactor of the asylum, were fearful of incurring "the odium of an unpopular cause."[83] The Colored Orphan Asylum was destroyed by an anti-draft mob in 1863 and was later moved to Riverdale, New York.

During the 1830s, at least one black woman served as matron of the asylum; Rachel Johnson was employed as matron until 1839, when poor health apparently led to her dismissal. Black leaders Samuel Cornish and

James McCune Smith, physician for the asylum, expressed opposition to Johnson's replacement by a white person, finding it "somewhat strange they could not find a colored woman to fill that important position."[84] During the 1840s, the managers of the asylum established a school for the orphans. The asylum functioned under the direction of prominent free black women such as Mrs. Charles B. Ray and Mrs. A. N. Freeman, whose husbands were black abolitionist leaders in New York City.

Black spokesmen expected the women of their race to expand their efforts to establish orphanages for black children "in all towns and cities of our happy country where colored orphans are denied the benefits of their institutions." In 1838 Cornish expressed hope that the New York Orphan Asylum would set an example for other female reformers, that "the good ladies whom God has blessed with friends and plenty . . . will follow the example of the good ladies of New York."[85] Inadequate funding, however, sometimes thwarted such efforts. In Boston, Nancy Gardner Prince had called a meeting for the establishment of a black orphanage, after she encountered in 1833 "a poor little orphan destitute and afflicted, and on account of color shut out from all the asylums for poor children." But after devoting seven months to setting up a board of "twelve gentlemen of standing" as supervisors, the project fell through due to lack of funds.[86]

In 1833 black women in Salem, Massachusetts, organized the Colored Female Religious and Moral Society of Salem to address a wide range of moral issues. The president of this society was Clarissa C. Lawrence, who also served as vice-president of the all-Black Salem Female Anti-Slavery Society before its reorganization as a racially mixed society. A group of black women in Troy, New York, joined with men in 1836 to form the Moral Reform Society among "the people of color." The officers of the new organization included one woman, Clarissa Jefferson.[87]

Black women clearly perceived anti-prostitution and temperance as part of their moral reform activities. Hetty Reckless of Philadelphia was well-known for her work with prostitutes. In 1849 Reckless, "an untiring and most excellent colored lady" and a member of the Philadelphia Female Anti-Slavery Society and the Vigilant Association, opened a boardinghouse in Philadelphia, the Moral Reform retreat, designed to reform "illicit" females.[88]

Black women also participated in the drive to promote "entire abstinence from all that can intoxicate." Several leaders in the temperance movement who were also abolitionists made concerted efforts to encourage black-white cooperation in ridding society of drunkenness. In 1833, Garrison published a notice of a state temperance convention and encouraged blacks to attend, since "there is no exception made to colored skins in the notice, and we hope our colored friends in this city [Boston], who have united in the Temperance Reform, will take measures to secure a representation in the Convention."[89] Black men and women perceived alcohol as a threat to the survival of the black community, and like white temperance advocates, they identified men as the perpetrators and women as the victims of an intemperate community. Male leaders of the New England Temperance Society of Colored Americans expressed this attitude at the society's 1838 meeting in Boston, in arguments that alcohol was the source of "physical debasement and misery as well as the degradation and suffering, entailed upon unoffending wives and innocent children by cruel husbands and unnatural fathers."[90]

In the black Canadian communities, abolitionist Samuel Ringgold Ward observed that women as well as men were intemperate, noting to Frederick Douglass in 1852 that drinking alcoholic beverages was "so fashionable that ladies who profess religion, minister's wives included, drink without blushing."[91] He reported that among blacks in Canada, drinking was so common that abstention was the exception, not the rule.[92] In 1856 Mary Ann Shadd Cary charged that both black and white churches in Canada were actually the centers of the liquor traffic. Shadd's solution for curbing alcohol consumption was a suggestion that blacks establish alcohol-free boardinghouses. Black Canadians should establish "a good temperance house of high tone," she said, because "we do not know of a public boarding house that is not also a drinking house."[93]

As the moral protectors of the home and agitators for community improvement, black women participated in temperance organizations, some joining with male temperance advocates, while others formed all-female societies. During the 1830s many black temperance organizations were sexually integrated and held meetings open to all members of the black community, which received considerable attention in the black and white abolitionist newspapers and temperance journals, such as the *Genius of Temperance*. In July 1835 *The Liberator* published an announcement of an upcoming meeting of the Boston Colored Temperance Society for a discussion of "Total Abstinence," which invited both "ladies and gentlemen to attend." In the Hartford Colored People's Society in Connecticut, women outnumbered men forty-five to thirty-two when they established the society in 1832.[94]

Like other instances of male-female cooperation, sexually integrated black temperance activities placed men in leadership positions and women in supportive roles. Like the parallel white organizations, black societies were often headed by prominent male abolitionists and religious leaders. The Home Temperance Society, for example, was founded in Middletown, Connecticut, by "the colored population of Middletown."[95] Jehiel C. Beman, a respected Black abolitionist minister, served as president, and no woman served in any leadership position. Black women exercised greater autonomy when they formed all-female temperance societies in the 1840s, though they continued to support male leaders, as reflected in the names honoring prominent men in the temperance and abolition movements, which they gave their organizations: the Hudson Female Gerrit Smith Society in Lenox, Massachusetts, the Massachusetts Female E. C. Delavan Society, and the Edwin Jackson Society, for example. In these organizations, women filled all the leadership positions.

Black women often brought the temperance message to the public in their speeches and writings. Frances E. W. Harper published several poems on temperance and the evils of alcohol in abolitionist newspapers and included some in her own poetry collections. Her poems "The Drunkard's Child" and "Nothing and Something" focused on the family as the victim of alcoholism."[96] Speaking in public to mixed audiences, though generally contrary to women's "proper" place, could be justified when the topic was moral reform. Sarah Parker Remond included addresses on temperance in her speaking itinerary, and reports of her speeches suggest that women were considered particularly suited for temperance reform activities. During her tour in England, Remond delivered a lecture in 1861 on "Total Abstinence" to the Total Abstinence Society: "Miss Remond . . . at considerable length urged the importance of female efforts to promote the cause of abstinence, and showed the great influence which females might exert in the training of the rising generation in habits of total abstinence."

Black women's participation in moral and social reform raises questions regarding the mutability of the "true womanhood" model. For middle-class white women, moral superiority was equated with intellectual inferiority and served as a justification for excluding women from the male world of business and politics. In the free black community, however, such an equation was potentially dangerous: to have adopted this logic would have undermined attempts at dispelling stereotypes of black inferiority.

Moreover, the reality of black life in antebellum America had forced black women to gain a great deal of financial and political experience, for the sake of survival. Although in interactions with the men of their race black women were expected to defer to male authority, it appears that black men and women reshaped the dominant sexual ideology to accommodate black political goals, which recognized the contributions black female wage earners made to the movement. By the end of the 1840s, black leaders such as Martin Delany and Frederick Douglass retained much of the rhetoric of "proper" women's behavior, yet championed the efforts black women had made on behalf of the race, even though some of these activities were not traditionally ladylike.

Thus, contemporary notions of gender roles, as conceived by the free black community, served to define the place of women in the struggle for black liberation. Nonetheless, black women decided as individuals how they would contribute their time and talents to the cause. Community activism combined a commitment to the black community with efforts to end slavery, and participation in the movement alerted many black women to similarities between racism and sexism. As will be discussed in later chapters, a number of well-known black women abolitionists supported women's rights, a focus of activism that was emerging from abolition, but others supported women's circumscribed role in both the family and the community at large—which was also liberating, given the unique history of black women in slavery. But throughout their careers as activists, a commitment to the welfare of the community remained central. Whether they worked within or outside of organized abolitionism, black women activists stressed the importance of self-help. When slavery ended and many white abolitionists saw their work coming to a close, black women continued their work among their black neighbors, as educators, as participants in the black women's-club movement, as advocates for temperance, and as anti-prostitution activists. The next chapter traces black women's struggles to keep community work on the agenda of antislavery organizations.

4

Weathering the Storms

"We do not look up to the ladies of the American Antislavery Society," announced Frederick Douglass in 1848, "but should we desire assistance from any source, it will be mainly to the *colored* Anti-Slavery ladies we shall look for such assistance."[1] For Douglass and other black nationalists, the call for separatism from white-led abolition, for self-reliance and unity, illustrated the depth of disillusionment they felt toward Garrisonian abolition by the 1840s.

Although some nationalists, including Douglass, disagreed with the more radical views of nationalist-emigrationists, all agreed that separatism was an effective way to achieve black abolitionist goals and escape the racism that still existed in the racially mixed movement. The motivation for participating in self-help had clearly changed since the early 1830s, when Maria Miller Stewart and William Wells Brown had argued that black involvement in community improvement would eliminate race prejudice. By the 1840s it was evident that such efforts had failed to change racial attitudes—in fact, race discrimination actually seemed to have increased during the 1830s and 1840s.[2] And, of course, moral suasion had also failed to end slavery.

By 1848, Douglass encouraged self-help for the purpose of creating a self-sufficient black community, not as a means of changing white attitudes. Separation from whites, Douglass and other leaders hoped, would encourage blacks to promote self-sufficiency within their communities and thereby, obtain freedom and equality. Douglass, in his "Address to the Colored People," argued that self-help activities would reduce dependence on whites for economic survival: "Now it is impossible that we should ever be respected as a people, while we are so universally and completely dependent upon white men for the necessities of life. We must take white persons as dependent upon us, as we are upon them."[3] And as Douglass made clear, black women, not white women activists, were central to this effort.

Although organized abolition societies had provided black women with a structure, in addition to their own community organizations, through which they could participate in community activism at the same time that they joined in antislavery work, the movement served as center stage for conflict, as it became painfully obvious that cooperation between the races and the sexes had its limits. The public debate over agenda and tactics for abolition exposed underlying and overt racism and sexism within the movement. Black women, who were accustomed to confronting racism and sexism in their daily lives as well as within the movement, struggled to maintain an agenda that emphasized both anti-slavery goals and the survival and advancement of the race. For a number of these women, this agenda eventually included a black female perspective on women's rights.

Like white women, black women had formed antislavery societies that functioned as auxiliaries to local male organizations and, ultimately, to the state and national antislavery societies. During the early years, black and white women had supported Garrison, raising money for his organization, the American Anti-Slavery Society, and for his newspaper, *The Liberator*, and organizing petition campaigns, lecturing, and meeting for regular discussions on slavery. Combining the skills they had learned in the household with organizational skills developed through community activities, they organized sewing circles to make samplers and other "useful ornaments" that they sold, along with food, drink, and handmade trinkets, at annual Christmas bazaars. Throughout this period, they also continued to participate in and raise money for teaching, benevolence, and moral reform within their communities.

Black women had been involved in organized antislavery since February 1832, when a group of "females of color" in Salem, Massachusetts formed the first women's antislavery society in the United States, the Female Anti-Slavery Society of Salem, just one year after the emergence of Garrison and the establishment of the New England Anti-Slavery Society as the regional parent organization.[4] The existence of a variety of black women's antislavery societies was documented in the abolitionist press.

Some were affiliated with the members' churches, while others were secular groups. A few, such as the "colored females" of the Juvenile Anti-Slavery Society of Salem, Massachusetts, were made up of children and young girls.[5] Black female societies, including the Female Colored Union Society of Nantucket, Massachusetts; the Union Anti-Slavery Society of Rochester, New York; and the Female Wesleyan Anti-Slavery Society of the Methodist Episcopal Church in New York City, dotted the Northeast between 1833 and 1860.[6] One predominantly black female antislavery society in Manhattan may have reflected the exclusionary practices of the Ladies' New York Antislavery Society; Abby Hopper Gibbons commented: "Here I am, the only *white* female member of the Manhattan Anti-Slavery Society."[7]

Like black men, black women gave community improvement a prominent place in their societies' constitutions. In the constitution of the Female Anti-Slavery Society of Salem, members addressed the needs of all blacks: "We the undersigned, females of color, of the commonwealth of Massachusetts, being duly convinced of union and morality, have associated ourselves for our mutual improvement, and to promote the welfare of our color."[8] The constitution contained no explicit mention of slavery, but the women of this society determined that to achieve their "mutual improvement" and "to promote the welfare" of blacks they had to support Garrisonian abolitionism. In their first resolution, they pledged financial support to *The Liberator*, noting that Garrison's publication was "the means of enlightening the minds of many" by opposing African colonization and prejudice against "the free people of color."[9]

Two years after its founding, the Female Anti-Slavery Society of Salem reorganized as the Salem Female Anti-Slavery Society, a racially mixed organization. Several black members held leadership positions in the new society, including Clarissa C. Lawrence, president of the Colored Female Religious and Moral Reform Society of Salem. Sarah P. Remond also participated in society activities, though she may not have been a member; her mother and several sisters definitely were members and did participated in many activities. The transformation of the female antislavery society in Salem into a racially mixed organization in 1834 indicates that the interest of whites in abolitionism had increased during the early 1830s and that the original black members were willing to work with white women.

But the transformation ultimately resulted in alteration of the goals that black members of the original society had espoused. While the first organization had focused on the practical needs of the free black community, the second organization emphasized abstract Garrisonian ideas of the sinfulness of slavery, as reflected in its new constitution: "we are fully convinced that the system based upon it [slavery] is subversive of every precept of Christianity, and hostile to the best interests of all who are under its influence . . . injuring the morals and tending to destroy all the kind and noble affections of one class."[10] Abolition of slavery, which was not even mentioned in the constitution of the original, all-black Female Anti-Slavery Society of Salem, was now cited as the foremost objective, though the new society did continue the original group's anti-colonizationist stance and commitment to assisting the free black community. Perhaps black members had ensured that the new society included community improvement as a major goal.

The creation of biracial antislavery societies had both positive and negative consequences for black women. On the one hand, these societies attested to the willingness of many white and black women to personally challenge race segregation in antebellum America. In Salem, Boston, and Philadelphia, black and white women worked together to establish an antiracist, antislavery agenda and to organize fundraising projects and petition drives, activities that for many women resulted in the formation of lasting personal friendships. But on the other hand, however, not all white and black abolitionists shared the same goals. Some white women held a narrow view of abolitionism, maintaining money and energy ought to be concentrated on ending slavery via moral suasion, and thus that the society's finances should mainly be channeled toward the support of antislavery newspapers and lecturers. Many black members, however, wanted to direct much of their society's resources to the free black community.

The relative economic situations of black and white women may have accounted in part for black women's emphasis on community work, though some black women abolitionists did come from well-to-do families. Black members paid close attention to how they spent their dues, as Lydia Maria Child of the Boston Female Anti-Slavery Society discovered in 1841: "I have been crying like a fool, to day, because two colored members of the Ex. Committee, talked a great deal last night before me, about the necessity of cutting down my salary, saying they earned their money too hard to spend it so lavishly. My sensitiveness about taking money at all in the Anti-Slavery business makes this very painful to me."[11] The frank request from her black colleagues made the ever self-reflective Child dwell on the irony of receiving money from reform activities, but her anguish may have also reflected economic circumstances that set her apart from many black women members—for at the time, she and her husband were struggling financially on their sugar beet farm in Northampton, Massachusetts, a project intended to create a market for free produce to replace slave-grown cane sugar. But unlike many of her black colleagues, Child experienced poverty only because she and her husband had chosen such a course for the sake of the cause; both had come from well-to-do New England families and had enjoyed the accoutrements of wealth since birth.[12]

By combining community self-help with antislavery, black women had provided important links between abolition societies and the black community. Prominent free black women helped form both the Philadelphia Female Anti-Slavery Society and the Boston Female Anti-Slavery Society in 1833. At least eleven black women participated in the Boston Female Anti-Slavery Society, including Susan Paul, Louisa Nell, and Nancy Prince, along with lesser-known black members such as Eunice R. Davis, Margaret Scarlett, Eliza Ann Logan Lawton, Anna Logan, and Phillis Salem.[13] Other black women participated in the society's activities without becoming official members—such as Anna Murray Douglass, who participated in the annual antislavery fairs in Boston though her name never appears on membership lists. In Philadelphia, Charlotte Forten, her daughters Harriett, Margaretta, and Sarah, Grace and Sarah Douglass, and Hetty Reckless took active roles in the local society.

Although the societies in Philadelphia and Boston encouraged social interaction between whites and blacks, white members of other female antislavery societies retained conservative racial views and discouraged racial mixing. White members of antislavery societies in New York and Fall River, Massachusetts, attempted to exclude black women from membership. Their members opposed slavery and, in some cases, supported efforts to "uplift" the black community, but they drew the line at social equality between the races.

Throughout the "nominally free states" in the North, many whites, including some abolitionists, accepted prevailing racial assumptions of the inherent inferiority of blacks, believed that blacks and whites were too different to live together in harmony, and feared that social mixing between the races would result in intermarriages—racial amalgamation—which they believed would ultimately result in the degradation of the white race.[14] An anonymous writer for the *Hampshire Republican* expressed both abolitionist and anti-amalgamation sentiments: "Slavery is an evil of a great magnitude. . . . We do not believe it was the design of the Creator, that marriages should take place between negroes and whites, and certain we are, that such alliances will never be tolerated in New England."[15]

Among northern whites, of course, were people who were far more extreme in their opposition to intermixing as well as abolition, and who sometimes resorted to violence. But rioting by white mobs was probably rooted not only in an extreme aversion to interracial mixing but also in perceived threats to white job security and a general hatred of black people.[16] The English observer William Chambers said that the sufferings endured by blacks between 1835 and 1842 were "shocking." It was not unusual, he reported, for a black person to be "openly assaulted by white persons, for no cause whatever; and if his outcries attracted attention, no notice was taken when they were understood to come from 'only a nigger.'"[17]

In the case of the Ladies' New York City Anti-Slavery Society, which was organized in 1835, the commitment of white members to evangelical revivalism may have been the basis for rather conservative attitudes toward race relations. The religious movement that had swept the Northeast during the 1820s and 1830s had inspired some interest in abolition but was primarily devoted to preserving middle-class notions of the social order, family life, and morality; it has been argued that the New York group was more homogeneous in its constituency and ideology than were the Boston or Philadelphia societies, and, unlike them, it remained exclusively white.[18] Not surprisingly, its members opposed the social mixing of the races even in the antislavery movement. These women defined their mission in the movement as crusaders against an immoral institution. Many members had come to New York city from rural regions of the state, where the preachings of the leading revivalist, Charles Grandison Finney, had echoed loudly. Their abolitionist activity was an extension of their earthly duty to perform good works. They opposed the idea of enslavement and supported benevolent aid to blacks, which befitted their roles as women and as reformers, but their reformist vision did not include disturbing the structure of social relations, and they did not embrace equality between either the sexes or the races.[19] Although their constitution did not explicitly exclude any particular group of women from membership, a twenty-five-dollar membership fee was high enough to keep out most free blacks and working class whites.[20]

Several women from integrated antislavery societies in other cities expressed disapproval of such practices. In 1836 Anne Warren Weston, a member of the Boston group, denounced racism among some leaders of the New York society. In a letter to her sister, Deborah Weston, she specifically criticized Abigail Ann Cox: "Mrs. Cox is the life & soul of the New York Society and she is in a very sinful state—full of wicked prejudice about colour; they do not allow any coloured women to join their society." According to Weston, Lydia Maria Child also objected to the racial attitudes of the New York women: "Mrs. Child thinks [their racial policy] prevents a blessing on them, and they are very lifeless." Weston noted, however, that a few of the group's members objected to the policy, including Julianna Tappan and her family, who "have none of this prejudice [and] therefore they & Mrs. Cox are hardly on speaking terms."[21]

The exclusion of black women from the New York society, however, did not stop the members from proclaiming a "sisterhood" between themselves and slave women. Their first annual report in 1836 emphasized the bonds of womanhood that white and slave women shared:

> The thought is forced upon us . . . that all this and much more, if necessary, might be meekly borne by us, in such a cause, when we remember that the unspeakable injuries endured by our sex in slavery, and remember too how long we remained insensible to those injuries, and with an indifference that now shocks us in the retrospect, withheld from the poor heart-broken victims ever our sympathies and prayers.[22]

That the women of the New York society could believe in unity between themselves and slave women but still exclude black women from their organization reveals that the members clearly distinguished between the slave and the free black, between social equality with blacks and social obligation to the "poor heart-broken victims" of slavery. Unlike many other antislavery societies, male or female, and in an unusual show of independence from the parent male society in New York, the members of this group declined to include the "elevation" of the city's free black community among the goals mentioned in their constitution. A smaller group of New York women, the Chatham Street Society, declared in the

Constitution and Address that they would not "join in the hypocrisy to persecution by dictating to them [blacks] how they are to improve their character and their prospects,"[23] an unusual position for an antislavery society, many of which emphasized improvement as part of the agenda. Cutting out one of the more patronizing aspects of the predominantly white abolitionist agenda may have reflected the presence of black members, such as Eliza Ann Day, who participated in the Chatham Street organization.[24]

When twenty-seven women from respected white families in Fall River, Massachusetts, organized the Female Anti-Slavery Society of Fall River, the issue of race nearly destroyed the new organization. Elizabeth Buffum Chace, one of the founding members, reported in her diary that some white members, though committed to the antislavery cause, shunned association with blacks: "In some cases, persons who were opposed to slavery and were willing to work for its abolition, nevertheless strongly objected to any association with colored persons in their Anti-Slavery labors." The new society almost disintegrated that same year when three free black women, who had been attending the meetings, applied for membership. Chace noted that many of the white members did not mind that black women attended the meetings but believed that to accept them as members would mean accepting them as social equals:

> In the village of Fall River, were a few very respectable young colored women, who came to our meeting. One evening, Lucy [Buffum Lovell] and I went to see these negro women and invited them to join. This raised such a storm among some of the leading members, that for a time, it threatened the dissolution of the Society. They said they had no objection to the women attending the meetings, and they were willing to help and encourage them in every way, but they did not think it was at all proper to invite them to join the Society, thus putting them on an equality with ourselves. Lucy and I maintained our ground, however, and the colored women were admitted.[25]

Debates within several local female antislavery societies over racial integration were well known to members of integrated organizations. Phebe Matthews, a white abolitionist from Cincinnati, wrote to Theodore Weld about the racist attitudes of some members of her antislavery society:

> I said to Br. [Augustus] Wattles the other evening I shall be glad when Mrs. Mahan, Mrs. Gridley, Misses Dewey, Fletcher, etc. . . . are gone, for none of them are more than half-hearted abolitionists and I cannot endure to be shackled as they wish me to be. . . . I love these dear sisters, but they do wish us to stoop so often to race prejudice. . . . And they feel so bad if perchance we lay our hands on a curly head, or kiss a coloured face. It distresses me to be in the society of the coloured people with them. I am afraid I shall offend their nice taste.[26]

By the 1840s, abolitionists had still not resolved the question of interracial mixing. In upstate New York, the Western New York Female Anti-Slavery Society split over the admittance of blacks. Sarah Burtis, a white leader and manager of the Society, wrote to Abby Kelley in 1843 about the dissension, reporting that some women "had left us on account of our admitting colored persons to our society." She assured Kelley, however, that "we do not sacrifice principles to numbers, neither will colored people be rejected."[27]

Even the racially integrated Boston society had white members who wished to keep the races separate at meetings and public events, segregationist practices that underscored the tensions in the city over racial segregation by both custom and law. The period between 1820 and 1860 had seen slow, but generally positive, change in the Bay State. By the 1840s, racial barriers had been gradually lowered in the legal and political realm, with the abolition of anti-miscegenation laws, the desegregation of public schools, the enactment of personal liberty laws, and progress toward ending the prohibition of social intermixing between the races in restaurants, hotels, and theaters.[28] Such changes met with resistance, however, ranging from stubborn adherence to social custom to violence. Moreover, the difficulty of enforcing desegregation laws in public establishments that had customarily excluded black patrons undoubtedly made some black Bostonians skeptical about the success of such measures; enforcement often depended on the willingness and ability of the injured party to pursue the case—which many did, particularly in the area of public transportation—and a decision in favor of a black plaintiff was likely to depend on the size and influence of the business under investigation and the attitude of the local judiciary toward social mixing of the races, for the courts and the legislature in Massachusetts were at loggerheads over the segregation issue.[29]

At antislavery meetings in Boston, blacks and whites occupied separate sections of the hall. When Charlotte Coleman, a black woman, dared to sit in the white section at a meeting, she met with severe disapproval from Elisha Blanchard, a white women who was a life-member of the society. Blanchard informed Coleman that though whites were willing to help blacks, "traditions must not be violated." She quickly added, however, that Blacks "were very well in their place," implying that despite Coleman's indiscretion, most blacks behaved well and did not violate codes of propriety that kept them separate from whites.[30] Such attitudes must have provoked Maria Weston Chapman to address "Female Anti-Slavery Societies throughout New England," "On Behalf of the Boston Female Anti-Slavery Society." She encouraged white members to eliminate exclusory policies: "Let there be no exclusive system adopted in our societies. Ask no one's sect, rank, or color. Whoever will, let them come."[31]

In Philadelphia, as in Boston, black women helped found a racially integrated female antislavery society. Most of the white members in Philadelphia, and at least one black member, Grace Douglass, were Quakers. Names of ten black women appear regularly in the records: Grace Douglass, Sarah Douglass, Charlotte Forten, Margaretta Forten, Sarah Forten, Harriet Forten Purvis, Sarah Lewis, Sarah McCrummell, Hetty Reckless, and Hetty Burr. Sarah McCrummell and Margaretta Forten had attended a "meeting of Females convened at the school room of Catherine McDermot" in February 1833 "to take into consideration the propriety of forming a Female Anti-Slavery Society" in Philadelphia. McCrummell and Forten served on the committee to form the society and draw up a constitution, which they presented in December 1833. Of the eighteen women who signed the constitution, at least seven were black.

Black women consistently served in leadership capacities throughout the existence of the organization, though none ever served as president. Charlotte Forten and Grace Douglass had been founding members; Margaretta Forten usually served as recording secretary, and her younger sister, Sarah, often presented her original poems on slavery at meetings, as well as submitting them to the antislavery press. Grace Douglass occupied leadership positions in both the Philadelphia group and the Antislavery Convention of American Women, which held conventions in

1837, 1838, and 1839 for women representatives from antislavery societies throughout the free states. In 1837 and 1839, she served as convention vice president in New York. Her daughter Sarah joined the society shortly after its founding and served on its education committee in 1840, in addition to her own work as a schoolteacher.

According to the minutes of the Philadelphia organizational meeting, the founding committee set forth to "propose such measures as will be likely to promote the Abolition of Slavery and to elevate the people of colour from their present degraded situation, to the full enjoyment of their rights and to increased usefulness in society."[32] Black and white members cooperated on a number of issues relating to the black community and women's activism in the movement. The improvement of education for blacks was one of the priorities of the society, due in part to Sarah Douglass's involvement in black education. Before Douglass joined the education committee in 1840, other members had supported Douglass's effort to operate a school for black children. The members of the committee, which included Lucretia Mott, president of the society, committed the organization to assume responsibility for establishing Douglass's school in September 1836. In 1838, the society assumed financial support of the school when several members learned that it "does not yield a sufficient income to continue as she [Douglass] would wish."[33] After the committee decided to support Douglass's school, it had to seek final approval for funding from the parent society, the Pennsylvania Abolition Society, to which it petitioned in 1836: "The undersigned having seriously felt the want of a suitable room for a female coloured school under the care of Sarah Douglass . . . present the claims of this school for your consideration and ask of you to rent the room."[34] The petition was approved, and in return for funding, the schoolroom was used as a meeting place for the Philadelphia society.[35]

By 1840, the society was responsible for monitoring all the educational facilities for black children in the Philadelphia area. In the report of the sixth annual meeting of the society on January 1, 1840, members of the education committee criticized unnamed members for neglecting their duties. During the year, the committee had agreed to evaluate the progress of black schools in the area by assigning each member to "have the charge of a school, advise & instruct the teacher and report to the Committee the state of that school." Members pledged to visit the homes of black children in order to persuade their parents of the importance of education, but they believed such efforts would be useless unless they could hire "moral and intelligent teachers." The concern for morality and community responsibility was part of "woman's influence" that abolitionist leaders had expected of female activists. In the case of the Philadelphia women, however, several members apparently had failed to fulfill their duties. According to the annual report, "had the proposed plan been pursued by an *efficient* Committee, it might have been productive of good results, but many have been so neglectful that the report of the Condition of the schools cannot be (so full) as it might have been."[36]

Despite such lapses, members participated actively in the effort to improve education for blacks. Sarah Douglass, in fact, believed the society exerted too much control over her school. In March 1840, she submitted a letter to the board of managers "stating her wish to have her school under her own control." Although the board expressed regret over her request, it left no indication that the members harbored ill feelings. Mary Grew, a white member, offered a resolution in response to Douglass's letter: "Resolved, That this society deeply regret[s] the withdrawal of the school taught by S. M. Douglass from their charge, the supervision & maintenance of which has been a source of pleasure to them, & that they wish for it a continuance of prosperity & usefulness under her care."[37]

Although the board voted to relinquish control, it continued to provide financial support by appropriating an annual sum of $125.[38] Throughout the 1840s, the PFASS funded Douglass's school, despite periods of decreasing enrollment.[39] In 1841, the education committee, which included Douglass that year, reported a significant decline in enrollment in the school, for which members blamed the public school administrators in Philadelphia. The "controllers of Public schools" apparently fearful that their own enrollment was inadequate to keep the public schools open, had encouraged parents, blacks included, to remove their children from the private schools and enroll them in public schools. Douglass, with the aid of the society, managed to keep her school open until 1853, when she assumed the responsibility for the girls' primary department at the Institute for Coloured Youth. In 1847, the year Douglass served as librarian of the society, members agreed to purchase a stove for her schoolroom.[39] Until the summer of 1849, the society paid the rent for the schoolroom because the members often held meetings there.

Black member Hetty Reckless (sometimes listed as Hester or Esther Reckless) provided a link between the society and the black community.

Reckless encouraged the group to extend its aid to black education by supporting black Sabbath schools that blacks themselves had established in Philadelphia. In 1841, she reported on the progress of the Sabbath schools: "Hester Reckless informed [us] that through the exertions of the coloured people a Sabbath School had been (lately) established among the ignorant & despised colored population of Bedford St. & its neighborhood which had already effected some information among them. . . . The members of this Society were urged to give their countenance & aid to this work of benevolence. . . ."[40] Reckless also persuaded the society to provide aid to moral reform institutions in the black community, and in 1847, at the same meeting in which the members appropriated money for Sarah Douglass's stove, they also donated twenty-five dollars to the Moral Reform Retreat, the antiprostitution boardinghouse where Reckless served as the head matron.[41]

In 1846, Reckless spearheaded a drive to ally the society with the Philadelphia Vigilance Committee, a predominantly black female group that served as a conductor of the Underground Railroad in the city, providing food, shelter, and clothing to fugitive slaves. In July 1838, a group of black women had formed the Female Vigilance Associations, auxiliary to the Philadelphia Vigilance Committee, which was headed by prominent black men. Mary Bustill, Sarah Douglass's aunt, served on this committee.[42] Reckless's dual membership in both the black-led Vigilance Association and the racially integrated Philadelphia Female Anti-Slavery Society provided her with an opportunity to persuade the other society members of the Society to pledge financial assistance to the Vigilance Committee.[43] Reckless approached the society in September 1841 "on behalf of the Vigilant Committee" and "urged upon us their claims for our sympathy and pecuniary aid—She reported that since our last meeting they had assisted thirty-five fugitives in their escape to a land of liberty & that they now had three more under care." The PFASS members resolved to "more efficiently . . . bear in mind the wants of the Vigilance Committee."[44]

But despite verbal pledges of support, the society was reluctant to commit its funds to the Underground Railroad. Although the society had extended a great deal of assistance to the black community, at least one leading white member believed that it should limit its participation in black community activities, since the budget was limited and the foremost goal of the society was to destroy slavery. At the meeting in September 1841, the society agreed to provide aid to the Female Vigilance Association, but only according to the needs of individual cases, rather than donating a lump sum to an external organization. This approach apparently proved inadequate, and in May 1845, Reckless reported difficulties in obtaining funds to care for "several fugitives" who "have passed into this city lately." The following June, the Society agreed to pay Reckless ten dollars "for the benefit of fugitive slaves."[45]

The society's reluctance to extend too much aid to "these mere branches of the Anti-Slavery cause" represented a fundamental difference between black and white interpretations of abolitionism and reveals that some white abolitionists did not view the movement as broadly as did many blacks. In 1856, white activist Lucretia Mott noted that though aiding fugitive slaves was important, it was "not properly Anti-Slavery Work." According to the minutes of one meeting, "L.[ucretia] M.[ott] after acknowledging some contributions received for their [fugitive slaves'] benefit said it was impossible not to be interested & excited by such narratives [of fugitive slave experiences], but we must remember that relieving the necessities of these was not properly Anti Slavery work."[46] According to Mott, the primary goal of the society was to eliminate slavery, arguing that because those born into slavery in one year outnumbered the slaves who escaped to the northern states and Canada, the goal of antislavery women must remain "to destroy the system, root and branch, to lay the axe at the root of the corrupt tree."[47] Mott and others may have preferred to rely on private assistance for the Underground Railroad, because several society members and their families had been aiding fugitives in their own homes for many years. Thus, they probably saw no need to commit the society's limited funds to the Vigilance Committee and the Female Vigilance Association.

Commitment to the free black community and to the abolition of slavery raised questions about the extent to which the society should pledge financial support to outside organizations. The resignation of Esther Moore, a white member who served as the the first president and as a delegate of the American Moral Reform Society, indicates that the cause of the fugitive slave threatened to draw members away from the PFASS and its more narrow agenda. Moore resigned from the society in order to devote more time to the Vigilance Committee. Her decision forced the remaining members to consider the ties of the society to "these mere branches" of abolition, revealing that whites themselves did not always agree on limiting the agenda to ending slavery:

> A member stated that it was the wish of Esther Moore to have her name erased from the list of members of this society and incidently mentioned as her reasons that she was more interested in the Vigilance Com[mitee] operations and such like departments of the cause. This gave rise to a discussion as to how far these mere branches of the Anti-Slavery cause had claims on abolitionists for their support.[48]

Clearly, black women's influence in the society helped to shape its goals as an organization and raised questions about balancing commitments to both the black community and antislavery.

Debates about goals and tactics, however, extended beyond the confines of individual antislavery organizations and erupted on a national scale by the 1840s. Black women's commitment to community activism as well as antislavery led the majority of black women abolitionists in Boston and Philadelphia to support Garrison amid increasing criticism of his ideology and tactics. In 1837, when the Boston members informally divided into pro-Garrison and anti-Garrison factions, only a minority of the total membership still supported Garrison. The majority of black members, however, remained loyal. In support of Garrison, Eunice Davis made an appeal on behalf of the black members of the Boston Female Anti-Slavery Society for readers of *The Liberator* to renew their subscriptions.[49] The split in the Boston group signified disagreement over abolitionist ideology and tactics that had been brewing within white and black abolitionist circles since 1836.

During the first few years of Garrison's leadership, most abolitionists had supported his commitment to moral suasion, as well as his criticism of the government and the church. By the mid-1830s, however, Garrison had embraced a more radical view of abolitionism, arguing that abolitionists must fight not only for the end of slavery, but for the end of all evil in society through universal reform. *The Liberator* became a forum for a wide range of ideas. The responsibility of abolitionists, Garrison maintained, was to purify and perfect human society by engaging in all types of reform that would remove inequality and oppression. Supporters of Garrison agreed that abolitionists should not associate with the government or the churches, institutions that had traditionally condoned slavery. They also embraced nonviolence and promoted other reform movements, such as women's rights.

Opponents of Garrison argued that issues besides abolition were distractions from the original objective to end slavery. They also opposed Garrison's antigovernment, antichurch position, arguing that the most effective way for abolitionists to end slavery was to infiltrate the government and the churches and cleanse these institutions of corruption. Anti-Garrisonian leaders such as James G. Birney and Lewis Tappan even proposed the formation of a third political party that would espouse abolitionist goals. The division between supporters and opponents of Garrison finally resulted in a formal split in the American Anti-Slavery Society in 1840. While Garrisonians stayed with the AAS, anti-Garrisonians formed their own national organization, the American & Foreign Anti-Slavery Society. In 1840, most black abolitionists still supported Garrison, though several sided with the new organization.[50]

Debate over these issues also occurred within female antislavery societies. While the Philadelphia group remained loyal to Garrison, the Boston group formally split in 1840 into pro-Garrison and anti-Garrison factions. The majority of the Boston women, in fact, opposed Garrison. For conflict to arise within the Boston society over abolitionist ideology and tactics is not surprising, for Garrison's presence in the city may have created a conflict in abolitionist circles between principles of natural rights and Garrison's emphasis on sin and morality. Boston had been the center of political agitation during the revolutionary period in America, and the founders of the Boston society, influenced by the ideals of the revolution, approached abolitionism from the perspective that slavery threatened basic principles of human freedom and natural rights.[51] When Garrison's moral-suasion tactic failed to persuade slaveholders to free their slaves, the majority of white female abolitionists in the Boston society could readily abandon Garrison's position and adopt new approaches, as the anti-Garrison majority, led by Mary S. Parker, indicated in the society's Seventh Annual Report in 1840: "We are an antislavery society—not a non-resistance society."[52]

Conflict between the two factions manifested itself in 1839 with respect to fund-raising and election of officers. Maria Weston Chapman, a leading member and a supporter of Garrison, attempted to call a special meeting to raise one thousand dollars, the amount of the customary contribution to the AAS. But the anti-Garrison president, Mary Parker, declared Chapman's request unconstitutional. At the regular meeting, the members finally voted to collect the annual pledge and to gather subscriptions to

The Liberator. In the meantime, Chapman and fourteen other pro-Garrisonians had met on their own to arrange a fund-raising fair in October 1839, an annual event that Chapman, Lydia Maria Child, Louisa Loring, and their friends and relatives had organized since the founding of the society. The leader of the annual fair was clearly Chapman, who had, over the years, made it into a successful money-maker. Not surprisingly, the Chapman group protested when the society's board of managers decided to take control of the 1839 fair. Chapman and her supporters went ahead with their own fair in October, but the majority of the members held a fair in December.[53]

A heated dispute over the election of officers finally led to the formal dissolution of the society in 1840. In October 1839, at the meeting to elect officers for the upcoming year, Lucy Ball, as secretary, had recorded a majority voting for Mary S. Parker as president. Members of the pro-Garrison minority protested the election, claiming that Parker had not actually received a majority.[54] At least seven black women signed the certificate protesting Parker's election, and nine voted against the dissolution of the society in the spring of 1840, when the majority anti-Garrison faction voted to dissolve the organization. Chapman's faction protested the decision on procedural grounds, but the Parker faction left to form the Massachusetts Female Emancipation Society, which supported the political involvement of abolitionists. The Chapman faction regrouped to reconstitute the Boston Female Anti-Slavery Society. Both organizations vied for leadership of the female antislavery movement.

Most black men and women abolitionists still considered Garrison a true friend of the slave, despite the fact that moral suasion had not resulted in the end of slavery. For many black women in the Boston society, their work together within the black community probably factored into their decision to stay with the pro-Garrison group, since Garrison had consistently supported black community improvement as part of the abolitionist agenda. His support of a multifaceted program for his "perfect" society also signaled an ability to understand abolitionist goals broadly. Although he had not been immune from adopting a patronizing attitude toward blacks, he at least had not embraced the myopic vision of abolition accepted by many of his colleagues. Pro-Garrison members of the Boston black community showed support for the leader by withdrawing financial support from Martha and Lucy Ball's school for black girls at the Smith School (also called the African School), which the two had operated since

1833. The Ball sisters, who had backed the anti-Garrisonians from the beginning, were forced to close the school in 1839 despite continued funding from the new organization.[55]

Another factor probably influencing black women's decisions in the factional conflict was personal loyalty. Most of the black women who supported Garrison and voted against Mary Parker participated actively in the free black community, especially in black education, temperance, and local church activities. Susan Paul's primary school for black children in Boston and her Garrison Juvenile Choir were well known in abolitionist circles, and she maintained close personal ties with prominent white women members of the society who remained loyal to Garrison. Eunice R. Davis, Margarett Scarlett, Eliza Ann Logan Lawton, and Anna Logan worked together in fighting segregation in the Boston public schools. Church activities also bound black women abolitionists together; Eunice Davis, Anna Logan, and Caroline F. Williams, for example, all belonged to the Zion Church in Boston and participated together in various church functions. In 1843 Logan served as president of a committee hosting a fund-raising fair to "liquidate the debt" of the Zion Church.[56] Louisa F. Nell, mother of black abolitionist William Cooper Nell and wife of William G. Nell, supported Garrison, as did her son and husband.[57] Susan Paul, Jane Putnam and Nancy Prince participated in temperance activities, and Prince also worked outside the United States to improve the condition of blacks, especially in the area of education. Julia Williams had been a close associate of Garrison and often traveled with Garrison and other white abolitionists to antislavery conventions. For those black women who supported Garrison, then, community activism as well as antislavery-society activities had been central to their work in abolitionism. Two black members of the society had voted for dissolution in 1840, though their names do not appear in the dispute over Parker's election: Chloe Lee and C. L. Barbadoes. Barbadoes was probably related to black abolitionist James Barbadoes. Lee had participated in the fight against racial segregation in the Boston schools.

The rift within the Boston society is illustrative of infighting among abolitionists over issues of race, ideology, and tactics, regardless of gender. As in the male societies, female abolitionists wrangled over issues that, in the end, seemed impossible to resolve peaceably. In female antislavery societies, however, the particular issues around which larger disputes swirled related specifically to women's role in organized abolition—i.e., fund-raising. The Boston society's conflict over the annual fair illustrates the seriousness with which they took their role. Moreover, the incident also reflected most clearly the composition of leadership in the organization, for at center stage of the controversy were white women who had been leaders in the society since its formation seven years before.

In Philadelphia, no formal divisions occurred among members of the Philadelphia Female Anti-Slavery Society, despite Lucretia Mott's opinion that the agenda should focus on ending slavery, with only limited aid to the free black community. Until the late 1840s both black and white members in Philadelphia remained loyal to Garrison, a unity that reflected general agreement with Garrison over use of moral suasion as the best way to end slavery. Most of the Philadelphia women were Quakers, who equated political inequality with sin and immorality; in their constitution, members had declared that slavery was sinful and "contrary to the . . . principles of our Declaration of Independence.[58] Thus, most members probably found Garrison's ideas compatible with their own, despite the fact that he was a Congregationalist. Harriet Martineau, an English traveler, remarked upon meeting Garrison in 1835 that he had "a good deal of a Quaker air; and his speech is deliberate like a Quaker's."[59]

Black and white members of the Philadelphia society also supported the radical idea of granting women the right to vote, to occupy leadership positions in the AAS, and to perform traditionally male roles such as speaking in public. In 1836, for example, five black women signed a Certificate of Recommendation supporting Angelina E. Grimké's lecture tour. Black male leaders encouraged and supported black women who engaged in public speaking. Two black members expressed their support for Garrison.

In June 1839, almost a year before the split in the national society and the Boston Female Anti-Slavery Society, Sarah and Grace Douglass wrote to Garrison, offering sympathy and encouragement: "We have felt much for you. . . . Your enemies may say what they will of you; they can *never* convince us, that you are recreant to the cause of the crushed, degraded slave. . . . We don't believe that the cause of the slave will be injured by the dissension in the antislavery ranks. . . . You will please remember us affectionately to Mrs. Garrison."[60] Their feelings may have changed, however, by 1848, when Sarah Douglass helped organize the all-black Women's Association of Philadelphia, explicitly intended to support Frederick Douglass's cry for black nationalism. Even so, she gave no indication that she had given up on the idea of cooperating with white abolitionists. The commitment of the Philadelphia society to Garrisonian ideals led its members to remain loyal to Garrison despite increasing criticism from abolitionists who disagreed with his emphasis on moral suasion, his antigovernment and antichurch stance, and his willingness to embrace universal reform.

By the late 1840s, a growing number of black abolitionists, led by Frederick Douglass, Martin Delany, Mary Shadd, and others, had become disenchanted with an abolitionist movement that clearly was dominated by whites, exhibited racist attitudes, and had relied primarily on unsuccessful tactics. In their eyes, the passage of the Fugitive Slave Act in 1850 confirmed the failure of moral suasion and the prevalence of racism in the United States.

The new law made black efforts to mobilize for the protection of the community more urgent, as manifested in increased black migration to Canada. White male leaders as well as blacks condemned the law in the abolitionist press. But black men and women, freeborn and ex-slave alike, recognized the gravity of the measure in terms of its consequences for their own safety. At the fifteenth annual meeting of the Rhode Island State Antislavery Society in Providence in November 1850, Sojourner Truth had "thanked God that the law was made—that the worst had come to worst: now the best must come to best."[61]

Compounding the failure of moral suasion, in the eyes of many black abolitionists, was the persistent institutional racism in the state and national antislavery organizations. By the 1840s, a number of black men sat on committees and participated as voting members in the national organization, but white men still dominated the AAS, the American and Foreign Anti-Slavery Society, and the state organizations. Although black men participated in the proceedings as full members, they often were not included in policy decisions. Such racism among white leaders irritated many black abolitionists, several of whom eventually broke with the white-dominated movement.[62] Not surprisingly, black members looked suspiciously on any slight against them.

The case of Hester Lane in 1840 exemplifies the growing dissension over race, sex, and ideology in the national organization. Lane was an exslave who earned her living in New York by taking in laundry, had reportedly purchased ten blacks out of slavery. Despite her apparent support for the anti-Garrison faction, she had received high praise from pro-Garrisonian Lydia Maria Child, who described her as "diligent, capable, and laborious."[63] The election of Abby Kelly Foster to the Executive Committee of the AAS clearly opened the way for increased female participation in the affairs of the national society, but the victory was more for white Garrisonian women than for women who backed the "new organizationists." After the dissenters had walked out of the meeting, the remaining delegates nominated two white women and one black woman to serve on the executive committee. David Lee Child's nomination of Lucretia Mott and Lydia Maria Child carried, but Charles B. Ray's nomination of Lane was rejected.

A contributor to the *Colored American* blamed racism for Lane's exclusion from the Committee:

> He [David Lee Child] therefore nominated Lucretia Mott, of Philadelphia, as a member of the Executive Committee—carried. . . . Charles Ray, then moved, as there was still one vacancy in the committee, that the name of Hester Lane be added—lost. Hester Lane is well known in this city as a woman of good character and senses, and has been a slave, but the "principle" could not carry her color.—eh![64]

Further discussion, however, revealed that political factionalism, rather than overt racism, was at issue in this particular instance. Thomas Van Rensselaer, a black Garrisonian from New York, countered the charge of racism by arguing that he had stopped Lane's appointment for ideological reasons, because she had supported the Tappan faction. In a letter to *The Emancipator*, Van Rensselaer defended his action:

> HESTER LANE—A great outcry has been made about the individual, being rejected as a member of the Executive Committee of the National Society. . . . Reasons for objecting, because I had a conversation with Mrs. Lane a few days before on the woman question, and found her opposed to *us*, and strongly in favor of the new *organizationists*. With those facts before my mind . . . I rose and said the committee was full, although it was found afterwards that another person could have been constitutionally added, so that all the blame, if blame there is, ought to be attached to brother Ray,

for nominating a person who he knew, or ought to have known, was opposed to *us*.[65]

In the Lane case, charges of racism made little sense in light of Van Rensselaer's role. Moreover, if Lane was indeed a supporter of the new organizationists, it is not surprising that her nomination would be rejected by the Garrisonians. Nevertheless, the suspicion that Lane had been rejected on the basis of her color suggests that black disillusionment with the decision-making process of the national antislavery organization had begun to fester. The rejection of a black woman from the executive committee also reveals that though white women may have gained access to leadership within organized abolition, black women still had not.

Although black abolitionist men and women retained community improvement as an important abolitionist objective, the emphasis on community activism after 1840 was influenced more by the movement for black empowerment, nationalism, and unity than by the desire to overturn race prejudice. In his "Address to the Colored People" in 1848, Douglass supported interracial cooperation but also encouraged blacks to organize on their own: "Attend anti-slavery meetings, show that you are interested in the subject, that you hate slavery, and love those who are laboring for its overthrow. Act with white Abolition societies wherever you can, and where you cannot, get up societies among yourselves, but without exclusiveness."[66]

Douglass met with much resistance and opposition from abolitionist colleagues, many of whom were loyal Garrisonians and considered him ungrateful to his white benefactors. They also predicted that such a split would irrevocably divide and weaken the movement. A disappointed Garrison believed Douglass simply misguided, but others, such as black abolitionist William G. Allen, expressed anger over the former slave's action. Allen wrote in 1854: "To what depth of sliminess has Frederick Douglass descended=His last stupid article . . . proves that he has lost his senses as well as his conscience. His attempts to excite the prejudices of the Colored People against Mr. Garrison . . . is unparalleled in cruelty, ingratitude, and meanness."[67] In a letter to Amy Post, black abolitionist William C. Nell wrote that Douglass was "indefatigable in his abuse and misrepresentation of me. . . . He forgets that in this controversy there are blows to take as well as blows to give."[68]

Nevertheless, Douglass enjoyed support from many free blacks, who answered his call and formed all-black societies to support his newspaper, the *North Star*. The proceeds from black women's fairs helped sustain "a good and efficient newspaper," which he believed was important to the "elevation" of the community. Formation of these organizations reflected changes in black abolitionist goals and the growing momentum of nationalism within black abolitionist circles. In some cases, black antislavery societies existed side by side with white or racially mixed organizations. In Douglass's city of Rochester, for instance, black women organized the Union Anti-Slavery Society in 1850, which cooperated with white women in the organization of a mass antislavery festival.[69] In 1849, fourteen black women in Philadelphia met at the home of Rachel Lloyd to organize the all-black Women's Association, which in 1850 engaged Grace Douglass's nephew, Joseph C. Bustill, to act as agent for the *North Star*.[70] Although this organization remained separate from the Philadelphia Female Anti-Slavery Society, a number of members retained membership in the racially mixed society, which had been the center of black-white female cooperation since 1833. At least two Women's Association members, Sarah Douglass and Hetty Burr, held leadership positions in the old society as well as in the new organization.[71] Douglass served as corresponding secretary in 1849 and as a spokesperson for the fair in 1850. Burr served as association vice-president in 1849.

Several other association members were also well connected to the black abolitionist community. Amy Matilda (Williams) Cassey, the daughter of the Reverend Peter Williams of New York, had married Joseph Cassey, a respected black abolitionist in Philadelphia. Hetty Burr's husband, John P. Burr, was a barber who had served as an agent for the *Liberator* and the American Moral Reform Society and supported the Haitian-emigration and black-convention movements. Hetty's household of twelve people, which included the Burrs and their five children, entailed heavy responsibilities, but she managed to devote time to community activism.[72] Harriet Smith's husband, Stephen, was a prominent businessman, co-owner with William Whipper of a successful lumberyard in Columbia, Pennsylvania. Stephen Smith was one of the wealthiest black merchants in the Philadelphia area and provided financial assistance to the Underground Railroad. Whipper's wife, Mary Ann, was active in both the society and the Vigilance Committee.[73] Louisa, Lydia Ann, and Hester Bustill were cousins of Sarah Douglass. The names of association members Elizabeth Appo, Mary Barrott, Louisa Bristol, Hester Bustill, Lydia Ann Bustill, Helen Johnson, and Charlotte Mills do not appear in society records;[74] they may or may not have participated in society activities, but they never obtained formal membership.

The 1850 census data offers glimpses of some association women. Louisa Bristol, originally from Maryland, lived with her husband, six-year-old son, and two boarders. Elizabeth Appo, aged thirty-two, had moved from New York to Philadelphia some time between 1842 and 1849, with her husband William, aged forty-one, and their five children, ranging in age from two to thirteen. William Appo quickly gained prominence as a piano instructor. Johnson, thirty, who resided in a household with two other black women, was the young widow of Captain Frank Johnson, a reknowned bandleader and composer, who died in 1844.[75]

At the organizational meeting of the Women's Association, Delany addressed the members, encouraging them to maintain the "elevation of our people" as their foremost goal. He also wrote and presented a constitution for the association, which the women adopted.[76] The fact that male leaders had guided the formation of this organization and helped formulate its goals reflects the auxiliary status of the association, and its acceptance of male leadership. Nevertheless, the women exercised autonomy within the association, electing their own officers and organizing annual antislavery fairs to support the *North Star*.[77]

The association assumed the role of both an antislavery society and a community self-help organization. In the preamble to their constitution, the women embraced the responsibility of supporting self-help within the free black community and agreed that existing antislavery societies had not done enough to achieve the goals of black abolitionism:

> Whereas The Necessity of an efficient organization for the support of our cause has long been apparent and its absence deplored; and
>
> Whereas, Believing Self-Elevation to be the only true issue upon which to base our efforts as an oppressed portion of the American people; and believing that the success of our cause depends mainly upon Self-Exertion are the most powerful means by which an end so desirable can be attained: Therefore, we do agree to form ourselves into an Association, to be known as the Women's Association of Philadelphia.[78]

The members pledged to support the "Press and Public Lectures" by holding fairs, which resembled antislavery bazaars. The members of the fair committee, Harriet Smith, Rachel Lloyd, and Amy M. Cassey, appealed to "a benevolent public, and to the friends of the Slave everywhere" to purchase items.[79]

In the Women's Association of Philadelphia, as in other black female societies, members not only demanded the end of slavery but worked equally hard for their community, devoting themselves to the "Elevation of the Colored People in the United States by Self-Exertion." Such a statement reflects the shift in focus of many black activists, who became concerned more with encouraging self-sufficiency among free blacks than with changing the racial attitudes of whites.

Antislavery societies, whether all-black or integrated, provided the structure within which black women could continue their community work and still participate in the campaign to end slavery. Participation in self-help activities represented continuation of a tradition of black activism, but, with particular responsibilities within the black community as a result of their gender. Community activism was a responsibility that the black community perceived as particularly suitable for women, but black women shared with white women an auxiliary status that required them to assume a supportive role to male leaders. Like white women, black women organized regular fund-raising events to support the abolitionist press and antislavery lecturers, but within the racially mixed societies, as illustrated in the cases of the Philadelphia and Boston organizations, black women occupied a subordinate position to white leadership.

Their commitment to black community improvement remained consistent throughout the antebellum years, though the context of their activism changed. In the early years of the movement, black leaders had argued that self-help activities would eventually overturn prevailing stereotypes of black inferiority and lead toward racial equality. By the 1840s, however, as racism persisted in the North and slavery became more firmly entrenched than ever in the South, a number of black men and women turned away from the original hope of reforming whites, looking instead to black nationalism and achievement of self-sufficiency within the black community. Although many black women supported Douglass's nationalist scheme, they did not sever the personal and professional ties they had forged with white women abolitionists, for, despite the limitations of interracial cooperation, racially-mixed societies had extended valuable aid to their local free black community.

The fact that some black women formed their own antislavery societies, however, reveals that these limitations hindered the achievement of black abolitionist goals and the development of black unity. Both the Salem Female Anti-Slavery Society and the Women's Association of Philadelphia represented alternatives to racially integrated or all-white female antislavery societies. The histories of these two organizations reveal that black women's abolitionist goals differed from those of many whites; black women may have welcomed cooperation with whites, but all-black organizations clearly allowed them to map out their own agendas to pursue their own goals. Like black men, black women abolitionists emphasized the need to participate in community self-help efforts in addition to supporting antislavery and hoped that a separate all-black female society could better respond to the needs of their community.

The racism of some white women abolitionists also motivated the formation of all-black societies. Differences in the perception of abolitionist goals and prevailing racist sentiments not only prevented full interracial cooperation but, for women abolitionists, precluded the possibility of creating a sisterhood between black and white women. Participation in organized abolitionism exposed black women to conflict over reform issues besides slavery and, at times, forced them to choose sides.

Garrison and his followers upheld the right of women to become voting members of the national organization and to engage in public activities for the good of the abolitionist cause. Many black and white women abolitionists, especially in Boston and Philadelphia, supported the emerging demands for women's rights. Women's affiliation with organized abolition apparently gave them the political experience that eventually guided their campaign for suffrage. Many black women abolitionists also supported women's rights and engaged in activities that were considered untraditional, for both women and blacks. But their feminism embraced not only the rights of women but equal rights for all blacks. Black women who engaged in public abolitionist activity were continuing the struggle for equal rights.

5

Breaking Customs

For a number of black women, commitment to the movement for racial equality led to participation in activities that challenged nineteenth-century notions of acceptable behavior for women and blacks. When women wrote antislavery poetry and prose, spoke from public platforms, or signed and circulated petitions condemning slavery and northern racism, they defied customary codes of behavior. In the process, they, as individuals and as a group, reconstructed notions of respectability within the free black community regarding black female activism. Historians have examined the careers of white women abolitionists and have acknowledged the pathbreaking contributions of outstanding individual black women to the movement, including Sojourner Truth, Sarah Parker Remond, Maria Stewart, Frances E. W. Harper, and Mary Ann Shadd Cary. Valuable collections of their writings and speeches have been published.[1]

In varying degrees, black women's activism challenged prevailing assumptions of black female inferiority. As we know, such images were deeply rooted, complex, and often contradictory. Whites often perceived black women as more docile than black men, simply because they were women, but a "Mammy" stereotype depicting black women as strong and domineering also prevailed among whites, an image that was reinforced when women physically resisted slavery and racism. Black women's activism also carried important implications for sexual dynamics within their communities, defying both racist laws and customs meant to keep blacks illiterate and submissive and racial and gender boundaries helping to define acceptable behavior in nineteenth-century American free society.

With the exception of Sojourner Truth and Ellen Craft, many of the leading Black women who engaged in public speaking and writing shared a common background. Margaretta Forten, Sarah Forten, Maria Miller Stewart, Frances Harper, Mary Ann Shadd Cary, and Sarah P. Remond had all been born into free black families in which they enjoyed some measure of economic privilege and formal education. Their background of education, relative economic comfort, and family activism set them apart from both slaves and the majority of free blacks. Their personal and professional connections with abolitionist friends, in addition to their own talents, undoubtedly helped them gain access to abolitionist newspapers and the public platform.

Public speaking and writing had long been acceptable ways for men to engage in intellectual self-expression, but not until the 1840s had women, white or black, begun in any numbers to break the custom barring them from such activities. The president of the Detroit Female Benevolent Association, a Black organization, expressed a degree of self-consciousness about speaking at one of the group's meetings: "Sister members, you are aware of the fact that it is not customary for females to speak or read in public, but since it has fallen my lot, I sacrifice all feeling of diffidence, and yield to your request."[3]

Proclaiming the evils of slavery and the possibility of racial equality, on the antislavery lecture circuit, was risky for anyone. Like abolitionist writers and editors, who faced the destruction of their presses and physical violence at the hands of anti-abolitionist mobs, antislavery lecturers risked their personal safety in their travels. Black women speakers, like other abolitionist men and women, were often at the mercy of hostile audiences who harassed them physically as well as verbally. Frances Harper, for example, wrote of troubles she and her colleagues encountered when they lectured in small towns in Ohio. At Columbiana they were "interrupted by a manifestation of rowdyism," and when they traveled to Churchill they were met with an attempt at sabotage: "We had some more persons of the same spirit, who made a noise during the time of speaking, and removed some of the linch pins from our wagon. It was, however, discovered in time to prevent any injury to life or limb."[4]

Violence on the lecture tours, was an even greater threat for black women than for black men and white abolitionists. Physical and verbal attacks against black women activists could originate at any time or place from crowds motivated by three sources of hostility: anti-black feelings, anti-abolitionist sentiments, and hatred of "public" women. Unlike male abolitionists, women who spoke in public invited criticism from audiences who believed they had violated basic ideals of "proper" behavior for women.

Although black women enjoyed support from the men of their race for their writings and, eventually, for their speeches, they still found themselves bound by codes of proper behavior for women. As in the white community, social custom in the free black community still required women to act like "ladies." Black male leaders applauded black women speakers only so long as they did not criticize black men directly or assume a position of authority in gatherings where men were present.[5] The period between 1830 and the 1860s was one in which female public speakers gradually gained acceptance from both abolitionist leaders and their audiences. Writing to Amy Post in 1845, black leader Jeremiah Sanderson approved of the change:

> A few years ago, men in this city [New York] hissed at the mere idea of Women's speaking in public in promiscuous assemblies, now men come to Anti-Slavery Conventions attracted by the announcement that Women are to take part in the deliberations and they are often more desirous of having Women, than men——The world is becoming habituated to it. . . . Woman is rising up, becoming free."[6]

Even as late as the 1850s, however, audiences in some cities still objected to the presence of women speakers. The male delegates at the eleventh Colored National Convention in Philadelphia in 1856 resisted a proposal to allow Mary Ann Shadd Cary to deliver an address. After lengthy discussion, the delegates finally voted to allow her to speak.[7] In that same year, Shadd Cary wrote from Rockford, Illinois, that "the citizens are so conservative on the question [of Women's Rights], as not to tolerate lectures from women."[8]

Public speaking, more than any other abolitionist activity, seemed to spark the greatest conflict between the sexes. Public opinion was slow to accept female lecturers, regardless of race, because public speaking was an activity in which an individual assumed a role of authority long the domain of political leaders and a predominantly male clergy and forbidden to women by social and religious custom.[9] Much of the criticism of women who spoke in public came from clergymen, who consistently condemned this form of activism as not only improper for respectable women but also in violation of St. Paul's biblical order for women to "keep silent." In 1837, a group of clergymen from Andover, Massachusetts, denounced Sarah and Angelina Grimké for delivering public addresses, in a letter to the *New England Spectator:* "The public lectures of females we have discountenanced and condemned as improper and unwise," a violation of religious faith, and a "departure from propriety."[10]

During the 1820s and 1830s, a number of influential black men also made strong objections to female lecturers. In 1828, Samuel Cornish and John Russwurm expressed their disdain in *Freedom's Journal* for Frances Wright, a white British woman and reportedly the first woman to deliver public speeches in the United States: "This woman ought to get into pantaloons immediately, she is a disgrace to the fairer part of creation."[11] Wright was well known not only for her public speaking but for advocating radical social changes that may have seemed threatening to black male leaders, including miscegenation as a solution to race prejudice. She attacked the churches for supporting patriarchal social relations and wrote extensively on the sexual experience.[12] Despite her strong antislavery stance, Cornish criticized her again in 1839 in the *Colored American:*

> LADIES BEWARE. . . . Fanny Wright's first step toward scepticism were her masculine assumptions. Male speculations and male experiments addled her brain, and male achievements engrossed her soul. The fatal result was to be expected—she is now the leader in masculine infidelity—one of the grossest sceptical disorganizers that ever cursed the world. Ladies are lovely, truly lovely in their place, but alas! when they abandon it!![13]

Black male audiences were especially hostile when women speakers publicly criticized the behavior of black men. In 1831 in Boston, an audience of black men jeered and threw rotten tomatoes at Maria Miller Stewart when she delivered an address to black men that criticized them for failing to follow basic Christian principles of thrift, sobriety, and hard work.[14] After two years of public speaking, Stewart concluded that her appeals to her fellow blacks had accomplished little, and on September 21, 1833, she delivered a farewell announcing her decision to leave Boston. Her last speech revealed her bitterness and disappointment, noting that it was "no use for me as an individual, to try to make myself useful among my color in this city."[15]

The black itinerant preacher Zilpha Elaw, one of a very few female preachers during this period, fared only slightly better. She traveled to England in 1842 to preach to "large assemblies." Leading members of the British and Foreign Anti-Slavery Society apparently received her "rather coldly"—"probably because she was a woman, traveling in the capacity of public teacher or exhorter," Lucretia Mott speculated.[16] Such secondhand reports are difficult to corroborate. A number of pages are missing from Elaw's memoirs, and in the surviving portion she mentions nothing about her reception by the British abolitionists. She does, however, describe being negatively received at a small Methodist church in Liverpool in 1841, where the minister and his wife, "Mr. & Mrs. D," lectured her privately about the inappropriateness of preaching by women. They advised Elaw that she was better suited to the Quakers and did not belong to the Methodists.[17]

Black and white women speakers drew additional criticism when they spoke to audiences made up of both men and women, in defiance of traditional dictates that male and female audiences be kept separated, sometimes in different rooms. At the World Antislavery Convention in London in 1840, for example, male and female members of the audience sat in separate sections of the hall, with women in the back behind a curtain, where they were not allowed to participate in the proceedings. Despite strong support from some men for a proposal to include women as equal participants and not just as silent observers, the majority of men in the audience rejected it.

For white women, in particular, public speaking posed a threat to domestic tranquility. Writing poetry and essays did not require women to leave their households, and even women who attended local antislavery society meetings or antislavery sewing circles usually did not need to travel outside the neighborhood or town. But delivering speeches was another matter: it required women to leave their homes and towns and, hence, their domestic duties, threatening physical and psychological boundaries. Men and women who opposed the idea of women speaking in public feared that because it drew women away from their homes and into the political arena with men, they would abandon their domestic responsibilities altogether.

Free blacks may have had similar concerns when they saw the women of their race participating in lecture tours. Unlike middle-class white women, black women were often away from their families for most of the day, because most worked outside the home. Although it was clear that black women had not abandoned their family responsibilities when they left home to earn a wage and participate in community activism, some blacks were apprehensive about women who sought to leave their communities to engage in potentially dangerous activity. As a result, black women lecturers received mixed responses. Some black leaders perhaps understood too clearly the damage that racism and economic deprivation had already done to the ideals of manhood and womanhood in the free black community; it was bad enough that black women had to help support their families, and allowing them to be drawn further from home duties by participating in public-speaking tours might permanently damage the effort to create middle-class gender roles.

Abolitionists such as Frederick Douglass and Charles Lenox Remond, who gave wholehearted support to female lecturers, perceived the situation a bit differently. They put aside such notions of sex roles for the moment and saw these women as assets to the campaign to promote race pride, as well as a source of public opposition to slavery and racism. By the 1840s and 1850s, many male leaders argued that black women speakers, in particular, occupied an important place in the abolitionist movement. William C. Nell wrote to Garrison in 1858, for example, in praise of Frances (Watkins) Harper: "Miss Watkins's exertions in the lecturing field cannot but yield an abundant anti-slavery harvest. Her audiences during this campaign were always so impressed as to urge her continuance, or at least promise of her early return."[18] Mary Ann Shadd Cary also applauded Watkins's speaking abilities:

> Miss Watkins & Mr. Nell came back to Detroit and she is going west. a ways. Why the whites & colored people here are just going crazy with excitement about her. She is the greatest female speaker ever was here, so wisdom obliges me to keep out of the way as with her prepared lectures there would just be no chance of favorable comparison.[19]

Shadd Cary also noted that it would be impolitic for her not to support Watkins: "I puff her as strongly as any body in fact it is the very best for me to do so otherwise it would be put down to jealousy."[20]

The appeal to race pride, in particular, helped to justify black women's participation in public activities and made it more acceptable for black women than for white women to engage in non-traditional activities such as public speaking. Mary Ann Shadd Cary, for example, received praise from black colleagues for her speaking efforts. Her coeditors of the *Provincial Freeman* portrayed her in 1856 as a positive representative of the free black community: "Remember, that they [blacks] belong to a class denied all social and political rights, and after they had been listened to, will the people say they are inferior to ANY of the lecturers among white fellow citizens? O' why will the people not be just?"[21]

The fact that many black female speakers delivered effective lectures also helped make them more acceptable to their audiences. Black and white observers could not deny that many of the black women who gained prominence as speakers were actually talented orators who often expressed ideas that intrigued their audiences. In praise of Frances Harper, William Still noted that "perhaps few speakers surpass her in using language and arguments, more potently, in impressing and charming her audiences."[22] When the delegates at the eleventh Colored National Convention finally allowed Shadd to speak, at least one observer complimented her for her effort even though he opposed her stand on emigration:

> Her ideas seem to flow so fast that she, at times hesitated for words; yet she overcomes any apparent imperfections in her speaking by the earnestness of her manner and the quality of her thoughts. She is a superior woman; and it is useless to deny it; however much we may differ with her on the subject of emigration. She obtained the floor and succeeded in making one of the most convincing speeches in favor of Canadian emigration I ever heard.[23]

When Shadd delivered an address at Elkhorn, Indiana, an observer noted that despite a "nervous and hurried" speaking style her lecture was "replete with original ideas and soundest logic . . . and unmistakably showed that she is a woman of superior intellect, of high literary cultivation, and the most persevering energy of character."[24] Sarah Remond, who delivered most of her lectures in England, also received praise for the effectiveness of her speeches. Observers in Bury said she demonstrated a "very eloquent style of address" and delivered "a most impressive lecture" on "the horrors of slavery." Other English witnesses described her style as both "eloquent and thrilling."[25]

Finally, the fact that black women speakers exuded "feminine qualities" when they spoke from the public platform undoubtedly helped make them more acceptable to their audiences. William Still once described Frances Harper as "gentle," as well as an "earnest, eloquent, and talented heroine."[26] When Shadd Cary delivered an address at Elkhorn, Indiana, in 1856, one observer praised not only the content of her speech, but the manner of its delivery, which was termed "modest, and in strict keeping with the popular notions of the 'sphere of women.' "[27] In England, where codes of social propriety were even stricter than in the United States, Sarah Remond received praise for exhibiting feminine qualities when she spoke. In Bristol, she "spoke for an hour with the utmost readiness and clearness, with an admirable choice of words, and with a womanly dignity, which was the admiration of all who heard her." The editors of the *Warrington Times* described her as "one of the best female lecturers we have heard; her gentle and easy manner, combined with an animated and intelligent countenance, rivets the attention of her auditors."[28] Audiences perhaps expected that women should still retain feminine qualities if they insisted on expressing their opinions publicly. Over time, however, as women continued to speak in public, black and white men eventually became accustomed to the idea that women could participate in such activity and still retain their "femininity."

Both black and white women also challenged contemporary codes of appropriate behavior for women through the act of writing. White women writers found themselves limited primarily by gender expectations: they found a large, receptive audience only when they wrote on "feminine" subjects, such as female piety and domesticity, and only so long as they were not aggressive or political. Even within these bounds, however, the success of white women writers such as Catharine Maria Sedgewick and Lydia H. Sigourney led competition with male writers in the already crowded literary marketplace. To defend such obvious intrusion into a male domain, many white women writers felt obliged to argue that their writing would not lead them away from their homes and domestic duties.[29]

Black women writers struggled not only with contemporary views on women's "sphere" but with barriers of race. For them, the act of writing challenged prevailing stereotypes of black female intellectual inferiority, even though they were following in a tradition first charted by writers such

Sarah P. Remond, public speaker.
(Courtesy, Essex Institute, Salem, Mass.)

as Lucy Terry and Phillis Wheatley, who had established writing as a form of black female expression during the mid-eighteenth century.[30] Between 1830 and 1865, Sarah Forten, Margaretta Forten, Frances Harper, and Mary Ann Shadd Cary all continued to write, within the context of protest.

Race prejudice usually prevented black women from getting their works published.[31] Lucy Terry's poem, "Bar's Fight," for example, was not published until 1895, though it had been written in 1746. During the antebellum period, black women poets and essayists were able to publish their works only with the aid of prominent abolitionists, and they gained the most public attention when they wrote for abolitionist audiences. Lydia Maria Child, Garrison, and Still, for example, helped several black women writers publish collections of poetry and essays.

Readers often praised the women and their works as shining examples of black progress, which refuted racist stereotypes. In 1836, one reader, known to us only as "S. S.", praised Sarah Forten and her poem, "The Grave of the Slave": "We have here another proof of the folly of the assertion which ignorance and prejudice, united, have attempted to palm upon the world; viz,—that the colored race are incapable of intellectual and moral elevation."[32] Referring to Forten as "a colored female residing in Philadelphia," "S. S." refuted the claim that black women could not attain the status of "ladies": "I ought to have said *young lady,* even at the risk of exciting a sneer among certain doughfaces; her whole department bears testimony to the fact that she is truly such."[33]

Garrison, in his preface to Frances Harper's poetry collection, *Poems on Miscellaneous Subjects*, suggested that her work would help the black community gain respect and, eventually, equality. He described her as representing "intelligence, talent, genius, and piety" and said her poems would "deepen the interest already so extensively felt in the liberation and enfranchisement of the entire colored race." In a letter to Mary Ann Shadd Cary in 1854, Still described Harper as a "gifted" member of the "downtrodden class—in complexion and proscription" who, while working as a seamstress and a teacher, devoted her spare time to improving her skills as a writer. Her selection of poems, he said, demonstrated her ability to judge "of what kind of material is best suited to reach the heart."[31]

Mary Ann Shadd Cary, the first black female newspaper editor, also received praise for providing a vehicle for black voices and for expanding the role of black women in the movement. Shadd was well aware of the significance her position held for black women, and even congratulated herself for setting a precedent: "To colored women, we have a work—we have 'broken the Editorial ice' . . . for your class in America; so go on editing, as you are ready."[35] H. T. Williams, a black male abolitionist, commended Shadd for breaking the gender barrier in publishing: "Although this routine of business for a female looks masculine, in the eyes of some, and is sneered at by the same class . . . yet it is creditable and praisworthy, and never fails to produce a salutary effect. If Miss Shadd has gained any new plumes to her wreath, she is fully deserving of them, for her intrinsic value is not half known, nor appreciated by the people she has so faithfully served."[36]

Several common themes emerge from Black women's oral and written work: the sexual exploitation of slave women by white men and the impact of slavery on slave mothers, the hope for creating an alliance between black and white women, and the need for black community improvement. An examination of their speeches and writings reveals the particular contribution they made to abolitionist thought and rhetoric. Sarah Forten, Frances Harper, Sarah Remond, and Sojourner Truth described the harshness of slavery; though only Truth had actually been a slave, even the freeborn women related vivid descriptions of the black woman's experience under slavery. They probably gained their knowledge of slavery from contacts with fugitive slaves that can be traced to their families' involvement in the Underground Railroad and their connections with prominent abolitionists. In Sarah Forten's poem, "Grave of the Slave," she suggests that death might be preferable to life in bondage:

Poor slave! shall we sorrow that death was thy friend!
The last and the kindest that Heaven could send:—
The grave to the weary is welcome and blest;
And death to the captive is freedom and rest.[37]

Harper, Remond, and Truth argued that slavery was especially difficult for slave mothers, who often saw their children sold away from them, and their writings examined the breakup of the slave family and the sexual exploitation of slave women. Harper, one of the most prolific black woman writers of the nineteenth century, wrote several poems depicting the experiences of slave mothers. In "The Slave Mother," she described the powerlessness of slave parents to prevent the sale of themselves or their children:

She is a mother, pale with fear,
  Her boy clings to her side,
And in her kirtle vainly tries
  His trembling form to hide.

He is not hers, although she bore
  For him a mother's pains;
He is not hers, although her blood
  Is coursing through his veins!

He is not hers, for cruel hands
  May rudely tear apart
The only wreath of household love
  That binds her breaking heart.[38]

Sojourner Truth described her own trials as a slave mother in her now famous "Ain't I a Woman" speech in 1851: "I have born thirteen children, and seen them most all sold into slavery, and when I cried out with my mother's grief, none but Jesus heard me!"[39] In "Eliza Harris," Harper's central character is a slave mother who tries to escape with her child, risking death:

She was nearing a river—in reaching the brink,
She heeded no danger, she paused not to think!
For she is a mother—her child is a slave—
And she'll give him his freedom, or find him a grave.[40]

By emphasizing the experience of motherhood, perhaps Harper and Truth hoped to appeal to white women and to create a common bond between all women abolitionists and slave women. Black women writers and speakers, when addressing the public, often promoted the idea of a cross-racial "sisterhood," even though they knew that racism existed openly within the movement as well as in society at large. The writings of Sarah Forten reflect this effort to emphasize the shared experiences of women of both races. In 1836, writing under the pseudonym "Ada," Forten recalled her own acceptance of women's "appropriate sphere" in a poem entitled "Lines":

> Yes, this is woman's work,
> Her appropriate sphere; and nought should drive
> Her from the mercy seat, til mercy's work be finished.[41]

At the Antislavery Convention of American Women held in New York City in 1837, she contributed a poem in which she links her belief in a female alliance to ties of womanhood and Christianity:

> We are thy sisters. God has truly said,
> That of one blood the nations he has made.
> O, Christian woman! in a Christian land,
> Canst thou unblushing read this great command?
> Suffer the wrongs which wring our inmost heart,
> To draw one throb of pity on thy part!
> Our skins may differ, but from thee we claim
> A sister's privilege and a sister's name.[42]

Forten's belief that "women's influence" was essential to the success of abolitionism and that women of both races should unite in the cause was typical of nineteenth-century expectations of women reformers. Her cry for unity among women of all races also suggests that white women had not always accepted black women as sisters.

Sarah Remond, in her speech in 1859 on the differences between slave women and white women, drew on the theme of sexual exploitation to suggest common bonds of womanhood between black and white women: "If English women and English wives knew the unspeakable horrors to which their sex were exposed on southern plantations, they would freight every westward gale with the voice of their moral indignation, and demand for the black woman the protection and rights enjoyed by the white."[43] In a report on Remond's speech, a writer for the *Anti-Slavery Advocate* argued that by emphasizing the sexual exploitation of slave women Remond intended to evoke sympathy and cooperation from white women in England:

> She called especially on the women of England to sympathize in the atrocious wrongs of the colored women of America, who are sold for their basest purposes, their value on the auction block being raised by every quality of beauty, talent, piety, and goodness which should have commanded the respect and tenderness of their fellow-creatures.[44]

Remond's theme of sexual exploitation and motherhood emphasized the shared experience of womanhood, it also suggests that slave status for black women precluded the creation of a universal sisterhood: "There was this unmeasurable difference between the condition of the poorer English woman and that of the slave woman—that their persons were free and their progeny their own, while the slavewoman was the victim of the heartless lust of her master, and the children whom she bore were his property."[45] She perceived both the commonalities of gender oppression linking black and white women, and the inseparability of gender and race in the lives of black women. In the United States, race was the determining factor that allowed some women freedom and placed others in bondage—even the poorest white women were at least free, though, as Remond admits, planters sometimes treated poor whites "with more contempt than the slaves themselves."[46] Her suggestion that sexual and reproductive exploitation characterized the lives of slave women pointed to a crucial distinction between their lives and those of white women.

Remond apparently was optimistic, at least in public, about breaking down racial barriers at least within abolitionist circles. her own treatment in England may have heartened her to this possibility. In February 1859, when she addressed an all-female audience at the Red Lion Hotel in Warrington, the Englishwomen at the meeting gave her a watch. The inscription read: "Presented to S. P. Remond by Englishwomen her sisters, in Warrington, February 2nd, 1859." Remond responded, "I have been received here as a sister by white women."[47]

Another topic of much concern to black women writers and speakers was the encouragement of free black men and women to participate in community-improvement activities. Not all audiences, of course, appreciated this advice, as Maria Stewart discovered more than twenty years earlier when she attempted to advise black men on "proper" conduct. Like other reformers of her generation, Stewart promoted middle-class values of thrift, sobriety, and hard work, and argued against gambling and dancing, which she believed undermined efforts to achieve black self-sufficiency: "I would implore our men, and especially our rising youth, to flee from the gambling board and the dance-hall; for we are poor, and have no money to throw away." Contemporary newspapers note that her advice met with hostility.[48]

Stewart also argued that improved education in the free black community would help end racial prejudice by convincing whites of the "moral worth and intellectual improvement" of blacks. During the early 1830s, Stewart predicted that "prejudice would gradually diminish, and the whites would be compelled to say—Unloose those fetters! Though Black their skins as shades of night, Their hearts are—pure—their souls are white."[49] Using widely accepted Christian imagery in her arguments, Stewart, like most thinkers of her time, referred to sin as black and righteousness as white.

Nearly a generation later, Frances Harper maintained that education in "virtue and morality" as well as in practical skills was necessary for improving the condition of free blacks and would result in their reception "as citizens, not worse than strangers."[50] She added that material wealth among free blacks, though important for improving the community, entailed a special responsibility to the slave. In an essay submitted to the *Anglo-African Magazine* in May 1859, Harper urged blacks to use their time and money to support the movement to end slavery: "We have money among us, but how much of it is spent to bring deliverance to our captive brethren? Are our wealthiest men the most liberal sustainers of the Anti-slavery enterprise? Or does the bare fact of our having money, really help mould public opinion and reverse its sentiments?"[51]

Although these writers and lecturers often received praise from black male abolitionists, social custom within the black community still required them to act like "respectable ladies." The career of Mary Ann Shadd and her tumultuous relationship with Henry Bibb suggests that as late as the 1850s such ideas prevailed, even when black male leadership supported female public activism. The feud between Shadd and Henry Bibb over "caste" schools and the Refugee Home Society contributed to Shadd's decision to establish her own abolitionist newspaper, symbolic of the rift between them. Her newspaper, the *Provincial Freeman*, published articles on a variety of subjects, including anti-colonization, emigration, slavery, self-help, and moral improvement. The project, however, was more than simply a vehicle for opposing the Bibbs; it was intended in part to open the way for black women who desired careers in editing and publishing. White abolitionist women, such as Elizabeth Chandler and Lydia Maria Child, already had broken the white gender barrier in newspaper editing.[52] Shadd's claim that she had "broken the Editorial Ice" for the women of her race reveals that she clearly identified herself with her female readers, whom she urged to pursue careers in writing and publishing.

Shadd's plainspoken and direct style contrasted markedly with the eloquent poetry and prose of Sarah Forten and Frances Harper. Shadd never hesitated to criticize persons and institutions she considered harmful to herself, to the antislavery cause, or to the progress of the free black community. For example, she attacked churches in Canada and the United States for allegedly supporting slavery, arguing that the "American church is the pillar of American slavery." In 1856, she expressed disdain for Frederick Douglass in an article for the *Provincial Freeman:* "Having been permitted so long to remain in our tub, we would rather that the great Frederick Douglass, for whose public career we have the most profound pity, would stay out of our sunlight."[53] In the same issue, she despaired that a number of leading white and black abolitionists (including, in her opinion, Douglass) could still support colonization:

> An abolitionist . . . remarked to us recently, that it was very easy to be an abolitionist and a colonizationist at the same time—that Mrs. H[arriet] B[eecher] Stowe—and that many others confessed to like views can be held, but we feel quite sure, that the "Uncle Tom" fever struck down many a brave man and woman from the abolition ranks . . . and we have reason to fear that the epidemic is raging among "leading" colored men. Mrs. Stowe . . . Miss Miner at Washington . . . Frederick Douglass of evangelical memory.[54]

Her outspokenness sometimes bordered on personal attack and inevitably invited criticism from those who already disagreed with her opinions.

Black women abolitionists' use of the pen and the public platform to articulate their opinions demonstrated an individual independence and a willingness to challenge prevailing expectations of gender and race. The act of public speaking and writing among black women, by defying racist expectations of black docility and intellectual inferiority, led black male leaders as well as many white abolitionists to accept black women writers and speakers as symbols of black success and resistance. Unlike white women, they could be perceived as assets to both the black community and the abolitionist movement. Their writings and speeches, as explicit forms of black protest and self-expression, provided fuel for abolitionist propaganda even as they continued a tradition of writing established by black female authors a century earlier. For black women, public speaking gradually became socially acceptable, as long as they stopped short of direct criticism of black men or challenges to male authority.

Male and female abolitionists of both races had frequently used the petition as a way to protest slavery and race discrimination in the "nominally free states." They flooded Congress and their state legislatures with antislavery petitions throughout the antebellum period, demanding the end of slavery and race discrimination in the District of Columbia and the United States. The onslaught of petitions so incensed southern congressmen that they succeeded in passing a gag rule, which, until its repeal in December 1844, tabled any discussion of slavery on the floor of the House.

For woman and black men, however, the petition was more than an abolitionist tactic. Political disfranchisement was a condition they shared until 1869, when the passage of the Fifteenth Amendment left women as the only adult group without the right to vote. Although anyone could circulate and sign a petition, this form of political expression reflected their exclusion from the American political system. For disfranchised groups—but not, of course, for white men, who had the right to vote—the petition was the only legal means to make their voices heard and seek changes in the law. In 1840, several white male abolitionists formed an antislavery political party in hopes of overthrowing the "Slave Power" in Congress. For women and most black men, who could not vote, the formation of political parties held little meaning. A contributor to the *Colored American*, known only as "A Friend", expressed support for women's involvement in petition drives: "I think as they are identified with us in our sufferings . . . they are the aggrieved with us, and being aggrieved with us, certainly ought to have the right to petition also to have these grievances removed."[55]

Many male observers considered women's participation in petitioning campaigns an improper intrusion into a traditionally male domain. One defender of female petitioners described some of these criticisms: "The New York Sun is very severe upon the 'Eastern women' who are getting up petitions against the admission of Texas [as a slave state], and thinks they had better be shaking bed ticks rather than politics."[56] Supporters of women petitioners combined ideas of women's "nature" and patriotism as justification for participation in a political activity. In 1837, one contributor wrote a lengthy defense in *The Liberator:*

> But now that our attention is called to the most dreadful scenes which are daily occurring in our own country, where the female slave murders her infant . . . that it may never know the horrors of slavery; where husband and wife, parents and children, are separated under the hammer of the auctioneers . . . and we have formed societies for the dissemination of light on this subject, and petitioning Congress to abolish the soul-destroying system; at least so far as they have the exclusive power to do it—why we immediately overstep the bounds of female delicacy and propriety![57]

The *New York Sun* writer supported women petitioners by arguing that women's influence would help to purify the nation: "if our 'State Laws' exclude them from Voting, they ought not to be excluded from exerting an influence upon the morals and prosperity of the nation."[58]

Supporters also argued that these women were merely following in the patriotic traditions of their foremothers in the War for Independence. "A Female Petitioner" wrote: "Well remember their [Revolutionary-era women's] readiness to aid their husbands, fathers, and brothers. Now loading fire arms; now moulding bullets, now exposing deep laid schemes of treachery. . . . Did they overstep the bounds of female delicacy and propriety?"[59] One writer for the *Boston Times*, responding to the *New York Sun* article, argued that "Our grandmothers of the revolution did not confine themselves to 'shaking bed ticks.' . . . When those good grandmothers assisted in shaking the redcoats we had no squeamish editors . . . to cry out against it."

Female antislavery societies and activist groups within the black community provided black women with opportunities to participate in abolitionist petition drives. Between 1834 and 1850, for example, the members of the Philadelphia Female Anti-Slavery Society sent petitions to the state legislature of Pennsylvania and to Congress, demanding the end of slavery. To Congress, they wrote: "The undersigned respectfully ask that you will . . . abolish everything in the Constitution or Laws of the U.S. which in any manner sanctions or sustains slavery."[60] In the society's 1836 annual report, members wrote of their commitment to petitioning:

> Since the year 1834, we have annually memorialized Congress, praying for the abolition of slavery in the District of Columbia and the Territories of the United States. We are frequently asked what

> good have petitions done: The full amount of good produced by them, is yet to be revealed. . . . We knew that our petitions were not ineffectual, when the wise men of the South, sent back to us the cry, 'Impertinent intermeddlers! incorrect devils! &c.'[61]

Black women members of the society frequently served on committees to coordinate petition drives in the Philadelphia area. Committee members drew up detailed maps of the city and assigned individuals and groups of women to cover specific neighborhoods. In 1835, for example, Sarah Forten and Hetty Burr were the two black members appointed to a committee to "obtain signatures to a petition to Congress."[62]

In Boston, members of the Female Anti-Slavery Society also signed and circulated petitions. In 1837, Maria Weston Chapman, representing the society, coordinated women's petitions protesting the annexation of Texas as a slave state. In addition to petitioning against slavery, members also circulated petitions protesting race discrimination against free blacks. Black and white abolitionists petitioned, in particular, against discrimination on railroads, racial segregation in public schools, and the state marriage law, which outlawed interracial marriages.

In 1839, black members Susan Paul, Eunice R. Davis, Lavinia Hilton, Chloe Lee, Jane Putnam, and Julia Williams joined with the other "undersigned women of Boston," in submitting a petition to the Massachusetts legislature denouncing the law that forbade interracial marriage. This protest revealed a radical side to the predominantly white, middle-class group. It has been argued that the movement to abolish the marriage law, which was repealed in 1843, was primarily the result of white initiative, because blacks, recognizing the sensitivity of the issue, approached it cautiously.[63] Additional evidence, however, indicates that although the movement for repeal had been a pet project for white abolitionists since the emergence of Garrison, the black community may also have felt strongly; in February 1843, a group of "Colored Citizens of Boston" met to draw up resolutions supporting *The Liberator*, and denouncing the state marriage laws and race discrimination on railroads. The group agreed to circulate these resolutions within the black community in Boston, and antislavery-society member Eunice R. Davis was one of three black women appointed to a committee to obtain signatures for the petitions.[64]

Strong voices emanated from both sides over whether to keep the old colonial anti-miscegenation law on the books, and both sides questioned the authenticity of the petitions and counter-petitions that made their way to the Massachusetts legislature. Not long after the resolutions of the "Colored Citizens of Boston" appeared, another petition was presented to the legislature, apparently signed by twenty "colored ladies" in Boston, which supported the effort to end race discrimination on railroad cars but denounced the attempt to abolish the state law prohibiting interracial marriages. Regardless of whether this petition was forged or legitimate, whoever wrote it used language that reflected contemporary ideas about the role of men as protectors of the home and family. But instead of the standard anti-miscegenation argument—that interracial marriages were unnatural and went against God's intentions—the argument chosen appeared to look out for the best interests of black women by claiming that repeal of the marriage law would deprive them of their "natural protectors and supporters," without whom they would be "thrown upon the world friendless and despised, and forced to get our bread by our own vile means that may be proposed to us by others, or that despair may teach us to invent."[65] While members of the anti-repeal group used the petition as proof of the law's benefit to blacks, Garrisonians denounced the document as a "low device of white blackguards" and a "worthless hoax."[66]

The fear that black men would choose to marry white women instead of black women if the existing marriage law were abolished probably reflected the thinking of whites more than of blacks. After the legislature repealed the law in 1843, and interracial marriages did increase in Boston over time, approximately 91 percent of all black men were married to black women in 1850. The increase in marriages between blacks and whites was undoubtedly the result of residential patterns among Boston's poor population, in which poor whites, mostly Irish, sometimes boarded with blacks.[67]

Despite the fact that the legislators never mentioned the petition again after the initial debate, the incident is significant. The submission of the counter-petition, whether faked or authentic, illustrates the visible role that free black women played in the petition campaign. If the document was real, it suggested that not all free black women in Boston supported the drive to abolish the existing law, a position based, perhaps, on the historical experience of black men and women. Outright opposition or silence on the issue may reflect knowledge of the history of exploitation and abuse in slavery and, hence, the desire to ensure solidarity between black men and women in freedom. If the document was a fake, it was produced by people who knew that black women were active in the petition drives that protested racial discrimination, and thus that submission of such a document by black women would not be unusual.

Black women also participated in the drive to eliminate racial discrimination in the private and public education of free blacks. In Boston and Philadelphia, centers of abolitionist activity, black women participated so actively in petition campaigns that their names made up a large portion of black signatures on some of the petitions circulated within the free black community. In both New Haven and Middletown, Connecticut, black women outnumbered black male signers against the 1833 "Black Law" prohibiting education of "colored persons" who came to Connecticut from another state without the permission of local officials. In March 1838, the newly organized Connecticut State Anti-Slavery Society passed a resolution urging inhabitants of the state to sign and circulate petitions requesting repeal of the law. Perhaps in response to the society's appeal, eighty-five black women and fifty-four black men in New Haven and thirty-six black women and twenty-six black men in Middletown, signing themselves "the colored inhabitants," submitted petitions requesting the repeal of the "Black Law" to the Connecticut legislature, which did repeal the law in May 1838.[68]

In addition to working with their local anitslavery societies, black women abolitionists also coordinated petition drives within the black community protesting racial segregation in the public school system. In 1844 black women in Boston signed a petition to prevent the establishment of separate schools for black children. In the "Petition on Separate Schools to the Boston Committee," Eunice R. Davis, Margarett Scarlett, Eliza Ann Logan Lawton, and Anna Logan identified themselves as "the undersigned, colored citizens of Boston," rather than as representatives of the Boston Female Anti-Slavery Society. In the petition, they argued that "the establishment of separate schools for the coloured children of this city appears to us inexpedient."[69] The decision of these women to identify with their community rather than the female antislavery society indicates that their commitment to the community existed apart from organized abolitionism.

The movement for school desegregation in Boston flourished in the free black community by the 1840s, reversing the position taken more than a generation before, when black parents had vigorously campaigned for the establishment of separate black schools. Over the decades, it had become evident that separate schools under the authority of the all-white Board of Education and Primary School Committee had not resulted in the equal education of black and white children in Boston. The inadequate supplies in the African Schools and neglect of building maintenance led to increased absenteeism and a decline in interest in the schools.[70] Moreover, black leaders and parents expressed resentment over their lack of autonomy with respect to education of their children and were rebuffed several times by the Board of Education, whose members saw the black schools as solely under the jurisdiction of the board. Black parents found they had no say over the hiring and firing of teachers, most of whom between 1818 and 1848, with the exception of John B. Russwurm, were white men.[71] For black women, this situation was particularly precarious, as is illustrated by the case of Miss Woodson, a black teacher. Fired after teaching five years in the black primary school, Woodson had been judged incompetent by the board, despite the praise she had received from black parents for her literary qualifications. The board explained that they would have ousted Woodson earlier, except that they had wanted to "experiment" with a "colored teacher" and give her a "long and fair trial," so as not to "wound the feelings of the colored people." The board subsequently hired a Miss Symmes, a white teacher, to replace Woodson.[72] Black parents and leaders of the black community registered numerous protests against what they saw as heavy-handedness at best and racism at worst. The board viewed such protests in terms of routine conflict with parents over autonomy, rather than as the racism that was implicit in their judgments of black teachers.

Black women as well as black men in Boston were an integral part of the movement to wrest control of black education from whites, even if it meant desegregating the public school system. But a number of black men and women maintained support for separate black schools, which they saw as legitimate as long as black parents had control over the education of their children and their schools received the same treatment as did white schools. Dominating the structure and administration of public education in Boston were white men whose policies reflected racist and sexist assumptions. Integrationists won their battle in 1855, after more than a decade of petitions and picketing of the Smith School by black parents.[73]

Black women also took part in the third major area in the fight against segregation, campaigning against segregation in public transportation. Black women as well as men, regardless of class, routinely suffered public humiliation from railway conductors and ticket collectors. They were often forcibly removed and verbally abused when attempting to board segregated trains and carriages. In San Francisco, one writer for the black newspaper, *Pacific Appeal,* noted that such incidents were not exceptional: "We often hear of gross insults being offered to respectable and well dressed colored ladies by the conductors of the horse railroad cars."[74] Deborah Lancaster, a black woman traveling from Alliance to Lima, Ohio, in 1859 refused the head brakeman's order to leave the ladies' car. After he barred her way into the car and ordered her into the forward car, Lancaster went into the ladies' section anyway. When she sat down, the brakeman entered, threatening to stop the train and eject her. Fortunately, Lancaster received the support of several white passengers and was able to remain on the train. Another black woman, Elizabeth Jennings, sued the Third Avenue Railroad Company in New York for being ejected from a car on her way to church. In the well-publicized case, Jennings eventually won $225 for damages as well as the right of blacks to ride the cars unmolested.[75] In another well-publicized case, Charlotte L. Brown of San Francisco sued the Omnibus Rail Road Company in 1863 after the conductor refused to take her ticket and then ejected her from the car, claiming that "colored persons are not allowed to ride." As was revealed in the testimony, the conductor had acted on his own accord, for the company had rescinded its previous policy of excluding blacks.[76] As is well known, female resistance to race discrimination in public conveyances continued well into the twentieth century.

Although they failed to convince Congress to abolish slavery and prevent its extension into the territories of the Southwest, black and white petitioners did succeed in obtaining repeal of some discriminatory laws on the state and local levels. For Black women, petitioning served as a way both to protest slavery and race discrimination and to participate in a political system that excluded them from full citizenship on the basis of race and sex.

Petitioning provided black women with their only opportunity to appeal to the state and federal governments for the end of slavery and race discrimination. Like writing and speaking, it was a way to make their voices heard in a society in which they, as blacks and as women, had been expected to keep silent. The public work that many women performed for the sake of abolition, however, quickly raised questions about the "proper" role of women in public reform. For black women abolitionists, this "woman question" held important implications for the black abolitionist agenda, because women's rights would, in some ways, directly contradict black goals for the creation of a truly free community.

6

Sowing the Seeds of Black Feminism

During the 1830s, the "woman question" had opened animated discussion about the possibility of achieving sexual as well as racial equality, given the extensiveness of female activism in the battle against slavery. The abolitionist movement had provided the setting in which both black and white women challenged their subordinate status as females and campaigned for an equal voice for women in antislavery organizations and in society at large.[1] Black women interested in rights for women continued the struggle against racism, no doubt because experience had made them painfully aware of contradictions between rhetoric and reality in the struggle for equality. White feminist-abolitionists had proclaimed a sisterhood between themselves and black women, likening their own oppression to that of the slave and using as a favorite rhetorical device the image of the black woman as a victim of double oppression—but white women, as a group, could not always be trusted to evaluate their own complicity in racism or even to understand black women's concerns.[2] In fact, only a few white women had publicly addressed the problem of racism among white reformers.

Studies on the history of feminism in the United States have generally referred to the struggle for sexual equality as "the" women's movement, as if only one such movement ever existed. While acknowledging the existence and reproduction of racism in American feminism, the focus has been primarily on white women's activities as well as on their participation in the systematic and conscious exclusion of black women. It is well known that white women did create a white women's movement in the 1840s, and that as the campaign developed into an independent movement they paid less and less attention to black women and often discouraged them from joining or participating in predominantly white suffrage organizations. Such attitudes continued throughout the nineteenth century, as white leaders worried that associating with blacks might jeopardize an alliance with southern white women who had not supported abolition. They knew that although abolitionist women were an active and vocal lot, they represented a numerical minority of the American population. Moreover, abolition had been unpopular among many northern as well as southern whites, who feared that ending slavery and promoting racial equality would result in racial amalgamation. But a failure to perceive race and class as essential to women's liberation shaped the agenda of the white women's movement and ultimately prevented the possibility of forging a biracial feminist alliance, a failure of vision that would remain problematic into the twentieth century.[3]

The movement that white women had created, however, was not the only movement, nor the primary one from the perspective of black women. To shift the focus away from white middle-class women—to bring women of color in from a marginal position to the center of discussion—opens the possibility of a fuller examination of women's rights.[4] Moreover, such an approach calls into question the existence of a single women's movement, when in fact at least two existed simultaneously. Black women, by virtue of a long history of activism, had also generated a movement for women's rights, one that pursued an even broader agenda than that of white feminists.

White feminists' adoption of overtly racist tactics led black women once again to establish their own pattern of activism by forming black suffrage organizations. When white feminists fought to dissociate the movement from its abolitionist roots, black women activists recognized the need to maintain black abolitionist goals. Separate participation in the struggle for sexual equality, however, was not simply a response to exclusion by whites; it was a continuation and expansion of a tradition of resistance and protest, in which the terms "liberation" and "equality" included the elimination of racism as well as sexism. Consequently, their agenda was the most dangerous and radical that this generation of reformers could formulate, for it represented the possibility of overturning two of the most firmly entrenched forms of oppression.

Ironically, white and free black women who had participated in reform activities shared similar experiences, because on every level of public activism, sexist conventions had helped define their roles. In their interactions with men, women as a group occupied the "female" role as supporters of male activities. For those women who engaged in antislavery activism, public opinion made them acutely aware of the consequences of engaging in "male" activities. It was in organized abolition that black and white women publicly demanded an equal voice with men in the proceedings of state and national antislavery conventions. Abby Kelley Foster's election to the executive committee of the AAS in 1840 represented progress for white women in the national organizational hierarchy. Nearly a decade later, black women in Columbus, Ohio, demanded equal voting rights with men in the proceedings of the black conventions.

Many white men, including members of the clergy, vigorously opposed women's rights, arguing that political equality for women would eventually draw them away from their domestic responsibilities. But many black male leaders sympathized with the women's rights campaign because they, like all women, had experienced political disfranchisement. These men tended to be more tolerant of equal rights for black women, in particular, because they had suffered race discrimination.[5] To black men, black women's suffrage was a means of achieving racial solidarity through self-improvement and black empowerment, despite tensions between the sexes, for though some black men supported women's rights in principle, leaders such as Frederick Douglass believed it should remain separate from the struggle for racial equality. Others, as illustrated in the black conventions, simply opposed the equal participation of women.

The desire to impose culturally dominant sex roles placed women's rights in direct conflict with the effort to create a self-reliant free black community, despite the sense in which women's rights represented another step toward racial equality for black women. In the black conventions, gender ideals were strong enough to prevent some black men from giving full support to women's equality. Although they expressed less opposition to women's rights than did white men, black men were sometimes reluctant to grant women an equal voice in black antislavery and self-help organizations, and by 1869, political expedience had led most of these men to abandon their support for women's rights in favor of universal manhood suffrage.

Efforts by several black and white women to engage in nontraditional antislavery activities during the 1830s produced debate over the extent to which women could participate as public activists without losing their femininity. Within the black community, the issue was particularly sensitive because women's rights seemed to contradict a central goal of black activism, which was to adopt separate sex roles.

Several years before the "woman question" became such a divisive issue, black activist Maria Stewart endured verbal and physical abuse from some of the black men in her audience when she publicly advocated economic independence and education for all women, regardless of race, and criticized the behavior of black men. In an address to the Afric-American Female Intelligence Society in 1832, Steward had urged women to save money and build their own businesses, arguing that economic independence would enable them to exercise their capabilities beyond the domestic realm. She advised all women to "unite and build a store of your own. We have never had an opportunity of displaying our talents; therefore the world thinks we know nothing." Although Stewart was unquestionably a strong supporter of women's rights, she, like many others, held forth male standards for behavior: "Possess the spirit of independence. . . . Possess the spirit of men, bold and enterprising, fearless and undaunted. Sue for your rights and privileges."[6] In the same speech, she criticized male social activities such as drinking and gambling.

The split in the AAS over the "woman question" had produced divisions among black as well as white male abolitionists.[7] Although most black men remained with Garrison, many others joined the new organization, primarily because they were disillusioned with moral suasion as a tactic and agreed with the Tappan wing that formation of an antislavery political party was the only realistic way of defeating the Slave Power in Congress and ending slavery. Although some black men may have supported women's participation in the movement, it was not a priority for many of the black male delegates.[8]

Not all black abolitionist men perceived equal rights for women as a way to achieve racial solidarity, and some openly opposed the equal participation of women. Samuel Cornish, who had always believed that women should engage only in "feminine" activities in the movement, supported the Tappan wing and served as a delegate to the new organization. Nearly a year after the split, Cornish wrote about the role of women in the breakup: "Whilst most, if not all of us differ with those ladies on the question of women's rights, we do not therefore undervalue their successful and arduous labors in the Anti-Slavery Cause."[9]

By the 1850s, the effort by many white feminists to dissociate women's rights from antislavery was self-evident. Discouraging black women from participating with white women in the movement was not difficult, because white feminists had ignored the concerns of black women from the beginning. In 1848, Lucretia Mott and Elizabeth Cady Stanton held the first women's rights convention at Seneca Falls, New York, where they outlined their goals in the Declaration of Sentiments. Motivated by their own experiences as white middle-class women, the framers of the Declaration of Sentiments concentrated on issues such as the oppression of women within the institutions of marriage and the family and discrimination in education and the professions. Marriage and family, they argued, denied them the power to control their own finances and prevented them from pursuing other, more worldly, interests. In addition, educational institutions and the professions had excluded women.

No black women attended the Seneca Falls convention. Frederick Douglass, who professed support for women's rights, was reportedly the only black person in attendance. The issues addressed by the delegates held little relevance for most black women's lives. Marriage did not restrict most black women from access to the public domain. Marriage for slaves was, of course, illegal, and unlike middle-class white women, most free black women worked outside of the home in low-paying domestic jobs in order to support their families. Many free black women even operated their own businesses. Discrimination against women in higher education and in the professions also meant little to most black women, since, as Sojourner Truth later noted, they "go out washing, which is about as high as a colored woman gets."[10]

Despite their alienation from white women's-rights organizations, black women fought for female equality either as independent spokeswomen or as participants in the black convention movements. All of the black women who supported women's rights before the Civil War, unlike many white women, retained their commitment to abolition. Mary Ann Shadd Cary and Sojourner Truth carried on the tradition of public speaking that Maria Stewart had established twenty years before. Shadd and Truth were two of the most outspoken black female proponents of both women's rights and abolition.

Mary Ann Shadd Cary displayed her willingness to engage in "unfeminine" activities for the sake of abolition by traveling unaccompanied by her husband on lecture tours in order to promote Canadian emigration and abolition, and to solicit financial support for the *Provincial Freeman* and destitute fugitive slaves in Canada. Her activities as a newspaper publisher and traveling lecturer demonstrated an independence and assertiveness that defied contemporary expectations of black docility and female submissiveness.

Sojourner Truth was one of the only black spokeswomen who attended predominantly white women's-rights meetings before the Civil War and spoke directly to white women about racism in American society and the ways that racism gave white women privileges denied to black women. The predominantly white women's-rights convention in Akron, Ohio, in 1851 revealed the anti-abolitionist and anti-black sentiment of some of the constituents, and Truth's experience as the only black women in attendance clearly illustrates the attitudes of many of the white delegates toward the presence of black women and their determination to keep women's rights separate from abolition. Despite hisses from the audience, Truth delivered her famous "Ain't I a Woman" speech, in which she pointed out the hypocrisy of "chivalry" and showed how racism had prevented black women from enjoying the respect and deferential treatment that white women received:

> Nobody ever helps me into carriages, or over mud-puddles, or gives me any best place! And ain't I a woman? Look at me! I have ploughed, planted, and gathered into barns, and no man could head me! And ain't I a woman? I could work as much and eat as much as a man—when I could get it—and bear the lash as well! And ain't I a woman? I have born thirteen children and seen most all sold into slavery, and when I cried out with my mother's grief, none but Jesus heard me! And ain't I a woman?[11]

Truth's legendary speech also addressed the racism of the white women in the audience, many of whom expressed discomfort when they saw her at the convention: "The leaders of the movement trembled on seeing a tall, gaunt black woman in a gray dress and white turban, surmounted with an uncouth bonnet, march deliberately into the church, walk with the air of a queen up the aisle, and take her seat upon the pulpit steps. A buzz of disapprobation was heard all over the house."[12] When they saw Truth enter the convention hall, several white observers assumed that the presence of a black woman meant that the women's-rights convention was turning into an antislavery meeting: "there fell on the listening ear, 'An abolition affair!' 'Women's rights and niggers!' 'I told you so!'"[13] Several of the delegates were so determined to dissociate women's rights from abolitionists that they begged Frances Dana Gage, the president of the convention, to stop Truth from delivering her speech: "Again and again, timorous and trembling ones came to me and said, with earnestness 'Don't let her speak, Mrs. Gage, it will ruin us. Every newspaper in the land will have our cause mixed with abolition & niggers, and we shall be utterly denounced."[14] Gage ignored their requests, despite expressions of disapproval from the audience. As Gage recounted the incident, Truth "moved slowly and solemnly to the front, laid her old bonnet at her feet, and turned her great speaking eyes to me. There was a hissing sound of disapprobation above and below. I rose and announced 'Sojourner Truth,' and begged the audience to keep silent for a few moments."[15]

The events of the Akron convention reveal a great deal about the state of the white women's-rights movement in 1851 and the attitudes of many white feminists, who in their attempt to attract a broader constituency, perceived abolition as detrimental to their movement. The attempt to silence Truth, the only black woman at the convention, demonstrates that for many white women, racism ran as deep as their feminist convictions. By entering the convention hall with the "air of a queen" and delivering a public address to whites, Truth defied prevailing expectations of black docility and female submissiveness.

The participation of black women in women's rights also revealed the tensions that existed between themselves and black men, which limited the degree of male-female cooperation in the struggle for freedom. In 1856, Shadd commented on the dearth of women's-rights sentiment in one of the towns she visited on her lecture tour. In her report to the *Provincial Freeman*, she noted that in Geneva, Illinois, "the cause of 'Women's Rights' does not flourish as it should."[16] She also suggested that black men may have helped to undermine women's-rights sentiment in Geneva: "strange enough, the monkey tricks of such colored men are said to injure it. An honest and venerable abolitionist of Geneva was free to express his fears for me and for women generally, because of the many 'failures' of colored *men* in that region. What absurdity next?"[17] In her speech at the Equal Rights Association meeting in 1867, Sojourner Truth argued that many black women shared with white working-class women the dual burdens of economic and domestic responsibilities and often lacked control over their own wages, for the domestic ideal dictated that men control the family finances: "and when the women come home, they [their husbands] ask for their money and take it all, and then scold you because there is no food. . . . I want women to have their rights."[18]

In addition to articulating their feminist views on lecture tours, in their writings, and at women's-rights meetings, black women also raised the issue of sexual equality at the black conventions. Most black conventions allowed only men to obtain membership, though the delegates usually allowed women to attend and perform "feminine" tasks. Black conventions had been meeting since 1830, functioning simultaneously with Garrisonian abolition but providing an organizational structure through which black men could maintain a distinct black leadership and pursue black abolitionist goals. In 1830, black male leaders organized the first national black convention at Bethel Church in Philadelphia. The following year, fifteen male delegates met in Philadelphia to attend the First Annual Negro Convention, which several leading white abolitionists attended as guests.[19] In addition to condemning slavery, racism, and colonization, delegates promoted both vocational and classical education for blacks, temperance, better employment opportunities for black men, and moral reform.[20] These racially based conventions, though they advocated some of the same goals as the white-dominated antislavery, also offered black men the chance to formulate their own goals and strategies for the antislavery movement, which they believed was, above all else, a black struggle.

Black women's interaction with black men in organized abolitionism provided the context in which they demanded an equal voice in predominantly male organizations. Like white women, black women abolitionists fought for the right to participate as full voting members, but unlike the white men who dominated the AAS, the black men at their conventions did not split over the "woman question."

The American Moral Reform Society, which had been born out of the black conventions in 1835, had welcomed women by 1839 to participate as full members. Led by prominent black abolitionist men such as James Forten, Sr., James McCrummell, Robert Purvis, William Watkins, William Whipper, and Jacob C. White, this organization reflected both the broad objectives of radical abolitionism and the radical principle defining slavery as a sin. Moreover, the organizers perceived their role as encompassing universal moral reform extending even beyond the boundaries of the United States:

> We therefore declare to the world, that our object is to extend the principle of universal peace and good will to all mankind, by

> promoting sound morality, by the influence of education, temperance, economy, and all those virtues that alone render man acceptable in the eyes of God or the civilized world.[21]

Home Corresponding Secretary William Whipper added to this general pronouncement more specific objectives, directed in particular to the black community. Although the Society would become racially mixed, the black leader testified that its goal was "to unite the colored population in those principles of Moral Reform," in order to "aid in effecting the total abolition of slavery" and "to effect the destruction of vice universally." Women were seen as an integral part of this huge enterprise but had not been included in the early decision-making process. They were admitted four years after the organization was established, with its rules and structure already in place. At the third annual meeting in August 1839, held at the Second African Presbyterian Church in Philadelphia, the members resolved to welcome women into the organization on the basis of supposed moral equality that existed between the sexes:

> Resolved, 'That what is morally right for a man to do, is morally right for women,' therefore, we earnestly and cordially invite women to co-operate with us in carrying out the great principles of moral reform.[22]

Female delegates included black women who were also active in antislavery societies and community activities. A number of these women served as delegates along with spouses and relatives. For example, in 1839, Grace Douglass was a delegate with her husband Robert and her sister, Mary Bustill. Mary Ann and William Whipper of Columbia, Pennsylvania, were delegates as were Amelia and John Lewis and Eliza and James J. G. Bias of Philadelphia.

In the larger state and national black conventions, however, black women met with a great deal of resistance from the men of their race when they demanded an equal voice in convention proceedings. Black women's first official proposal for equality in the conventions occurred in 1848, the same year as the Seneca Falls convention, at the annual meeting of the National Convention of Colored Freedmen in Cleveland. One black woman, joined by Martin Delany and Frederick Douglass, motioned to allow women to participate in the convention proceedings, to speak and vote as men did. Many black men, like their white counterparts, had not considered that black women might play more than an auxiliary role in the antislavery movement. After considerable debate, however, the business committee reclassified eligible voters by the designation "persons" and allow women to participate on an equal basis with men.[23]

One year after the Cleveland convention, black women who were attending the Ohio state convention, held in Columbus, threatened to boycott the meeting unless they were permitted to participate. A Mrs. Jane P. Merritt submitted a resolution to the chairman of the business committee at the evening session on Friday, January 17, 1849: "Whereas the ladies have been invited to attend the Convention, and have been deprived of a voice, which the ladies deem wrong and shameful. Therefore, Resolved, that we will attend no more after tonight, unless the privilege is granted."[24] After some debate, the committee adopted the resolution. Black women's demands for an equal voice in the proceedings, however, did not mean they had rejected contemporary notions of femininity—they had, after all, proclaimed the right to participate as "ladies."

Despite official admittance of women, black conventions did not develop consistent policies on the participation of black women; decisions varied from state to state and at individual meetings when the issue arose.[25] While local organizations may have been more welcoming of women's participation in decision-making and recruitment, the state and national conventions, in which hundreds of black male delegages participated, put up stiff resistance to women's equality. A sexual division of responsibility still prevailed in some black conventions even after the Ohio women had won their rights. In 1859, members of both sexes attended the New England Colored Citizens' Convention in Boston, along with several prominent white male abolitionists. But while the men voted and determined policy, most of the women arranged the flowers that adorned the delegates' tables. Two women served on the fifteen-member finance committee: Eliza Logan Lawton, a member of the Boston Female Anti-Slavery Society, and Ruth Rice Remond, sister-in law of Sarah Remond.[26] In Alliance, Ohio, that same year, however, Lavinia J. Hamlin, Sarah A. Holliday, and Rebecca Oliver served on an important committee with black men to recruit "young people of Ohio" for an upcoming black convention in August. As explained in its statement of purpose, the goal of this convention was to "concentrate our voices to act against the system of slavery, and to so move the people to oppose the fiendish prejudice against color, that one part of the citizens of Ohio shall no longer be deprived of the right of elective franchise."[27]

During the 1850s black men in at least two states continued to thwart black women's attempts to obtain an equal voice with men in the conventions on both the state and national level. In 1855, a New York black woman was expelled from a convention "for no other reason than her sex."[28] In Philadelphia that same year, delegates at the National Convention of Coloured Men excluded women from membership when they voted twenty-three to three against admitting Mary Ann Shadd as a member, although they allowed her to deliver an address. Frederick Douglass had been one of the three men who favored admitting Shadd. A male observer at the convention conceded that Shadd had made "one of the best speeches," but noted approvingly that the majority of the men at the convention had separated women's rights from black conventions and denied Shadd membership. He criticized those men who favored her admission: "Great men, however, are not always wise; and Mr. Douglass himself supplied an example, in advocating the Motion, that 'Miss Shadd should be elected a member,' a proposition which was actually entertained, although a few men of sense protested, that 'that was not a Women's Rights Convention.' "[29]

Frederick Douglass had been one of the most vocal advocates of women's rights, though he still held to the common belief in women's moral superiority and delicacy. According to Douglass, the differences between men and women did not justify political inequality. In an editorial entitled "LADIES," Douglass argued that women's intelligence, moral superiority, and benevolent nature were good reasons for granting them political rights:

> The almoners of the race of man, superior to the opposite sex in all the offices of benevolence and kindness, fully equal in moral, mental and intellectual endowments, in short, entitled to an equal participancy in all the designs and accomplishments allotted to man during his career on earth. May the accumulated evils of the past, and those of the present, which superstition and bigotry have prescribed for them as a test of inferiority, be buried forever.[30]

In July 1848, Douglass endorsed the Seneca Falls convention: "Our doctrine is that 'right is of no sex.' We therefore bid the women engaged in this movement our humble Godspeed."[31] But Douglass believed that ending slavery was of more immediate concern than achieving female equality, as he told the Rochester Ladies' Anti-Slavery Society in 1855:

> I may say, however, that the first grand division [in abolitionism] took place fourteen years ago, and on the very minor question—Shall a woman be a member of a committee in company with men? The majority said she should be; and the minority seceded. Thus was a grand philanthropic movement rent asunder by a side issue, having nothing, whatever to do with the great object which the American Anti-Slavery Society was organized to carry forward. . . . While I see no objection to my occupying a place on your committee, I can for the slave's sake forgo that privilege. The battle of Woman's Rights should be fought on its own ground.[32]

Thus, long before the debate over black male suffrage during Reconstruction, even the most enthusiastic black male supporters of women's rights believed that abolition and women's rights should remain separate, and that women's-rights agitation actually hurt the cause of abolition.

The racism of white feminists and the sexism of black male leaders manifested themselves in a political context after the Civil War, when feminists and former abolitionists debated the issues of citizenship and suffrage. The emphasis on these issues during Reconstruction set the direction of the white feminist movement for the rest of the nineteenth century; suffrage became the primary focus, especially after the passage of the Fifteenth Amendment in 1869. Both the Fourteenth and Fifteenth amendments had engendered conflict between those who wanted to grant citizenship and suffrage only to black men and those who believed women should also receive political rights. The Fourteenth Amendment, adopted in 1868, defined citizenship, but failed to guarantee the protection of civil rights. More importantly to feminists, however, the framers of the amendment had officially excluded women by inserting the word "male" in the amendment.

Although most former abolitionists had initially opposed the Fourteenth Amendment because it failed to commit the federal government to protect the civil rights of the freedmen, leaders eventually accepted the measure based on their fundamental support for the Republican party and its plans for Reconstruction. Acceptance of the measure also confirmed the American Anti-Slavery Society's commitment to obtaining civil and political rights for black men first and women second. White feminist leaders opposed the Fourteenth Amendment and pointed to the exclusion of black women as an argument against the measure. Elizabeth Cady Stanton, in an angry letter to Wendell Phillips, stated: "May I ask just one question based on the apparent opposition in which you place the negro and the woman? My question is this: Do you believe the African race is composed entirely of males?"[33]

The ensuing debate again revealed that white feminists had included the interests of black women only as a handy rhetorical device. The proposed suffrage amendment caused further conflict between former abolitionists who wanted to grant political rights to black men and feminist leaders who favored "universal suffrage" for all adults. The members of the predominantly white Equal Rights Association campaigned vigorously for universal suffrage between the formation of the association in 1866 and the passage of the Fifteenth Amendment in 1869. Ardent white feminists and several black women believed that the Fifteenth Amendment, which granted suffrage to black men, had betrayed women's rights.

White women and black men had both betrayed black women. Frederick Douglass, in a letter to white feminist Josephine White in 1868, attempted to explain why he believed political equality for black men was of more immediate importance than suffrage for women. He did not include black women in his plea for "Negro suffrage," even though he knew that black women had suffered as much as black men in both slavery and freedom, because to include black women in the suffrage package would have meant including all women, a move that he knew would have been too radical for Congress to accept. Douglass's letter to White in favor of "Negro suffrage" did not apologize for excluding black women: "I never suspected you of sympathizing with Miss Anthony and Mrs. Stanton in their course. Their principle is: that no Negro shall be enfranchised while woman is not. Now, considering that white men have been enfranchised always, and colored men have not, the conduct of these white women, whose husbands, fathers and brothers are voters, does not seem generous."[34]

Disagreement over the Fifteenth Amendment split the Equal Rights Association in 1869 into the American Woman Suffrage Association, which agreed to accept the amendment on the condition that the Republican party promise to support future campaigns for women's suffrage, and the National Woman Suffrage Association, which proposed the more radical universal suffrage amendment. When Elizabeth Cady Stanton, leader of the NWSA, lobbied for a sixteenth amendment that would enfranchise women, she represented the interests of white middle-class women and exploited prevailing fears and prejudices against nonwhites in the United States:

> American women of wealth, education, virtue and refinement, if you do not wish the lower orders of Chinese, Africans, Germans and Irish, with their low ideas of womanhood to make laws for you and your daughters, . . . to dictate not only the civil, but moral codes by which you shall be governed, awake to the danger of your present position and demand that women, too, shall be represented in the government![35]

The continuation of racist and sexist attitudes during the suffrage debate had indeed placed black women in a difficult position in the struggle for equal rights. Their exclusion from any serious consideration in the agendas of black male activists and white feminists did not mean, however, that black women were inactive. The debate over the Fourteenth and Fifteenth amendments forced black women to choose between racial and sexual equality, when they knew that equality would be meaningful only if sexism and racism were both abolished. Political expediency had led some black women to accept the Fifteenth Amendment, for they were well aware of the dilemma in which the public debate had placed them. Frances Harper, for example, had campaigned for women's suffrage and had been one of the few black women who regularly attended suffrage meetings. But during the debate over the Fifteenth Amendment, she threw her support behind the American Woman Suffrage Association. At the 1869 meeting of the Equal Rights Association, Harper had commented on the inability of white feminists to recognize racism and sexism as intertwined systems of oppression: "When it was a question of race, she let the lesser question of sex go. But the white women all go for sex, letting race occupy a minor position."[36]

Several prominent black feminist-abolitionists supported the National Woman Suffrage Association, even though its leaders used racist arguments, which suggests that they may have resolved to endure the racism they had always encountered from white women in order to achieve a common goal. Perhaps, also, these black women wished to keep the issue of racism alive in the faces of white feminists, despite the fact that black women were outnumbered in white women's organizations. Sojourner Truth, who had certainly had experienced racism from white feminists, supported the Stanton-Anthony branch of the women's movement and intensified her own support for economic and political equality for women after 1869. In a speech she delivered when she was more than eighty years old, Truth explained to the men in her audience that women needed to achieve economic equality in order to escape the power of man. Informed by her experience as a slave, Truth compared the power that men wielded with that of slaveholders: "What we want is a little money. You men know that you get as much again as women when you write, or for what you do. . . . You have been having your rights so long, that you think, like a slaveholder, that you own us."[37]

Truth's indictment of black men must have struck a raw nerve among some members of the audience, for she underscored the tensions between black men and women that ultimately limited the extent to which they could cooperate equally with one another both within the home and in public. In her lectures, Truth articulated a serious critique of the dominant social construction and definition of "maleness" and "power" in American culture, which shaped prevailing conceptions of freedom. As black women's experiences in public reform revealed, two levels of discourse articulated by black male leaders themselves had developed between black women and men regarding black female behavior. Many black men had praised black women's assertiveness and participation in public activism for the sake of the movement, but, in private, in the home, black women were expected to defer to the authority of men. Truth made plain her understanding of the contradictions inherent in black activist goals and the pervasiveness of patriarchal models of freedom. As an activist, she knew about black women's struggles to obtain voting rights in the black conventions, and as an ex-slave who had spent much of her adult life laboring for low wages, she also knew about the difficulties for most free blacks of attaining those "ideal" gender roles within their own families, and appreciated how the only way they approached these roles was through community-based activism. Truth had fully expected that political equality for women would accompany emancipation, and she clearly understood the precarious position of black women after emancipation. As a black woman, she saw her sex denied political rights while all men received voting rights.

For a few black women, disappointment over the passage of the Fifteenth Amendment turned into hope that equality for blacks and suffrage for women would eventually follow. Sojourner Truth expressed optimism that the end of slavery and suffrage for black men would bring equality for blacks: "Now colored men have the right to vote. There ought to be equal rights now more than ever, since colored people have got their freedom." In 1872, Mary Olney Brown, a black contributor to the *New National Era* in Washington, D.C., expressed her belief that black women had been betrayed by the Fourteenth and Fifteenth Amendments. In a letter to Frederick Douglass, Brown wrote: "It is a gross injustice that the colored women have so long been defrauded of their right to vote."[38] Harriet Tubman expressed hope that women would also receive political rights. In 1911, two years before she died, she attended a meeting of the suffrage club in Geneva, New York, where a white woman asked her: "Do you really believe that women should vote?" Tubman reportedly replied: "I suffered enough to believe it."[39]

Between 1830 and the 1860s, black women abolitionists had developed a collective feminist consciousness that reflected their particular experiences as black women as well as the aspects of sexism they shared with white women. While white women fought for female equality in predominantly white antislavery organizations, black women abolitionists campaigned for equal rights within the context of organized black abolitionism. But, though both black and white women supported women's rights, their experiences differed in several important ways. First, black women's participation in women's rights reveals the extent to which racism characterized the early stages of the white feminist movement. White feminist leaders had consciously ignored the concerns of black women, and very few black women, notably Truth, Tubman, and Harper, bridged the two movements by attending white feminist meetings.

Second, unlike many white feminists, black feminists continued to support both abolition and women's rights. Their commitment to both movements held important implications for their experience in the struggle for sexual equality. As Sojourner Truth had suggested at the Akron convention, black women brought a perspective on women's rights that

Sojourner Truth—ex-slave, lecturer, temperance activist, and feminist—is shown here in a painting with Abraham Lincoln.
(Library of Congress)

clearly differed from that of white women, and for black women, the abolition of slavery and racism were intimately related to women's rights.

This combined commitment to race and gender also affected relationships with black male reformers. Black women's continued participation in the fight to end slavery and racism led them to maintain cooperative ties with black men, unlike many white feminists, who perceived their interests as separate from those of men. Thus, while black women campaigned for women's rights, they also worked with black men in a variety of self-help activities in the black community. On the other hand, as it became evident that many black men had considered racial equality a higher priority than women's rights, black women continued their struggle for women's rights. The betrayal of black women during the postwar period and the dominance of racially conservative feminist organizations throughout the nineteenth century ultimately prevented the achievement of sexual or racial equality. Nevertheless, black women voiced their opinions even when white women and black men outnumbered them and ignored or denounced their claims, and a few attended suffrage meetings even when they knew they were not welcome.

After the Civil War, black women continued to support both women's suffrage and the struggle for racial equality. The strengthening of Jim Crow laws and the gradual disfranchisement of and increased violence against black men after the Civil War signified to black men and women that the struggle for racial equality was not over. Former black feminist-abolitionists established a tradition of activism for future generations of Afro-American women. During the post-Reconstruction period, a new generation of black women activists emerged, some of whom were the daughters of black feminist-abolitionists. The old and the new generations of activists immersed themselves in the continuing struggle for social and political equality for black men and women by supporting suffrage and improved employment opportunities for blacks through the black women's clubs. During the postwar period, black women's clubs provided the avenue through which they mobilized against the lynching of black men and, at the same time, promoted education, temperance, and moral reform in their community. Mary Church Terrell, Sarah Garnet, Ida B. Wells, and Josephine St. Pierre Ruffin, for example, were part of this new generation to carry on black women's organized struggle for equality.[40]

Their demand for equal rights with men in the black conventions provides the strongest evidence of a developing feminist consciousness among black women and the of seriousness of their claim for female equality. Their commitment to racial and sexual equality, influenced to a great extent by political events, reveals a continuity in the pattern of black female activism. After the Civil War, they retained a pattern of organization that black women had established since the late eighteenth century, when their foremothers organized beneficial societies through their churches. Although racism had placed black women on the periphery of the white-dominated women's rights movement, black feminists found their own ways of creating a movement that continued the struggle against racism and sexism—on behalf of, as Mary Ann Shadd Cary once confided to her journal, "namely the colored people of this country and the women of this land."[41]

Conclusion

This book opened with the image of Sojourner Truth standing before a predominantly white audience at the Equal Rights Association meeting in 1867, issuing a dire prophecy about the fate of her black sisters. "If colored men get their rights and not colored women theirs," Truth had warned, "the colored men will be masters over the women, and it will be just as bad as before." After two generations of struggle for abolition and women's rights, to which black women had constantly committed all the energies and resources at their command, they stood on the threshold of exclusion; the "victories" of the impending Fourteenth and Fifteenth amendments to the Constitution did not extend political rights to black women and threatened to cut them off from their allies among black men and white women. That black women found themselves in such a vulnerable position is not surprising, considering the breadth and depth of racism and sexism among their colleagues in the movement as well as in the general population. Black women's commitment to the survival and advancement of their race, which had brought black men and women together in a common cause, had not succeeded in overcoming the sexism that threatened those political and personal bonds. The white feminist movement, for all its talk of sisterhood, had clearly succumbed to racist fears and abandoned the possibility of forging a biracial feminist alliance. In the face of this double betrayal by their long-time abolitionist colleagues, an agenda for women's equality that would also embrace anti-racism seemed impossible.

A central theme that emerges from the story of free black women is the tension between the ideal and the reality in their lives. Responsibility to both their gender and their race, on an idealistic as well as a practical level, placed an enormous burden on many free black women. In addition to fulfilling their domestic responsibilities and, in many cases, earning a wage, free black women were expected to extend their "female influence" into their community. But the history of free black women is also about the contradiction inherent in the ideals themselves. Freedom had meant, in large part, the destruction of gender roles that had existed under slavery, to be replaced by the white ideal of a patriarchal family and community structure, in which men wielded most of the power and women were subordinate. As free black men and women strove to create a society that rejected the structure of slavery and truly reflected free status, they advocated ideals that middle-class white society had disseminated about "true" womanhood and manhood. The preservation and advancement of the black community had seemed dependent on gaining acceptance within the dominant culture, in the hope that acceptance might help end the violence against blacks and lead to political, social, and economic equality, at least for black men. Community institutions, such as the churches and the schools, facilitated both assistance to needy blacks and the perpetuation of the societal ideals. But the commitment to this concept of free status produced a contradictory relationship between black women and men, in which many black men supported black women's participation in public activism for the sake of the cause, but still expected women to defer to the men of their race and to adhere to notions of "proper" female behavior.

Although black women participated in many of the same activities as other abolitionists, their role in the movement was multilayered. For free black women, as for no other group of activists, the limitations and obligations of being both black and female shaped their participation in the movement. Economics, family, friendships, and their experiences as freeborn and ex-slave women helped determine their goals, motivations, and activities, and influenced the degree to which they were willing to accept "true womanhood" ideals. While some free black women struggled to meet middle-class standards of respectable womanhood in their daily lives and in their activism, others, such as Truth, Harriet Tubman, and Mary Ann Shadd Cary, essentially did what they pleased, abandoning any kind of sexual stereotypes and ignoring prevailing expectations of ladylike behavior. Thus, individual personalities and perceptions of their roles as activists made each woman distinctive in her own right, regardless of external circumstances.

The continued existence of racism and sexism together, though it threatened black women's survival, as it had for other women of color in the United States, did not render them completely powerless or silent. Rather, the strength of their commitment to ending the subjugation of their race led black women abolitionists to form their own patterns of participation, which they would carry forward into the twentieth century. Their struggles with racism and sexism also illuminate the pervasiveness of white, patriarchal, middle-class values throughout much of American history. Such values, however contradictory and illusory, ultimately shaped the goals of groups that fought for acceptance and survival. But at the same time, black women also sought to reclaim a community identity that existed apart from the dominant culture, and that recognized the achievements and particular needs of its members. In her speech to white feminists in 1867, Truth accurately predicted the future of black women's activism, as they struggled to survive, to shape their own lives, and to build their community for the generations to come.

Notes

Abbreviations

AAS	American Anti-Slavery Society
ADS	African Dorcas Society
AFASS	American & Foreign Anti-Slavery Society
AMA	American Missionary Association
AWSA	American Woman Suffrage Association
BAP	*Black Abolitionist Papers*
BFASS	Boston Female Anti-Slavery Society
BPL	Boston Public Library
DAS	Daughters of Africa Society
HSP	Historical Society of Pennsylvania
LCP	The Library Company of Philadelphia
LNYCASS	Ladies' New York City Anti-Slavery Society
NWSA	National Woman Suffrage Association
OBHS	Ontario Black History Society
PFASS	Philadelphia Female Anti-Slavery Society

Introduction

1. Stanton, et al., *History of Woman Suffrage* 2:152. See also Sterling, ed., *We Are Your Sisters*, 411.

2. Although one can make an argument for including slave women in this scenario, one must construct an analytical framework that incorporates slave resistance into the abolitionist movement.

3. See Quarles, *Black Abolitionists*, and Curry, *The Free Black in Urban America*, ch. 13.

4. Quarles, *Black Abolitionists*, viii, 18.

5. Lois E. Horton, "Community Organization and Social Activism": 183.

6. See Welter, "Cult of True Womanhood," 151–74.

7. In 1837, Garrison reported in *The Liberator* the number and locations of antislavery societies in the United States: Me., 33; N.H., 62; Vt., 89; Mass., 145; R.I., 25; Conn., 39; N.Y., 274; N.J., 10; Penna., 93; Ohio, 213. See *The Liberator*, Aug. 4, 1837, p. 127. See also Quarles, *Black Abolitionists*, 26–33; Dillon, *The Abolitionists*, 51; *The Liberator*, June 14, 1834, p. 90. For more discussion on nonabolitionist blacks, see Quarles, *Black Abolitionists*, 56, and William J. Brown, *The Life of William J. Brown*, 156–62.

8. Lewis Tappan to Theodore D. Weld, May 26, 1840, Barnes and Dumond, *Letters of Theodore Dwight Weld* 2:836.

9. Leonard Curry notes that between 1830 and 1860 the black population of New York City increased from 13,977 in 1830 to 16,358 in 1840, then decreased sharply to 13,815. Boston underwent similar shifts, though in a smaller proportion, from 1,875 in 1830 to 2,427 in 1840 and down to 1,999 in 1850. In Philadelphia, the number of Blacks grew steadily from 9,806 to 10,736, and Cincinnati's black population more than doubled during this period, from 1,090 to 3,237. See Curry, *The Free Black in Urban America*, 250.

10. *A Statistical Inquiry*, 34.

11. Leo F. Schnore and Peter R. Knights, "Residence and Social Structure: Boston in the Ante-Bellum Period," in *Nineteenth Century Cities*, eds. Thernstrom and Sennett, 252.

12. *A Statistical Inquiry*, 37.

13. Ibid., 41.

14. For more detailed discussions of free black residential patterns, see Horton and Horton, *Black Bostonians*, Curry, *The Free Black in Urban America*, and Nash, *Forging Freedom*.

15. Levesque, "Black Boston," 113–15.

16. Daniels, *Pioneer Urbanites*, 140–41. See also Bay Area black newspapers, such as *Pacific Appeal* and the *Elevator*.

17. See Lerner, ed., *Black Women in White America*, Loewenberg and Bogin, eds., *Black Women in Nineteenth Century American Life*, and Sterling, *We Are Your Sisters*.

Chapter 1

1. DuBois graded black families according to income and occupation, assigning the "better class" of families "Grade 1." See DuBois, *The Philadelphia*

Negro, 310–11. See also, Emma Jones Lapsansky, "Friends, Wives and Strivings," 9–11, for information on black community networking.

2. For an excellent description of the Forten family, see the introduction to Stevenson, ed., *The Journals of Charlotte Forten Grimké;* Delany, *Conditions*, 94.

3. The Population Schedule for the Seventh Census of the United States (1850), roll 824.

4. For a discussion of Purvis's involvement in Philadelphia politics, see Silcox, "The Black 'Better Class' Political Dilemma," 47–52.

5. The Schedule of the Seventh Census of the United States (1850), listed Robert Purvis, age 39, as a "farmer" and the members of his household: Harriett D. (Forten), 40, William P., 17, Harriett, Jr., 11, Charles Burleigh, 9, Henry W., 6, Granville S., 4, Georgiana B., 1, and a black servant, Emma Epps, 29. Two other sons, Robert, Jr., 18, and Joseph, 16, attended Sophia Lathrop's school in Cortland, N.Y., at the time the census was taken.

6. Sallie Holley was the daughter of abolitionist Myron Holley. Sallie Holley to Caroline F. Putnam, Nov. 26, 1852, in Chadwick, ed., *A Life for Liberty*, 101–2.

7. Abraham Doras Shadd was the seventh son of Amelia and Jeremiah Shadd. Jeremiah Shadd's father was Hans Schad, a Hessian soldier who had fought in Gen. Edward Braddock's army during the American War for Independence. In 1756, Schad had married Elizabeth Jackson, a "young Negro woman" from Pennsylvania. The spelling had changed from "Schad" to "Shadd" by 1814. Elsie Lewis, untitled, Howard University, ca. 1959, from manuscript record prepared by Amelia C. Shadd Williamson, St. Catherine's, and son A. T. Williamson, 1905, OBHS, box 2, file 2.

8. James and James, *Notable American Women* 1:300; Delany, *Conditions*, 131.

9. Abraham Shadd held a seat on the Raleigh Town Council. Winks, *Blacks in Canada*, 215.

10. The other children of Abraham and Harriet Shadd were: Elizabeth J., Harriet, Joseph, Emeline, Garrison, Sarah M., Ada, and Gerrit S. Shadd. OBHS, box 2, envelope 9.

11. Ullman, *Martin Delany*, 182, 186–87; Delany, *Conditions*, 122.

12. Mary Ann Shadd Cary to G[eorge]. Whipple, Boston, Nov. 3, 1859, AMA Coll., OBHS, box 2, envelope 4.

13. The Population Schedule for the Seventh Census of the United States (1850), lists John Remond's assets at $3,600, roll 312. The census of 1870 lists John Remond, Sr., then 82 (though listed as 83 years old), as a "dealer in wines" with real estate totaling $19,400 and personal assets at $2,000.

14. Nancy Lenox Remond was originally from Newton, Mass.

15. Sterling, *We Are Your Sisters*, 97. Other children of John and Nancy L.

Remond were Nancy Remond Shearman, who was married to oyster dealer James Shearman, and John Lenox Remond, married to Ruth Rice Remond of Rhode Island. Stevenson, *Journals*, 574 (n. 13), 566 (n. 57).

16. See Rev. Daniel A. Payne's eulogy on Mary Woods Forten in the *Colored American*, Aug. 29, 1840; also Stevenson, ed., *Journals of Charlotte Forten Grimké*, preface; Sterling, ed., *We Are Your Sisters*, 198.

17. Billington, "James Forten: Forgotten Abolitionist," 290.

18. Stevenson, *Journals*, June 17, 1854, July 2, 1854.

19. Chester's writings indicate that his support of Liberian emigration was influenced not by colonizationists but by emigrationist arguments for the creation of an independent black community outside the U.S. See Blackett, *Thomas Morris Chester*, 7, 11.

20. Ibid., x, 4–5.

21. See Nash, *Forging Freedom;* Litwack, *North of Slavery;* and Curry, *The Free Black in Urban America*, ch. 5.

22. Anna Douglass Mapps was the daughter of Ruth Bustill Douglass, Grace Bustill's oldest sister, and William Douglass; Grace A. Mapps graduated from college in McGrawville, N.Y. in 1852. Cadbury, "Negro Membership," 190–94; Smith, "The Bustill Family," 639.

23. William Penn Douglass, the youngest child of Robert and Grace, had died in 1839 at the age of 23. *National Reformer*, Nov.–Dec. 1839, 176.

24. Sarah Grimké to Gerrit Smith and Mrs. (Ann Carroll Fitzhugh) Smith, Belleville, N.J., July 11, 1842. Gerrit Smith Papers, reel 10.

25. Her brothers, Nathaniel and Benjamin, both of whom were Baptist preachers, were also active in black community work in the Wilberforce settlement, where they were embroiled in conflicts over financial mismanagement. Winks, *Blacks in Canada*, 158–61; Horton, *Black Bostonians*, 41.

26. Anne Warren Weston to Deborah Weston, Boston, April 18, 1837, BPL. Anne W. Weston and Deborah Weston were sisters of Maria Weston Chapman.

27. Lydia Maria Child to Jonathan Phillips, Jan. 23, 1838. Schlesinger Lib.

28. Southwick, *Reminiscences*, 29.

29. Anne Warren Weston to Mr. and Mrs. H(enry) G. Chapman, Weymouth, May 18, 1841. BPL.

30. Harriet Hayden to Maria Weston Chapman, New York, Nov. 27, 1843, *BAP*, reel 4, fr. 0705. Maria Weston Chapman (1806–1885) was the eldest of six children born to Warren and Anne Bates Weston, one of the wealthiest families in Boston. Maria was educated in England and later married within her social circle to Henry Grafton Chapman, abolitionist and prosperous merchant.

31. Martin Delany and *The Liberator* note the address as Cambridge St. See Delany, *Conditions*, 106, and *The Liberator*, July 20, 1849. Contemporary histo-

rians, however, list the address as Phillips St. See Horton, *Black Bostonians*, 54–55 and Levesque, *Black Boston*, 108.

32. Population Schedule of the Seventh Census of the United States (1850), roll 336. See also Horton and Horton, *Black Bostonians*, 104.

33. Horton and Horton, ibid., 23–24.

34. *Frederick Douglass' Monthly*, Sept. 17, 1858, *BAP*, reel 11, fr. 0368.

35. Lois E. Horton, "Community Organizations and Social Activism," 186.

36. John Edward Bruce, "Noted Race Women I Have Known and Met," Woman's Day Address, Baptist Church, Cambridge, Mass., Sept. 1, 1923.

37. Blackett, *Beating Against the Barriers*, 288–89.

38. Richards, *'Gentlemen of Property and Standing,'* 28–29.

39. Blackett, *Beating Against the Barriers*, 289.

40. An elder son contributed to the family income through his work on ships. Ibid., 289.

41. Ibid., 290.

42. Harriet Tubman to Wendell Phillips, Aug. 4, 1860, *BAP*, reel 12, fr. 0944.

43. Sojourner Truth to Gerrit Smith [written by Caroline E. Sherman], June 25, 1863, *BAP*, reel 14, fr. 0932.

44. Child, Lydia Maria, ed., Harriet Brent Jacobs, *Incidents in the Life of a Slave Girl*.

45. Hewitt, *Women's Activism*, 241.

46. According to slave law, slaves could not legally marry because they were considered property.

47. "Report of the Great Anti-Slavery Meeting," April 9, 1851, Bristol, England, *BAP*, reel 6, fr. 0884.

48. Craft, *Running a Thousand Miles for Freedom*, 25.

49. James and James, *Notable American Women* 1:396–98.

50. "Report of the Great Anti-Slavery Meeting," April 9, 1851, *BAP*, reel 6, fr. 0884.

51. Blackett, *Beating against the Barriers*, 103.

52. Loewenberg and Bogin, *Black Women in Nineteenth Century American Life*, 178; *The Liberator*, Nov. 11, 1864.

53. James and James, *Notable American Women* 1:396–98.

54. William Still, *The Underground Railroad*, 755–57.

55. Margaret Hope Bacon, "'One Great Bundle of Humanity,'" 21–23.

56. Ibid., 25.

57. Ibid., 31.

58. Nancy Gardner Prince became an ardent evangelical by 1820. She had been baptized by the Rev. Thomas Paul in 1819. Gates, gen. ed., *Collected Black*

Women's Narratives, "Narrative of the Life and Travels of Mrs. Nancy Prince," 8, 17. See also Ronald G. Walters's description of Prince's career in Prince, *A Black Woman's Odyssey*, ix–xxii, and Sterling, ed., *We Are Your Sisters*, 95.

59. Ibid., 8–11.

60. Ibid., 19–20.

61. Nero Prince had intended to follow his wife, but died in Russia. See "Narratives of the Life and Travels of Mrs. Nancy Prince," in Gates, gen. ed., *Collected Black Women's Narratives;* Sterling, *We Are Your Sisters*, 93–95; Loewenberg and Bogin, *Black Women in Nineteenth Century American Life*, 201–8; *The Liberator*, Nov. 22, 1839, p. 187.

62. *The Liberator*, Nov. 5, 1841, p. 179.

63. DeCosta-Willis, "Smoothing the Tucks in Father's Linen, 30.

64. Ibid., 31; Render, "Afro-American Women," 308.

65. William Wells Brown to Amy Post, Plymouth, July 16, 1848, *BAP*, reel 5, fr. 0711–0712; Farrison, *William Wells Brown*, 107–8; 168–70.

66. *New York Daily Tribune*, March 12, 1850, cited in Farrison, *William Wells Brown*, 169.

67. Clara Brown to Wendell Phillips, March 31, 1851, *BAP*, reel 6, fr. 0867. Harvard Univ. Crawford Blagden Coll. of the Papers of Wendell Phillips (hereafter cited as PWP).

68. Josephine Brown, *Biography of an American Bondman*.

69. Sterling, *We Are Your Sisters*, 145.

70. Elizabeth Remond to Wendell Phillips, Aug. 2, 1868, Greenwood, PWP.

71. Mrs. Putnam may have been Charles Remond's sister, Carolina Remond Putnam. Elizabeth Remond to Wendell Phillips, Salem, Mass., Dec. 19, 1863, *BAP*, reel 15, fr. 0122. Elizabeth Remond to Wendell Phillips, Sept. 27, 1864, PWP.

72. E. Remond to Phillips, Aug. 2, 1868.

73. Mary Ann Shadd Cary from Thomas Cary, Toronto, Jan. 21, 1858.

74. Sterling, *We Are Your Sisters*, 174.

75. Sarah Grimké to Sarah Douglass, Newark, N.J., June 19, 1855, in Sterling, *We Are Your Sisters*, 132.

76. William Still to Mary Ann Shadd Cary, Philadelphia, Feb. 2, 1854, *BAP*, reel 8, fr. 0634.

77. See Sterling, *We Are Your Sisters*, 130.

78. (Sarah Parker) Remond from M(aria) W(eston) Chapman, Sept. 4, 1859, Weymouth Landing (Mass.), *BAP*, reel 12, fr. 0013–14.

79. Sarah (Parker) Remond to (Samuel) May (Jr.), Oct. 18, 1860, London, England, *BAP*, reel 12, fr. 1041–42.

80. Sarah Forten to Angelina Grimké, April 15, 1837, in Sterling, *We Are Your Sisters*, 125.

81. Barnes and Dumond, eds., *Letters of Theodore Dwight Weld* 2:830.

82. Sarah Douglass also attended the Ninth and Spruce meeting. Cadbury, "Negro Membership," 192.

83. Grace Douglass to the Rev. Gloucester, Philadelphia, Feb. 22, 1819, in "Brief Historic Sketch of the First African Presbyterian Church of Philadelphia."

84. Sterling, *We Are Your Sisters*, 131.

85. Sarah P. Remond to Abby Kelley Foster, Salem, Mass., Dec. 31, 1854, Stephen and Abigail Kelly Foster Papers. Also in Sterling, *We Are Your Sisters*, 176.

86. *Provincial Freeman*, April 26, 1856, *BAP*, reel 10, fr. 0118.

87. Anne Warren Weston to Deborah Weston, July 13, 1842, Groton, Mass., BPL.

88. Billington, ed., *Journal of Charlotte Forten*, 123.

Chapter 2

1. Until recently, scholars interested in women's roles have focused on the impact of gender ideals on the lives of white middle-class men and women. See Welter, "The Cult of True Womanhood, 1820–1860" and Smith–Rosenberg, "Beauty and the Beast and the Militant Woman." Two of the most widely circulated works on women's "proper" roles were *Ladies Magazine* (1828–36), edited by Sarah Hale, and *Godey's Lady Book*, published by Louis Godey and coedited by Hale.

2. See Horton, "Freedom's Yoke."

3. Linda Perkins offers this perspective in "Black Women and Racial 'Uplift' Prior to Emancipation" in Filomina Chioma Steady, ed., *The Black Woman Cross-Culturally* (Cambridge, Mass.: Schenkman), 317–34.

4. For more detailed discussions of slave women's dual economic function, see Jones, *Labor of Love, Labor of Sorrow*, ch. 1 and Deborah Gray White, *Ar'n't I a Woman? Female Slaves in the Plantation South* (New York: Norton, 1985).

5. For labor patterns among slaves, see Eugene D. Genovese, *Roll, Jordan, Roll*, 289–322; Jones, "'My Mother Was Much of a Woman' and *Labor of Love, Labor of Sorrow;* Lerner, *Black Women in White America*, ch. 2; Lebsock, "Free Black Women and the Question of Matriarchy: Petersburg, Virginia, 1784–1820"; Palmer, "White Women/Black Women."

6. See Scott, *The Southern Lady*, and Clinton, *The Plantation Mistress*.

7. Kemble, *Journal*, 39; *The Liberator*, May 9, 1845, p. 75.

8. See Moynihan, *The Negro Family*.

9. See Davis, *Women, Race, and Class*, ch. 1; Palmer, "White Women/Black Women," 157–58; Wallace, *Black Macho;* Frazier, *The Negro Family in the*

United States; Gilbert Osofsky, *Harlem: The Making of a Ghetto: The Negro in New York, 1890–1930* (New York: Harper & Row, 1966).

10. Henry Foster to (Frederick) Douglass, *North Star,* Oct. 20, 1848, *BAP,* reel 5, fr. 0808.

11. The phenomenon of interracial sexual relations in southern society was complex. Clearly, not all sexual alliances between white men and slave women resulted from coercion, nor did interracial relationships occur only between white men and black women. See Gutman, *The Black Family in Slavery and Freedom,* 388–93; Eugene Genovese, *Roll, Jordan, Roll,* 417–19, 422; Robert W. Fogel and Stanley L. Engerman, *Time on the Cross: The Economics of American Negro Slavery* (Boston: Little, Brown, 1974), 134–35.

12. John Blassingame, ed., *Slave Testimony: Two Centuries of Letters, Speeches, Interviews, and Autobiographies* (Baton Rouge: Louisiana State Univ. Press, 1977), 506, 540; Northup, *Twelve Years a Slave,* 31.

13. *The Pro-Slavery Argument,* 119–20.

14. Hammond, "The Morals of Slavery," in *The Pro-Slavery Argument,* 230.

15. Chesnut, *A Diary From Dixie,* 21–22.

16. An example of this can be found in ex-slave Linda Brent's autobiography, in which she describes the severe recriminations she suffered at the hands of her mistress for being the "favorite" slave of her master. See Child, ed., *Incidents in the Life of a Slave Girl,* 29–35.

17. Litwack, *North of Slavery,* 20–22; Jordan, *White Man's Burden,* ch. 5. See also *The Pro-Slavery Argument,* in which Chancellor Harper, James Henry Hammond, and Thomas Dew argue that slavery was necessary for maintaining civilization and that blacks, because of their innate inferiority, were incapable of living productive lives outside of slavery.

18. *Weekly Advocate,* Feb. 11, 1837, *BAP,* reel 1, fr. 0945. Robert Banks was a graduate of Gerrit Smith's manual labor school and worked as an agent for Frederick Douglass's *North Star.* Banks earned a living as a fabric and clothing dealer in Detroit, Delany, *Conditions,* 139–40. See Katzman, *Before the Ghetto,* 32.

19. *Weekly Advocate,* Dec. 22, 1860, *BAP,* reel 13, fr. 0063.

20. *Freedom's Journal,* July 7, 1827, p. 79.

21. Ibid., April 20, 1827, p. 24.

22. *North Star,* Aug. 24, 1849.

23. *Pacific Appeal,* March 5, 1864, *BAP,* reel 15, fr. 0268. Bell maintained a successful business in New York. See Delany, *Conditions,* 103.

24. *Colored American,* April 13, 1837, cited in Sterling, *We Are Your Sisters,* 221–22.

25. Ibid., 222.

26. Mary Still, "An Appeal to the Females of the African Methodist Episcopal Church," 6–7.

27. "Ellen" to the *Colored American,* 1836, *BAP,* reel 2.

28. *Freedom's Journal,* April 8, 1838, p. 10.

29. See Woody, *A History of Women's Education in the United States;* Linda K. Kerber, *Women of the Republic: Intellect and Ideology in Revolutionary America,* (Chapel Hill: Univ. of North Carolina Press, 1980); Rury, "Vocationalism for Home and Work."

30. See Charles C. Andrews, *The History of the New York African Schools*. For more recent works on black education, see Mabee, *Black Education,* 21; Rury, "The New York African Free School, 1827–1836," and "Philanthropy, Self-Help, and Social Control."

31. *Freedom's Journal,* Feb. 29, 1828, p. 194.

32. Mabee, *Black Education,* 22.

33. *Freedom's Journal,* Sept. 21, 1827, p. 12; April 13, 1827; *The Liberator,* Feb. 1, 1834, p. 19; May 24, 1834.

34. *Freedom's Journal,* Aug. 29, 1828, p. 183.

35. *The Liberator,* March 15, 1834, p. 43; April 19, 1834, p. 63; Feb. 1, 1834, p. 19.

36. Samuel Cornish, et al., "First Annual Report of the American Anti-Slavery Society," 39–61, May 6, 1834, New York, *BAP,* reel 1, fr. 0423.

37. Samuel J. May and Lucy B. Williams to Lucretia Mott, Philadelphia, June 25, 1834, Pennsylvania Abolition Society Papers, HSP (hereafter cited as PASP).

38. *Colored American,* Nov. 1839, reel 3, fr. 0281.

39. *Freedom's Journal,* April 13, 1827, p. 20.

40. Ibid., Aug. 10, 1827, in Aptheker, ed., *A Documentary History,* 89.

41. Ibid.

42. Charles B. Ray, "Female Education," *Colored American,* March 18, 1837, *BAP,* reel 1, fr. 1008.

43. *The North Star,* March 17, 1848.

44. *Colored American,* Nov. 1839, reel 3, fr. 0281.

45. Elizabeth Douglass Bustill was the eldest daughter of David and Mary Bustill and granddaughter of Cyrus and Elizabeth Bustill. Smith, "The Bustill Family," 641.

46. Sterling, *We Are Your Sisters,* 181–82.

47. Cornish, *Colored American,* Nov. 23, 1839, *BAP,* reel 3, fr. 0281.

48. Horton and Horton, "Freedom's Yoke," 60–62.

49. Charles C. Andrews, *The History of the New York African Schools,* 117–18.

50. See W. Jeffrey Bolster, "'To Feel Like a Man': Black Seamen in the

Northern States, 1800–1860," *Journal of American History* 76 (March 1990): 1181–83.

51. Levesque, *Black Boston*, 109.

52. Between the late eighteenth century and the present, black women, married and unmarried, far more than white women, have worked outside the home, usually in low-paying domestic labor. See Jones, *Labor of Love, Labor of Sorrow*, and Sterling, *We Are Your Sisters*, 89–104.

53. Quaker abolitionists founded the Pennsylvania Society for Promoting the Abolition of Slavery, for the Relief of Free Negroes Unlawfully held in Bondage, and for Improving the Condition of the African Race in 1775. Anti-slavery societies sometimes studied the condition of the free black community in their areas, reporting population statistics, work patterns, and the numbers of churches, benevolent societies, and reform organizations. See Sterling, *We Are Your Sisters*, 89.

54. *A Statistical Inquiry*, 18.

55. Ibid., 92.

56. Ibid., 91–92.

57. *Freedom's Journal*, May 9, 1838, p. 55; *The Liberator*, Oct. 27, 1843, p. 17. See also James and James, *Notable American Women* 1:511; *North Star*, July 6, 1849.

58. *Freedom's Journal*, May 16, 1828.

59. For explanation of class distinctions within the free black community, see Kronus, *The Black Middle Class*, and Rabinowitz, *Race Relations in the Urban South, 1865–1890*.

60. Studies on female factory workers later in the century demonstrate that racism in the workplace segregated women according to race and assigned black women to the lowest paying tasks. Lerner, *Black Women in White America*, 252–60; Suzanne Lebsock, *The Free Women of Petersburg: Status and Culture in a Southern Town, 1784–1860* (New York: Norton, 1984), 182–85.

61. Billington, "James Forten: Forgotten Abolitionist," 199–300; Winch, *Philadelphia's Black Elite*, 6.

62. Cornish does not indicate the racial makeup of these societies, but they probably were black organizations. *Colored American*, Dec. 7, 1839, *BAP*, reel 3, fr. 0299.

63. *Frederick Douglass' Paper*, Sept. 22, 1854, *BAP*, reel 9, fr. 0104.

64. *Weekly Advocate*, Feb. 11, 1837, *BAP*, reel 1, fr. 0945. See Delany, *Conditions*, 139–40, re Robert Banks.

65. Editorial for the *Colored American*, Nov. 17, 1838, *BAP*, reel 2, fr. 0655.

66. Catharine Beecher had written "Treatise on Domestic Economy," which codified the Cult of True Womanhood ideology. She was the eldest daughter of the well-known preacher, Lyman Beecher. For an in-depth study of Catharine

Beecher, see Kathryn Kish Sklar, *Catharine Beecher: A Study in American Domesticity* (New York: Norton, 1974).

67. See "Appeal of the Abolitionists of the Theological Seminary" at Andover, Mass., *The Liberator,* Aug. 25, 1837, p. 139.

68. Carol V. R. George, *Segregated Sabbaths* (New York: Oxford Univ. Press, 1973), 96; Sobel, *Trabelin' On,* 207.

69. Zilpha Elaw, Jarena Lee, and Julia Foote fought for the right to speak from the pulpit and confronted resistance to their ministerial goals from a predominantly male hierarchy. Julia Foote became the first female deacon in the A.M.E. Zion Church in 1894. See William L. Andrews, ed., *Sisters of the Spirit.*

70. Payne, *History of the African Methodist Episcopal Church,* 301.

71. *Colored American,* Nov. 11, 1837, *BAP,* reel 2, fr. 0265. *Palladium of Liberty,* Oct. 2, 1844, *BAP,* reel 4, fr. 0923. *The Liberator,* May 2, 1845, p. 71. For more information on church activities of black women in Pittsburgh, Detroit, and San Francisco, see the *Weekly Anglo-African,* Jan 1, 1861, *BAP,* reel 13, fr. 0193, *North Star,* Aug. 4, 1848, *BAP,* reel 5, fr. 0725, and *Pacific Appeal,* April 19, 1862, *BAP,* Reel 14, fr. 0251.

Chapter 3

1. Watkins to William Still, 1852, in Sterling, *We Are Your Sisters,* 159.

2. *Voice of the Fugitive,* 1852.

3. Miller, *The Search for a Black Nationality,* 98.

4. From Stewart's speech on Sept. 21, 1832, in Franklin Hall, reprinted in *The Liberator,* Nov. 17, 1832; Still on a speech delivered by William Wells Brown in Philadelphia, *The Provincial Freeman,* Nov. 11, 1854, *BAP,* reel 9, fr. 0206. For detailed discussion on Black initiative in education, see Mabee, *Black Education,* ch. 4.

5. Cross, *The Burned-Over District.*

6. "D" to the "Females of Color," *Weekly Advocate,* Jan 7, 1837, *BAP,* reel 1, fr. 0888.

7. Woodson, *History of the Negro Church.* For more recent works, see George, *Segregated Sabbaths,* Levesque, "Inherent Reformers," and Sobel, *Trabelin' On.*

8. John B. Vashon from William Lloyd Garrison, Boston, Dec. 8, 1832, *BAP,* reel 1, fr. 0228, Villard Papers, Harvard Univ. (hereafter cited as VP). See also Merrill and Ruchames, eds., *The Letters of William Lloyd Garrison* 1:193–95.

9. *Colored American,* Oct. 13, 1838, *BAP,* reel 2, fr. 0615.

10. Theodore S. Wright was active in the New York Vigilance Committee and the United Anti-Slavery Society of New York City, which attempted to coordinate

the work of black organizations. Wright was a firm believer in political action and, in 1840, sided with the Tappan wing of the American Anti-Slavery Society. Wright also believed in black unity. Thus, when the AAS split in 1840, Wright tried to keep all groups of blacks in New York City united in pursuing their abolitionist goals and "the practical needs of the colored people." See Sorin, *The New York Abolitionists*, 84. Oberlin College in Ohio, founded in 1826, was the first college to admit blacks and women.

11. *Colored American*, Oct. 31, 1840, *BAP*, reel 3, fr. 0682.

12. Perlman, "Organizations of the Free Negro in New York City," 190.

13. *The Liberator*, July 21, 1832, p. 114.

14. Sarah M. Douglass to William Lloyd Garrison and Isaac Knapp, Dec. 6, 1832, BPL.

15. *The Liberator*, Jan. 7, 1832, p. 2.

16. Ibid., July 21, 1832, p. 114.

17. *Genius of Universal Emancipation*, 1832, p. 163.

18. William Lloyd Garrison to Sarah M. Douglass, Secretary of the Female Literary Association of Philadelphia, March 5, 1832, BPL: Rare Books and Manuscripts.

19. *The Liberator*, Dec. 1833; Ibid., March 1, 1834, p. 36.

20. (Samuel Cornish) to (Charles B. Ray), *Colored American*, Dec. 2, 1837, *BAP*, reel 2, fr. 0290.

21. *Weekly Anglo-African*, July 23, 1859, *BAP*, reel 11, fr. 0869.

22. "A Tribute of Respect to the Veteran Teacher" ca. 1898, Slaughter Coll., Trevor Arnett Library, Atlanta Univ. Center Library.

23. *The Liberator*, Jan. 4, 1834, p. 3.

24. Ibid.

25. Lydia Maria Child to Jonathan Phillips, Jan. 23. 1838, Schlesinger Library.

26. See Landon, "The Buxton Settlement in Canada," "Henry Bibb," and "Negro Migration to Canada," 22. See Henry Bibb, *Narrative*, 190–91, and Delany, *Conditions*, 132, re Mary Bibb.

27. *Voice of the Fugitive*, Feb. 26, 1851, *BAP*, reel 6, fr. 0836.

28. *Anti-Slavery Bugle*, April 12, 1851, *BAP*, reel 6, fr. 0899.

29. Landon, "Negro Migration to Canada," 24.

30. Mary Ann Shadd to George Whipple, Oct. 27, 1852, Windsor, Canada, *BAP*, reel 7, fr. 0160–0161. Dillard Univ., Amistad Research Center (hereafter cited as ARC), AMA Coll.

31. *Provincial Freeman*, Nov. 3, 1855, *BAP*, reel 9, fr. 0915.

32. Ibid., July 26, 1856, *BAP*, reel 10, fr. 0238.

33. Mary Shadd to Whipple, Nov. 27, 1851, Windsor, AMA Coll., OBHS, box 2, envelope 4.

34. *Voice of the Fugitive*, July 15, 1852, *BAP*, reel 7, fr. 0657.

35. Alexander McArthur to George Whipple, Dec. 22, 1852, Windsor, AMA Coll., OBHS, box 2, envelope 4. Although McArthur may have truly supported Shadd, his attestation may be exaggerated. According to Robin Winks (*The Blacks in Canada,* 207), McArthur's testimony was unreliable, because Hiram Wilson, a friend of Bibb, had convinced the AMA to refuse McArthur's appointment as an agent.

36. Mary Ann Shadd Cary to G[eorge] Whipple, Dec. 28, 1852, Windsor, C[anada] W[est], *BAP,* reel 7, fr. 1039.

37. Shadd to Whipple, Windsor, June 21, 1852, AMA Coll., OBHS, box 2, envelope 4.

38. Ibid., June 21, 1852.

39. Ibid., Jan. 12, 1853, *BAP,* reel 8, fr. 0095.

40. *Voice of the Fugitive,* July 15, 1851, *BAP,* reel 7, fr. 0657.

41. Mary Ann Shadd to George Whipple, Dec. 28, 1852, Windsor, C(anada) W(est), *BAP,* reel 7, fr. 1039.

42. Ibid., July 21, 1852, *BAP,* reel 7, fr. 0688.

43. *Provincial Freeman,* Jan. 28, 1859, *BAP,* reel 11, fr. 0553.

44. Reports on the progress of her school consistently referred to her "colored" school or her "colored" students.

45. *Provincial Freeman,* Jan. 28, 1859, *BAP,* reel 11, fr. 0553.

46. Mary Ann Shadd Cary to George Whipple, June 21, 1859, Chatham, Canada, *BAP,* reel 11, fr. 0795–0796, Dillard Univ., ARC-AMA Coll.

47. Mary Ann Shadd to The Executive Committee of the AMA, Windsor, 1852, AMA Coll., OBHS, box 2, envelope 2.

48. Mary Shadd to [George] Whipple, Aug. 18, 1852, Windsor, AMA Coll., OBHS, box 2, envelope 4.

49. Perlman, "Organizations of the Free Negro in New York City, 1800–1860," 181–82.

50. Horton and Horton, *Black Bostonians,* 28–29. The historian for the Society, black activist John Zuille, asserted that several other black men's benevolent societies in New York City eventually sprang from the African Society. Zuille claimed that the many members of the African Society eventually broke to form the Clarkson Society, the Wilberforce Benevolent Society, and the Woolman Society of Brooklyn; see John T. Zuille, "Historical Sketch of the New York African Society for Mutual Relief," (New York, 1892), 20, cited in Perlman, "Organizations of the Free Negro in New York City, 1800–1860," 184.

51. In 1787, Prince Hall, a black mason and Methodist preacher founded the first black masonic lodge, the African Lodge #459 in Boston. Horton and Horton, *Black Bostonians,* 29; Meier and Rudwick, *From Plantation to Ghetto,* 90–91.

52. James T. Holly to Lewis Hayden, Jan. 9, 1857, New Haven, Conn., *BAP,* reel 10, fr. 0485.

53. Berg, *The Remembered Gate;* Boylan, "Women in Groups"; Hewitt, *Women's Activism;* Smith-Rosenberg, "Beauty and the Beast and the Militant Woman"; Mary P. Ryan, "The Power of Women's Networks," in Judith L. Newton, Mary P. Ryan, and Judith R. Walkowitz, eds., *Sex and Class in Women's History* (London: Routledge and Kegan Paul, 1983), 167–86.

54. *Freedom's Journal,* Jan. 25, 1828, p. 175.

55. Ibid., Feb. 1, 1828, p. 179.

56. Ibid., March 7, 1828, p. 197.

57. Ibid., Feb. 7, 1829, p. 355.

58. John J. Mitre to [Samuel E.] Cornish, *Colored American,* April 1, 1837, *BAP,* reel 2, fr. 0007.

59. Henry Highland Garnet, *Colored American,* Feb. 28, 1838, *BAP,* reel 2, fr. 0433.

60. *The Liberator,* March 12, 1831.

61. Ibid., Dec. 29, 1832, p. 207.

62. Still, "Appeal," 5.

63. Ibid., 4.

64. "Register of Pennsylvania," 7 (March 12, 1831): 163–64.

65. Mitre to Cornish, *Colored American,* April 1, 1837, *BAP,* reel 2, fr. 0007.

66. Wicks, "Address," 11, LCP.

67. Ibid., 14.

68. Ibid., 6.

69. Mary Bibb to Oliver Johnson, *Antislavery Bugle,* April 12, 1851, *BAP,* reel 6, fr. 0898.

70. Winks, *Blacks in Canada,* 205.

71. J(ames) C. Brown, J(ohn) W. Menard to *Toronto Globe,* Dec. 24, 1861, *BAP,* reel 13, fr. 1002a.

72. Mr. [Horace] Hallock to Mr. C. C. Foote, Detroit, Jan. 12, 1853, AMA Coll., OBHS, box 2, envelope 4.

73. H. Hallock to Wm Harned, Detroit, Jan. 24, 1853, AMA Coll., OBHS, box 2, envelope 4.

74. Winks, *Blacks in Canada,* 207.

75. Mary Ann Shadd to George Whipple, June 21, 1852, Windsor, AMA Coll., OBHS, box 2, envelope 4.

76. *Provincial Freeman,* April 7, 1855, *BAP,* reel 9, fr. 0522; *Pine and Palm,* Sept. 7, 1861, *BAP,* reel 13, fr. 0743.

77. DAS, Minutes, June 5, 1832.

78. Ibid., Nov. 3, 1835.

79. Ibid., June 3, 1823, Aug. 5, 1823, May 11, 1824. HSP.

80. A.M.E. Church Records, Minute & Trial Book, HSP.

81. Ibid.

82. The asylum was later renamed the Riverdale Children's Association. Shotwell served on the Board of Managers for more than thirty years, as secretary for twenty-eight of those years. According to the story, Shotwell and Murray had found two black orphans sitting on steps but discovered that the Long Island Farm (public nursery for white orphans) and the three other orphanages in New York excluded blacks. *Riverdale Children's Association's 120th Anniversary, 1836–1956*. Pamphlet. Schlesinger Lib.

83. *Colored American*, Dec. 15, 1838, *BAP*, reel 2, fr. 0681.

84. Cornish to James McCune Smith, *Colored American*, Jan. 19, 1839, *BAP*, reel 2, fr. 0979.

85. Ibid.

86. Gates, *Collected Black Women's Narratives*, "Narrative of the Life and Travels of Mrs. Nancy Prince," 41–42.

87. J(ohn) Miter to (Amos A.) Phelps, *The Emancipator*, *BAP*, reel 1, fr. 0705; *Friend of Man*, Sept. 29, 1836.

88. Martin R. Delany to Frederick Douglass, *North Star*, March 9, 1849, *BAP*, reel 5, fr. 0998.

89. *The Liberator*, Aug. 3, 1833, p. 114.

90. Ibid., Nov. 9, 1838, p. 180.

91. *Frederick Douglass's Paper*, Feb. 12, 1852, *BAP*, reel 7, fr. 0405. Ward was a black Congregationalist minister for a white congregation in Courtlandville, N.Y., editor of a religious newspaper, and an orator. See Delany, *Conditions*, 112.

92. Temperance advocates in white communities also perceived a serious alcohol problem. By 1851, the American Tract Society had flooded American communities with nearly five million pamphlets and circulated copies of the annual reports of the American Temperance Union. See Rorabaugh, *The Alcoholic Republic*, 196–97.

93. *Provincial Freeman*, March 28, 1857, *BAP*, reel 10, fr. 0597; Dec. 6, 1856, *BAP*, reel 10, fr. 0393.

94. *The Liberator*, Feb. 22, 1834, p. 32.

95. Ibid., May 11, 1833, p. 74.

96. See *Poems on Miscellaneous Subjects* and *Atlanta Offering Poems*, 43.

Chapter 4

1. *North Star*, Aug. 14, 1848.

2. See Dillon, *The Abolitionists*, 22. In 1832, for example, members of the state legislature of Pennsylvania proposed a law that would require all blacks to carry passes. Modeled after slave passes, these documents would mark the destination of the bearer and the time he or she expected to return home. Such a

proposal, though never passed, signified the desires of whites to limit the movements of free blacks. See Sterling, ed., *We Are Your Sisters*, 126.

3. *North Star*, Sept. 29, 1848; Foner, ed., *Life and Writings of Frederick Douglass* 1:335.

4. *The Liberator*, Nov. 17, 1832, p. 183.

5. This group donated fifteen dollars to the state antislavery society to sponsor a white abolitionist as a life member. *The Liberator*, July 12, 1839, p. 111.

6. Hewitt, *Women's Activism*, 42; *The Liberator*, July 5, 1839, p. 107; July 12, 1839, p. 111.

7. Emerson, ed., *Life of Abby Hopper Gibbons* 1:99. Abigail Hopper Gibbons (1801–93) was the daughter of Quakers Isaac Hopper and Sarah Tatum Hopper in Philadelphia. Her father, a tailor and bookseller, was also a reformer who opened a shelter for female convicts in New York. Unlike many of her white Quaker colleagues, Hopper and her family lived on a modest income, which Abby later supplemented by helping in her mother's teashop. The family later moved to New York. She married James Sloan Gibbons, a successful banker whose income enabled his wife to join the ranks of other middle-class white women in social reform. In addition to her antislavery work, she also devoted much of her career to prison reform for women and to charitable activities in New York City's tenements. Hersh, *Slavery of Sex*, 164–65, and James and James, *Notable American Women* 2:28–29.

8. *The Liberator*, Nov. 17, 1832, p. 183.

9. Ibid.

10. Ibid., June 21, 1834, p. 1.

11. Lydia Maria Child to Ellis Gray Loring, May 17, 1841, Lydia Maria Child Papers, Schlesinger Lib., Radcliffe College and Clements Lib., Univ. of Michigan.

12. Lydia Maria Francis Child was the daughter of David Convers Francis, a prosperous baker in Medford, Mass. In 1828, she married abolitionist David Lee Child, who had begun his career as a lawyer but gave up his occupation to participate in reform movements. See James and James, *Notable American Women* 1:330–33.

13. Louisa Nell was the mother of black abolitionist William C. Nell. Salem worked as a servant in the home of Sarah Southwick for twenty-five years. Hansen, "Bluestockings and Bluenoses," 216.

14. Litwack, *North of Slavery*, chs. 1–2.

15. *The Liberator*, Feb. 28, 1839, p. 21.

16. Litwack, *North of Slavery*, 100–102, 159.

17. Chambers, American Slavery and Colour," 128.

18. All of the members of the LNYCASS were Protestant. The organizers of the society had recruited one antislavery woman from every Protestant church in

the city to serve on the Board of Managers. They apparently had not considered recruiting non-Protestants. Unlike the Boston Female Anti-Slavery Society and the Philadelphia Female Anti-Slavery Society, the New York City society did not include women from all denominations, as the founding members had claimed. The BFASS consisted of Unitarians, Congregationalists, Quakers, Episcopalians, Methodists, and several Swedenborgians. Although the religious makeup of the PFASS was primarily Quaker, the Quaker members of the PFASS had advocated racial equality and welcomed black friends into their social circles. See Swerdlow, "Abolition's Conservative Sisters," 2–4.

19. Ibid., 9–11.

20. Ladies' New York City Anti-Slavery Society, First Annual Report, 1836, Art. 3.

21. Anne Warren Weston to Deborah Weston, Oct. 22, 1836, BPL. Julianna Tappan's father was Lewis Tappan, a leader in the evangelical and abolitionist circle in New York City. Lewis Tappan and his brother, Arthur, were wealthy textile merchants who provided a great deal of financial support for the abolitionist cause. They eventually broke with Garrison over abolitionist ideology and tactics and spearheaded the formation of the American & Foreign Anti-Slavery Society in 1841. Julianna Tappan, a leader in the women's petition drive in New York City, never challenged the idea of maintaining separate codes of behavior for women.

22. LNYCASS, First Annual Report, 1836, p. 6.

23. Swerdlow, "Abolition's Conservative Sisters," 6.

24. See ref. to Eliza Day, ch. 1, above.

25. Lovell, ed., *Two Quaker Sisters*, 118–19. Elizabeth Buffum Chace (1806–99), the daughter of abolitionist Quaker Arnold Buffum and Rebecca Gould Buffum in Providence, R.I., was married to Samuel Chace, also an abolitionist. See Hersh, *Slavery of Sex*, 129, 132, 228–229, and James and James, *Notable American Women* 1:317–19.

26. Phebe Matthews to Theodore Weld, Cincinnati, March 1835, Barnes and Dumond, *Letters of Theodore Dwight Weld* 1:217.

27. Sarah Anthony Burtis to Abby Kelley, Jan. 17, 1843; Stephen and Abigail Kelley Foster Papers, American Antiquarian Society; See also Hewitt, *Women's Activism*, 117.

28. Levesque, *Black Boston*, 92; Horton and Horton, *Black Bostonians*, 92.

29. Levesque, *Black Boston*, 126–27.

30. Horton and Horton, *Black Bostonians*, 94.

31. Maria Weston Chapman to "Female Anti-Slavery Societies throughout New England," Boston, June 7, 1837, in Barnes and Dumond, *Letters of Theodore Dwight Weld* 1:397.

32. PFASS, minutes; PASP.

33. James and James, *Notable American Women* 1:511.
34. PFASS, minutes, 1833–48, Sept. 29, 1836, PASP.
35. Ibid., April 19, 1841.
36. Ibid., Jan. 1, 1840. Sixth Annual Meeting.
37. Ibid., March 12, 1840.
38. Ibid.
39. Ibid., Jan. 14, 1847.
40. Ibid., Oct. 14, 1841.
41. Ibid., Jan. 14, 1847.
42. Mary and David Bustill were brother and sister of Grace Bustill Douglass. The census of 1850 (roll #810) lists Mary Bustill as 61 years old and her brother, a "plaisterer," as 66. The ages as listed are mistaken. Anna Bustill Smith marks David's birth in 1787, which would have made him 63 at the time the census was taken; he was the youngest child. In 1850, they resided in the Northern Liberties ward of Philadelphia with five of his nine children and two other plasterers, Edward Pierce and Lewis Parker; see also Smith, "The Bustill Family."
43. *Pennsylvania Freeman*, July 5, 1838.
44. PFASS, minutes, Sept. 9, 1841.
45. Ibid., June 12, 1845.
46. Ibid., April 10, 1856.
47. Ibid. Lucretia Coffin Mott (1793–1880) was a leading white antislavery woman and women's rights advocate. Mott, her mother, and her sisters were active in Philadelphia antislavery activities. She was married to wealthy Philadelphia wool merchant and abolitionist, James Mott.
48. Ibid., Oct. 8, 1846.
49. *The Liberator*, Jan. 18, 1839; Hansen, "Bluestockings and Bluenoses," 32.
50. For more detailed discussions of the organizational split in 1840, see Dumond, *Antislavery: Crusade for Freedom;* Dillon, *The Abolitionists*, 124–26; Kraditor, *Ends and Means in American Abolitionism*, 10, 51–52. For analysis of Black reactions to the split, see Quarles, *Black Abolitionists*, ch. 3.
51. "Address of the Boston Female Anti-Slavery Society to the Women of New England," BPL; Swerdlow, "Abolition's Conservative Sisters," 7.
52. BFASS, Seventh Annual Report, Oct. 14, 1840.
53. Hansen, "Bluestockings and Bluenoses," 178–79.
54. *The Liberator*, Nov. 15, 1839, p. 183.
55. Hansen, "Bluestockings and Bluenoses," 121.
56. In 1844 they signed a petition to prevent the establishment of separate schools for black children. See Josiah Smith, et. al., "Petition on Separate Schools to the Boston Committee," Boston, 1844, *BAP*, reel 4, fr. 0723–0726, BPL. In 1845, Davis and Williams served on a committee at a "meeting of

colored citizens of Boston" to appropriate money for a monument in memory of the late white abolitionist Charles T. Torrey. See Horton and Horton, *Black Bostonians*, 91. For Logan's association with the Zion Church, see *The Liberator*, Oct. 20, 1843, p. 168.

57. William C. Nell had briefly supported Frederick Douglass's campaign for black nationalism and separatism from white abolitionist leadership and had joined Douglass's staff in Rochester, New York, as publisher of the *North Star* in 1852. Nell left Douglass one year later after disagreeing over the issue of separatism. In 1853, he returned to Boston as an ardent supporter of Garrison and racial cooperation in the antislavery effort. See Delaney, *Conditions*, 123.

58. Swerdlow, "Abolition's Conservative Sisters," 8.

59. Martineau, *Retrospect* 3:255.

60. *The Liberator*, June 21, 1839, p. 98.

61. *National Anti-Slavery Standard*, Nov. 13, 1850, *BAP*, reel 6, fr. 0671.

62. Quarles, *Black Abolitionists*, 12; Dillon, *The Abolitionists*, 71.

63. *National Anti-Slavery Standard*, Dec. 2, 1841, Schlesinger Lib., Lydia Maria Child Papers.

64. *The Colored American*, May 30, 1840.

65. Thomas Van Rensselaer to Joshua Leavitt, *The Emancipator*, June 25, 1840, *BAP*, reel 3, fr. 0649.

66. *North Star*, Sept. 29, 1848, cited in Foner, *The Life and Writings of Frederick Douglass* 1:333.

67. William C. Nell to Amy Post, Boston, Feb. 19, 1854, *BAP*, reel 8, fr. 0655.

68. William C. Nell to Amy Post, Boston, Dec. 19, 1853, *BAP*, reel 8, fr. 0513.

69. Hewitt, *Women's Activism*, 42.

70. *North Star*, Jan. 25, 1850.

71. Winch, *Philadelphia's Black Elite*, 81, 105, 64, 94.

72. Ibid., 193 (n. 59). The Population Schedules of the Seventh Census of the United States (1850), roll #809, lists John P. Burr, 58, as head of household and included Hetty (listed as Hedy), 55, Elizabeth, 21, Lewise (probably Louise), 17, Mathilde, 15, Ellen, 13, and Walther H., 25. Another family, the Darrons, also lived at the Burrs': Nathaniel (a barber), 28, Sarah, 27, Francis, 2, and Eveline, 8 months. Hanna West, 60, also was a resident.

73. Delany, *Conditions*, 95–96, and Walker, "Prejudices, Profits, and Privileges," 404–5.

74. Hester and Lydia Bustill were cousins of Grace and Sarah Douglass.

75. The Census of 1850 (roll #817, New Market ward, Bristol) listed Bristol, 29 years old, as head of the household and the owner of $1,500 real property in Philadelphia, probably her house; the household included her 6-year-old son,

Charles, husband Andrew, age 31, and Henry Johnson, a bartender, and his wife, Margaretta. According to the Census, the Appos' fourth child, William, age 8, was born in New York, and their fifth child, John, age 2, was born in Pennsylvania (Roll #813, Pine ward). Helen Johnson resided with Mary Jane Peters, 30, and Sarah Girard, 64, occupations unknown (Roll #813, Pine ward). See Delany, *Conditions*, 126, 141–42.

76. Delany did not become an advocate of emigration until several years after this address. During the early 1850s, he supported emigration only within the western hemisphere and criticized emigrationists who supported the Liberia colony. According to Wilson J. Moses, Delany changed his stand by 1859 and began to encourage blacks to leave the United States and establish self-sufficient black communities in Africa. Miller, *The Search for a Black Nationality,* and Moses, *The Golden Age of Black Nationalism*.

77. *North Star,* March 3, 1849.

78. Ibid., July 13, 1849, *BAP,* reel 6, fr. 0044, and Sterling, ed., *We Are Your Sisters,* 117–18.

79. *North Star,* March 3, 1849.

Chapter 5

1. See Hersh, *Slavery of Sex;* DuBois, *Feminism and Suffrage;* and Lerner, *The Grimké Sisters*. See also Margaret Hope Bacon, *I Speak For My Slave Sister* (New York: Crowell, 1974); Lerner, *Black Women in White America;* Sterling, *We Are Your Sisters;* Loewenberg and Bogin, *Black Women in Nineteenth Century American Life;* Bogin, "Sarah Parker Remond: Black Abolitionist From Salem"; Porter, "Sarah Remond, Abolitionist and Physician", Noble, *Beautiful, Also, Are the Souls of My Black Sisters;* and Bearden and Butler, *Shadd*.

2. Lerner, ed., *Black Women in White America,* xxii.

3. *Signal of Liberty,* Feb. 6, 1843, *BAP,* reel 4, fr. 0535.

4. Frances Ellen Watkins [Harper] to Marius R. J. Robinson, reprinted in the *Anti-Slavery Bugle,* Nov. 13, 1858, *BAP,* reel 11, fr. 0404.

5. James O. Horton, "Freedom's Yoke," 62–63.

6. Jeremiah Sanderson to Amy Post, May 8, 1845, New York, NY, *BAP,* reel 5, fr. 0002.

7. *Provincial Freeman,* March 29, 1856, *BAP,* reel 10, fr. 0097.

8. Mary Ann Shadd Cary to Isaac Shadd, *Provincial Freeman,* March 8, 1856, *BAP,* reel 10, fr. 0075.

9. William Lloyd Garrison and his followers had advocated equality between both the races and the sexes in an effort to rid society of injustice.

10. Reprinted in *The Liberator,* Aug. 25, 1837, p. 139.

11. *Freedom's Journal,* Dec. 12, 1828, p. 291.

12. Eckhardt, *Fanny Wright*, 1–4.
13. *Colored American*, May 18, 1839, *BAP*, reel 3, fr. 0067.
14. See Stewart's address in Sterling, ed., *We Are Your Sisters*, 157.
15. Sterling, ed., *We Are Your Sisters*, 157–58; *Notable American Women* 3:378.
16. Lucretia (Coffin) Mott? to Lydia Maria Child (editor), *National Anti-Slavery Standard*, April 7, 1842.
17. *Memoirs of Zilpha Elaw*, in Andrews, ed., *Sisters of the Spirit*, 150–53.
18. *The Liberator*, Nov. 12, 1858, *BAP*, reel 11, fr. 0403.
19. Mary Ann Shadd Cary to Thomas F. Cary (n.d.), OBHS, box 2, folder 6.
20. Ibid.
21. *Provincial Freeman*, March 29, 1856, *BAP*, reel 10, fr. 0097.
22. Ibid., March 7, 1857, *BAP*, reel 10, fr. 0571.
23. Sterling, *We Are Your Sisters*, 170–71.
24. *Provincial Freeman*, March 29, 1856, *BAP*, reel 10, fr. 0097.
25. *Anti-Slavery Standard*, October 1859, *BAP*, reel 12, fr. 0072–0073; *Anti-Slavery Advocate*, Nov. 1, 1859, *BAP*, reel 12, fr. 0187; *Warrington Times*, Jan. 29, 1859, *BAP*, reel 11, fr. 0557.
26. *Provincial Freeman*, March 7, 1857, *BAP*, reel 10, fr. 0571.
27. Ibid., March 29, 1856, *BAP*, reel 10, fr. 0097.
28. *Warrington Times*, Jan. 29, 1859, *BAP*, reel 11, fr. 0557.
29. Wood, "'Scribbling Women' and Fanny Fern," 4–6.
30. Little biographical information exists on Lucy Terry (1730–1821), who wrote one widely known poem, "Bars Fight, August 28, 1746," about an Indian raid, in which she depicts whites as the losers. It was not published until 1895. Phillis Wheatley (ca. 1753–84) was a slave who arrived in North America when she was about eight years old. She received an extensive education from the family who owned her and later published several collections of poetry. See Stetson, ed., *Black Sister*, 3–5, 12–15.
31. Stetson, ed., *Black Sister*, xiii.
32. *Philanthropist*, March 11, 1836, *BAP*, reel 1, fr. 0650.
33. Ibid.
34. *Provincial Freeman*, Sept. 2, 1854, *BAP*, reel 9, fr. 0060.
35. Ibid., June 30, 1855, *BAP*, reel 9, fr. 0727.
36. Ibid., March 1, 1856, *BAP*, reel 10, fr. 0069.
37. *Philanthropist*, March 11, 1836, *BAP*, reel 1, fr. 0650.
38. Ibid., 7–8.
39. Loewenberg and Bogin, *Black Women in Nineteenth Century American Life*, 235; See also Stanton, *History of Woman Suffrage* 1:116. The speech was recorded in part by Frances D. Gage, who presided over the meeting.
40. Watkins, *Poems on Miscellaneous Subjects*, 9–10.

41. *The Liberator,* Oct. 6, 1836; see also Stetson, *Black Sister,* 18.

42. PFASS; Proceedings, Anti-Slavery Convention of American Women, 1837.

43. Bogin, "Sarah Parker Remond," 139.

44. *Anti-Slavery Advocate,* Sept. 1, 1859, *BAP,* reel 12, fr. 0001.

45. Bogin, "Sarah Parker Remond," 139.

46. *Frederick Douglass' Paper,* Feb. 17, 1860, *BAP,* reel 12, fr. 0496.

47. *Warrington Times,* (Feb. 5, 1859), in Bogin, "Sarah Parker Remond," 131.

48. Sterling, ed., *We Are Your Sisters,* 157.

49. From Stewart's speech on Sept. 21, 1832, in Franklin Hall, Boston, reprinted in *The Liberator,* Nov. 17, 1832.

50. *Anti-Slavery Bugle,* Ohio, July 9, 1859, *BAP,* reel 11, fr. 0852.

51. *Anglo-African Magazine,* May 1859, *BAP,* reel 11, fr. 0721.

52. Elizabeth Chandler edited the "Ladies Department" in Benjamin Lundy's *Genius of Universal Emancipation,* and Lydia Maria Child edited the *Anti-Slavery Standard* in Boston.

53. Shadd's obvious disgust with Douglass was probably based on his opposition to emigration. Although Douglass had been a staunch supporter of black nationalism, race pride, and separatism, he had argued that for blacks simply to leave the country that oppressed them was no solution to the problems of race prejudice or slavery. See *Provincial Freeman,* July 19, 1856, *BAP,* reel 10, fr. 0226.

54. Ibid.

55. *Colored American,* Nov. 13, 1841.

56. *The Liberator,* Sept. 15, 1837, p. 152.

57. Ibid.

58. Ibid.

59. Ibid.

60. PFASS, Minutes, Oct. 12, 1843, PASP, reel 30.

61. Ibid.

62. Ibid., Sept. 10, 1835, PASP, reel 30.

63. Horton and Horton, *Black Bostonians,* 70.

64. *The Liberator,* Feb. 10, 1843, p. 22.

65. Ibid., Levesque, *Black Boston,* 134, 137–44.

66. Ibid., 134; *The Liberator,* Feb. 24, 1843, p. 30.

67. Horton and Horton, *Black Bostonians,* 21–22.

68. 1838 Petitions re: Repeal of the Act Prohibiting the Education of Colored Persons, courtesy of the Conn. State Lib., box 27.

69. Smith, "Petition on Separate Schools to the Boston Committee," Boston, 1844, *BAP,* reel 4, fr. 0723–0726, BPL.

70. Horton, *Black Bostonians*, 71–72; Levesque, *Black Boston*, 168.

71. Levesque, *Black Boston*, 170.

72. Ibid., 172–73.

73. Horton, *Black Bostonians*, 75.

74. *Pacific Appeal*, April 4, 1863, *BAP*, reel 14, fr. 0788.

75. *Provincial Freeman*, March 10, 1855, *BAP*, reel 9, fr. 0476; Sterling, ed., *We Are Your Sisters*, 223.

76. *Charlotte L. Brown v. the Omnibus Rail Road Company*, District Court of the 12th Judicial District (1863), *BAP*, reel 14, fr. 0806; *Elevator*, April 7, 1865, *BAP*, reel 15, fr. 0809.

Chapter 6

1. Hersh, in her study of feminist-abolitionists, excluded black women from her profile of leading women, arguing that black women had played a "peripheral" role in the organized women's rights movement, "although they were important as abolitionists." See Hersh, *Slavery of Sex*.

2. DuBois, *Feminism and Suffrage*, 32; Yellin, *Women and Sisters*, 13–15; Davis, *Women, Race, and Class*, 33, 39.

3. DuBois, *Feminism and Suffrage*, 69–71; Terborg-Penn, "Discrimination Against Afro-American Women in the Woman's Movement, 1830–1920," in Harley and Terborg-Penn, eds., *The Afro-American Woman*, 17–27; Lerner, *The Majority Finds Its Past*, 33, 68; and Aptheker, *Woman's Legacy*, 9–52. For earlier studies of the women's movement, see Eleanor Flexnor, *A Century of Struggle: The Woman's Rights Movement in the United States* (New York: Atheneum, 1968).

4. See hooks, *Feminist Theory: From Margin to Center* (Boston: South End Press, 1984).

5. Quarles, *Black Abolitionists*, 177; Terborg-Penn, "Black Male Perspectives on the Nineteenth-Century Woman," in Harley and Terborg-Penn, eds., *The Afro-American Woman*, 29; Horton and Horton, *Black Bostonians*, 66.

6. Loewenberg and Bogin, *Black Women in Nineteenth Century American Life*, 189.

7. Thomas Van Rensselaer, David Ruggles, and Charles B. Ray, for example, stayed with Garrison. Many black men who defected with the Tappan faction were members of the clergy, who had encouraged women activists to remain within their "proper" sphere. The eight black men who attended the meetings that created the American & Foreign Anti-Slavery Society included the Rev. Samuel E. Cornish, Amos G. Beman and the Rev. Jehiel C. Beman, and the Rev. Theodore S. Wright.

8. Quarles and Bell have shown that many black men in the movement supported the political approach to fighting the Slave Power in Congress by

joining with the faction of the Tappan wing that favored formation of an antislavery party. Quarles, *Black Abolitionists*, 46–47.

9. *The Emancipator*, Feb. 25, 1841, *BAP*, reel 3, fr. 0904, 0906–7.
10. Stanton, *History of Woman Suffrage* 2:193.
11. Ibid. 2:235.
12. Ibid. 1:115–16.
13. Ibid.
14. Ibid.
15. Sterling, ed., *We Are Your Sisters*, 158.
16. *Provincial Freeman*, April 26, 1856, *BAP*, reel 10, fr. 0118.
17. Ibid., April 26, 1856, *BAP*, reel 10, fr. 0118.
18. Ibid., 193.
19. Aptheker, *A Documentary History*, 114.
20. Bell, *A Survey of the Negro Convention Movement*, 1–2.
21. *National Reformer*, Sept.–Oct. 1838, p. 13.
22. Ibid., Sept.–Oct. 1839, p. 42.
23. Coleman, "Keeping the Faith and Disturbing the Peace," 18.
24. Colored Citizens of Ohio, State Convention. Columbus, January 10–18, 1849, Minutes and Addresses, 15.
25. Coleman, "Keeping the Faith," 20.
26. Proceedings of the New England Colored Citizens' Convention, Boston, Aug. 1, 1859, in Foner and Walker, eds., *Proceedings of the Black State Conventions*, 2:207–08. Ruth Rice Remond was married to John Lenox Remond, brother of Charles Lenox Remond and Sarah Remond.
27. *Antislavery Bugle*, Aug. 6, 1859, *BAP*, reel 11, fr. 0921.
28. The *Troy Daily Times*, Sept. 6, 1855, p. 2, in Coleman, "Keeping the Faith," 20.
29. *British Banner*, Nov. 20, 1855, *BAP*, reel 9, fr. 0938.
30. *North Star*, Aug. 10, 1848; see Foner, ed., *Frederick Douglass on Women's Rights*, 49.
31. *North Star*, July 28, 1848.
32. Lecture delivered before the Rochester Ladies' Anti-Slavery Society, Jan. 1855, Foner, *The Life and Writings of Frederick Douglass* 2:349–50.
33. Elizabeth Cady Stanton to Wendell Phillips, May 25, 1865, in DuBois, *Feminism and Suffrage*, 60.
34. "Griffing Papers," Columbia Univ. Lib., pub. by Joseph Borone in *The Journal of Negro History* (1948), 469–70; see also Aptheker, *A Documentary History*, 627–28.
35. Stanton, *History of Woman Suffrage* 2:391; See also DuBois, *Feminism and Suffrage*, 178.
36. Stanton, *History of Woman Suffrage* 2:391.

37. Ibid. 2:194.

38. *New National Era* (Washington), Oct. 24, 1872, cited in Aptheker, *A Documentary History*, 628.

39. Stanton, *History of Woman Suffrage* 2:193; Sterling, ed., *We Are Your Sisters*, 411.

40. The women were active in the National Association of Colored Women, which promoted woman suffrage. Garnet, the wife of black abolitionist Henry Highland Garnet, also organized the all-black female Equal Suffrage League, and Wells led the fight among black women against lynching. Aptheker, *Woman's Legacy*, 65.

41. Mary Ann Shadd Cary, April 6, Sunday Evening, n.d., Shadd Family Papers, OBHS, box 2, envelope 3.

Bibliography

Manuscript Collections

African Methodist Episcopal Church Records (Mother Bethel). Philadelphia, 1822–51. Minutes & Trial Book. Historical Society of Pennsylvania.

Anti-Slavery Collection. Department of Rare Books & Manuscripts, Boston Public Library

Black Abolitionist Papers. Ed. C. Peter Ripley and George Carter. 17 reels.

Daughters of Africa Society. Philadelphia, 1822–1838. Minutes & Order Book. Historical Society of Pennsylvania

Daughters of Tapsico Society of Mother Bethel A.M.E. Church, 1837–47. Philadelphia. Minute Book. Historical Society of Pennsylvania.

Mary Ann Shadd Cary Papers. Moorland-Spingarn Research Center, Howard University.

Lydia Maria Child Papers. Sophia Smith Collection, Schlesinger Library, Radcliffe College.

Connecticut State Archives, State Library of Connecticut, Hartford.

Stephen and Abigail Kelley Foster Papers. American Antiquarian Society, Worcester, Mass.

Garrison-Villard Papers. Houghton Library, Harvard University.

New York Manumission Society Papers. New York Historical Society.

Pennsylvania Abolition Society Papers. Philadelphia, Historical Society of Pennsylvania.

Philadelphia Female Anti-Slavery Society. Annual Reports, 1839, 1845, 1851, 1852, 1860, 1862. Philadelphia Historical Society of Pennsylvania.

Salem Female Anti-Slavery Society Records, 1834–66. Essex Institute, Worcester, Mass. Henry P. Slaughter Collection, Trevor Arnett Library, Atlanta University Center Library, Atlanta.

Bibliography

Shadd Family Papers. Robbins Collection, Ontario Black History Society, Toronto.

Gerrit Smith Papers. Sterling Memorial Library, Yale University.

Newspapers

The Antislavery Examiner (1835–37)

The Anti-Slavery Record (New York: 1835–37)

Colored American (New York: 1837–42; published Jan.–Feb. 1837 as *Weekly Advocate*.

Elevator (San Francisco)

Freedom's Journal (New York: 1828–30)

Friend of Man

Douglass' Monthly (1859–63)

Genius of Universal Emancipation (1821–39)

The Liberator (Boston: 1831–65)

National Anti-Slavery Standard (New York: 1840–60)

The National Reformer

North Star (Rochester, N.Y.: 1847–51)

Pacific Appeal (San Francisco)

Provincial Freeman (Toronto, Ontario: 1852–ca. 57)

Voice of the Fugitive (Toronto, Ontario: 1851–53)

Published Primary Sources

American Anti-Slavery Society. Second Annual Report. New York: William S. Dorr, 1835.

"An Appeal to Women of the Nominally Free States Issued at the Anti-Slavery Convention of American Women." Boston, 1838.

Andrews, Charles C. *The History of the New York African Schools From their Establishment in 1787 to the Present Time*. New York: Nahlon Day, 1830; reprint ed., New York: Negro Universities Press, 1969.

Anti-Slavery Convention of American Women. New York, 1837, Proceedings.

Anti-Slavery Record. 3 vols., 1835–37. New York: American Anti-Slavery Society, 1836–38.

Anti-Slavery Records and Pamphlets, 1834–44; reprint ed., Westport, Conn.: Negro Universities Press, 1970.

Aptheker, Herbert, ed. *And Why Not Every Man? Documentary History of the Fight Against Slavery in the United States*. New York: International Publishers, 1960.

———. *A Documentary of the Negro People*. New York: Citadel Press, 1951.

Bacon, Benjamin C. *Statistics of the Colored People of Education and published by Order of the Board of Education of "The Pennsylvania Society for Promoting the Abolition of Slavery."* 1859.

Barnes, Gilbert Hobbes and Dwight L. Dumond, eds. *Letters of Theodore Dwight Weld, Angelina Grimké Weld, and Sarah Grimké, 1832–1844*. 2 vols. New York: Appleton-Century, 1934.

Billington, Ray, ed. *The Journal of Charlotte Forten*. London: Collier, 1953.

Blassingame, John W., ed. *The Frederick Douglass Papers*. 2 vols. New Haven: Yale Univ. Press, 1979.

Blassingame, John W., and Mae G. Henderson, eds. *Antislavery Newspapers and Periodicals*. 3 vols. Boston: G. K. Hall, 1980–81.

"Brief History of the First African Presbyterian Church of Philadelphia, Pa. Along with Rev. Wm. Catto's History and Discourse from 1807–1940," 1944.

Brown, Josephine. *Biography of An American Bondman, By His Daughter*. Boston: 1855.

Brown, William J. *The Life of William J. Brown of Providence, R.I. With Personal Recollections of Incidents in Rhode Island*. 1883; reprint ed., Freeport, N.Y.: Books For Libraries Press, 1971.

Chadwick, John W., ed. *A Life For Liberty: Anti-Slavery and Other Letters of Sallie Holley*. New York: G. P. Putnam's Sons, 1899.

Chambers, William. *American Slavery and Colour*. London: W. & R. Chambers, 1857.

Chapman, Maria Weston. *Right and Wrong in Massachusetts*. Boston: Dew & Jackson Anti-Slavery Press, 1838; reprint ed., New York: Negro Universities Press, 1969.

Chesnut, Mary Boykin, *A Diary from Dixie*, ed. Ben Ames Williams. Boston: Houghton Mifflin, 1947.

Child, Lydia Maria, ed. Harriet Brent Jacobs, *Incidents in the Life of a Slave Girl: An Authentic Historical Narrative Describing the Horrors of Slavery as Experienced by Black Women*. San Diego: Harcourt Brace Jovanovich, 1973

Craft, William. *Running A Thousand Miles For Freedom; or, the Escape of William and Ellen Craft from Slavery*. London, 1860.

Delany, Martin Robison. *The Condition, Elevation, Emigration, and Destiny of the Colored People of the United States*. Philadelphia, 1852. Reprint ed., New York: Arno Press, 1968.

Douglass, Rev. William. *Annals of the First African Church*. Philadelphia: King & Baird, 1862.

DuBois, Ellen C., ed. *Elizabeth Cady Stanton/Susan B. Anthony: Correspondence, Writings, Speeches*. New York: Schocken, 1981.

Dumond, Dwight L., ed. *Letters of James Gillespie Birney, 1831–1857*. 2 vols. New York: Appleton-Century, 1938.

Bibliography

Emerson, Sarah Hopper, ed. *Life of Abby Hopper Gibbons, Told Chiefly Through Her Correspondence*. 2 vols. New York: G. P. Putnam's Sons, 1897.

Faust, Drew Gilpin, ed. *The Ideology of Slavery: Pro-Slavery Thought in the Antebellum South, 1830–1860*. Baton Rouge: Louisiana State Univ. Press, 1981.

Foner, Philip, ed. *Frederick Douglass on Women's Rights*. Westport, Conn.: Greenwood, 1976.

———, ed. *The Life and Writings of Frederick Douglass*. 4 vols. New York: International, 1950.

Foner, Philip, and George Walker, eds. *Proceedings of the Black State Conventions, 1840–1865*. 2 vols. Philadelphia: Temple Univ. Press, 1979.

Garnet, Henry Highland. *The Past and Present Condition and Destiny of the Colored Race: A Discourse Delivered at the Fifteenth Anniversary of the Female Benevolent Society of Troy, New York, February 14, 1848;* reprint ed., Miami: Mnemosyne, 1969.

Gates, Henry Louis, Jr., gen. ed. *Collected Black Women's Narratives*. New York: Oxford Univ. Press, 1988.

Gilbert, Olive, and Frances W. Titus. *Narrative of Sojourner Truth and Book of Life*. Battle Creek, Mich., 1878.

Hardy, J. P., ed. *The Political Writings of Dr. Samuel Johnson*. New York: Barnes & Noble, 1968.

Harper, Frances Ellen Watkins. *Atlanta Offering Poems*. Philadelphia: George S. Ferguson, 1895; reprint ed., Miami: Mnemosyne, 1969.

———. *Iola Leroy, or Shadows Uplifted*. College Park, Md.: McGrath, 1969.

———. *Poems*. Philadelphia, 1895; reprint ed., Freeport, N.Y.: Books For Libraries Press, 1970.

———. *Poems on Miscellaneous Subjects*. Philadelphia: Merrihew & Thompson, Printers, 1857.

Jacobs, Donald M., ed. *Antebellum Black Newspapers*. Westport, Conn.: Greenwood, 1976.

Kemble, Frances Anne. *Journal of a Residence on a Georgian Plantation in 1838–1839*. New York: Harper & Brothers, 1863.

Lerner, Gerda, ed. *Black Women in White America: A Documentary History*. New York: Pantheon, 1972.

Loewenberg, Bert James, and Ruth Bogin. *Black Women in Nineteenth Century American Life*. University Park: Pennsylvania State Univ. Press, 1976.

Love, Rev. E. K. *History of the First African Baptist Church*. Savannah: The Morning News Print, 1888.

Lovell, Malcolm, ed. *Two Quaker Sister: From the Original Diaries of Elizabeth Buffum Chace and Lucy Buffum Lovell*. New York: Liveright, 1937.

Martineau, Harriet. *Retrospect of Western Travel*. 3 vols. London: Saunders & Otley, 1838.

Merrill, Walter, and Louis Ruchames, eds. *The Letters of William Lloyd Garrison*. 6 vols. Cambridge: Belknap Press of Harvard Univ. Press, 1971–81.

Murray, Pauli. *Dark Testament and Other Poems by Pauli Murray*. Norwalk, Conn.: Silvermine, 1970.

New England Anti-Slavery Society: First Annual Report of the Board of Managers. Boston: Massachusetts Anti-Slavery Society, 1833; reprint ed. Westport, Conn.: Negro Universities Press, 1970.

Northup, Solomon. *Twelve Years a Slave*. Ed. Sue Eakin and Joseph Logsdon. Baton Rouge: Louisiana State Univ. Press, 1968.

Payne, Daniel R. *History of the African Methodist Episcopal Church*. Nashville: Publishing House of the A.M.E. Sunday School Union, 1891.

The Pro-Slavery Argument; as Maintained by the Most Distinguished Writers of the Southern States, Containing the Several Essays, on the Subject, of Chancellor Harper, Governor Hammond, Dr. Simms, and Professor Dew. Walker & Richards & Co., 1852; reprint ed., New York: Negro Universities Press, 1968.

Register of Pennsylvania. Vol. 7, 11 (March 12, 1831), 163. List of Expenditures of Beneficial Societies.

Richardson, Marilyn, ed. *Maria W. Stewart: America's First Black Woman Writer, Essays and Speeches*. Bloomington: Indiana Univ. Press, 1987

Rossi, Alice S., ed. *The Feminist Papers: from Adams to de Beauvoir*. New York: Columbia Univ. Press, 1973.

Schoolcraft, (Mrs.) Henry Rowe. *Plantation Life: The Narratives of Mrs. Henry Rowe Schoolcraft*. Orig. published. 1852–1860; reprint ed., New York: Negro Universities Press, 1969.

Seabury, Samuel. *American Slavery Distinguished from the Slavery of English Theorists and Justified by the Law of Nature*. New York: Mason Brothers, 1861.

The Social and Economic Status of the Black Population in the United States: An Historical View, 1790–1978. Current Population Reports. Special Studies Series, P–23. No. 80. U.S. Department of Commerce, Bureau of the Census, 1980.

"Society of Friends in the United States: Their Views of the Anti-Slavery Question, and Treatment of the People of Color." Darlington, England: John Wilson, 1840.

Southwick, Sarah H. *Reminiscences of Early Anti-Slavery Days*. Macon, Ga.: The Kingsley Press, 1893.

Stanton, Elizabeth Cady, et al. *History of Woman Suffrage*. 6 vols. Rochester, N.Y., 1881.

A Statistical Inquiry into the Conditions of the People of Colour, of the City and Districts of Philadelphia. Philadelphia: Kite & Walton, 1849.

Sterling, Dorothy, ed. *We Are Your Sisters: Black Women in the Nineteenth Century*. New York: Norton, 1984.

Stetson, Erlene, ed. *Black Sister: Poetry By Black American Women, 1746–1980*. Bloomington: Indiana Univ. Press, 1981.

Still, Mary. "An Appeal to the Females of the African Methodist Episcopal Church, 1857." Philadelphia: Peter McKenna & Son, 1857.

Still, William. *The Underground Railroad: A Record of Facts, Authentic Narratives, Letters, &c*. Philadelphia: Porter & Coates, 1872.

Stevenson, Brenda, ed. *The Journals of Charlotte Forten Grimké*. New York: Oxford Univ. Press, 1988.

Wayman, Rev. A. W. *My Recollections of African M.E. Ministers, or Forty Years' Experience in the African Methodist Episcopal Church*. Philadelphia: A.M.E. Book Room, 1881.

Webb, Samuel, ed. *History of Pennsylvania Hall, Which was Destroyed by a Mob on the 17th of May, 1838*. Philadelphia: Merrihew and Gunn, 1838.

Wicks, Elizabeth. "Address Delivered Before the African Female Benevolent Society of Troy." Troy, N.Y.: R. Buckley, 1834.

Willson, Joseph. *Sketches of the Higher Classes of Colored Society in Philadelphia, By a Southerner*. Philadelphia: Merrihew and Thompson, Printers, 1841.

Woodson, Carter, G. *Free Negro Heads of Families in the United States in 1830*. Washington, D.C.: The Association for the Study of Negro Life and History, Inc., 1925.

———. *Negro Orators and Their Orations*. New York: Russell & Russell, 1969.

———. *The Mind of the Negro As Reflected in Letters Written During the Crisis: 1800–1860*. New York: Negro Universities Press, 1929; reprint ed., 1969.

———, ed. *The Works of Francis James Grimké*. 3 vols. Washington, D.C.: The Associated Publishers, Inc., 1942.

Wyman, Lillie B. C., and Arthur C. Wyman. *Elizabeth Buffum Chace, 1806–1899: Her Life and Its Environments*. Boston: W. B. Clarke Co., 1914.

Books, Articles, and Dissertations

William L. Andrews, ed. *Sisters of the Spirit: Three Black Women's Autobiographies of the Nineteenth Century*. Bloomington: Indiana Univ. Press, 1986.

Aptheker, Bettina. *Woman's Legacy: Essays on Race, Sex, and Class in American History*. Amherst: Univ. of Massachusetts Press, 1982.

Aptheker, Herbert. *The Negro in the Abolitionist Movement*. New York: International, 1941.

Bacon, Margaret Hope. "'Our Great Bundle of Humanity': Frances Ellen Watkins Harper." *The Pennsylvania Magazine of History & Biography* 113 (Jan. 1989):21–43.

Ballard, Allen B. *The Education of Black Folk: The Afro-American Struggle for Knowledge in White America*. New York: Harper & Row, 1973.

Barnes, Gilbert Hobbes. *Antislavery Impulse, 1830–1844*. New York: D. Appleton-Century, 1933.

Bearden, Jim, and Linda Jean Butler. *Shadd: The Life and Times of Mary Ann Shadd Cary*. Toronto: NC Press, 1977.

Bell, Howard. "American Moral Reform Society, 1836–1841." *Journal of Negro History* 27 (Winter 1958):34–40.

———. "Expressions of Negro Militancy in the North, 1840–1860." *Journal of Negro History* 45 (Jan. 1960):11–20.

———. "National Negro Conventions of the Middle 1840's: Moral Suasion vs. Political Action." *Journal of Negro History* 42 (Oct. 1957):247–60.

———. *A Survey of the Negro Convention Movement, 1830–1861*. New York: Arno, 1969.

Berg, Barbara J. *The Remembered Gate: Origins of American Feminism, The Woman and the City, 1800–1860*. New York: Oxford Univ. Press, 1978.

Berlin, Ira. *Slaves Without Masters: The Free Negro in the Antebellum South*. New York: Pantheon, 1974.

———. "The Structure of the Free Negro Caste in the Antebellum U.S." *Journal of Negro History* (Spring 1976):297–318.

Billington, Ray Allen. "James Forten: Forgotten Abolitionist," in August Meier and Elliott Rudwick, eds., *The Making of Black America: Essays in Negro Life & History*. 2 vols. New York: Atheneum, 1969.

Blackett, R. J. M. *Beating Against the Barriers: Bibliographical Essays in Nineteenth Century Afro-American History*. Baton Rouge: Louisiana State Univ. Press, 1986.

———. *Thomas Morris Chester, Black Civil War Correspondent: His Dispatches from the Virginia Front*. Baton Rouge: Louisiana State Univ. Press, 1989.

———. *Building an Antislavery Wall: Black Americans in the Atlantic Abolitionist Movement, 1830–1860*. Baton Rouge: Louisiana State Univ. Press, 1983

Bogin, Ruth. "Sarah Parker Remond: Black Abolitionist From Salem." *Essex Institute Historical Collection* 110 (April 1974):120–50.

Boylan, Anne. "Women in Groups: An Analysis of Women's Benevolent Organizations in New York & Boston, 1797–1840." *Journal of American History* 71 (Dec. 1984):497–523.

Bracey, John H., August Meier, and Elliott Rudwick, eds. *Blacks in the Abolitionist Movement*. Belmont, Calif.: Wadsworth, 1971.

Bibliography

Bragg, George Freeman. *History of the Afro-American Group of the Episcopal Church*. Baltimore: Church Advocate Press, 1922.

Brown, Ira V. "Cradle of Feminism: The Philadelphia Female Antislavery Society, 1833–1840." *Pennsylvania Magazine of History & Biography* 102 (April 1978):143–66.

———. "Racism and Sexism: The Case of Pennsylvania Hall." *Phylon* 37 (June 1976):126–36.

Cadbury, Henry. "Negro Membership in the Society of Friends." *Journal of Negro History* 21 (April 1936):151–213.

Clinton, Catharine. *The Plantation Mistress: Woman's World in the Old South*. New York: Pantheon, 1982.

Coleman, Willie Mae. "Keeping the Faith and Disturbing the Peace: From Antislavery to Women's Suffrage." Diss., Univ. of California, Irvine, 1982.

Cross, Whitney R. *The Burned-Over District: Social & Intellectual History of Enthusiastic Religion in Western New York: 1800–1850*. Ithaca: Cornell Univ. Press, 1950.

Curry, Leonard P. *The Free Black in Urban America, 1800–1850: The Shadow of a Dream*. Chicago: Univ. of Chicago Press, 1981.

Daniels, Douglas Henry. *Pioneer Urbanites: A Social and Cultural History of Black San Francisco*. Philadelphia: Temple Univ. Press, 1980.

Dannett, Sylvia G. *Profiles of Negro Womanhood, 1619–1900*. 2 vols. New York: M. W. Lads, 1964.

Davis, Angela Y. *Woman, Race, and Class*. New York: Vintage, 1981.

DeCosta-Willis, Miriam. "Smoothing the Tucks of Father's Linen: The Women of Cedar Hill." *Sage* 4 (Fall 1987):30–33.

Dick, Robert C. *Black Protest: Issues and Tactics*. Westport, Conn.: Greenwood, 1974.

Dill, Bonnie Thornton. "Race, Class, and Gender: Prospectives for an All-Inclusive Sisterhood." *Feminist Studies* 9 (Spring 1983):131–50.

Dillon, Merton L. *The Abolitionists: The Growth of a Dissenting Minority*. New York: W. W. Norton, 1974.

Dodd, Jill. "The Working Classes and the Temperance Movement in Ante-Bellum Boston." *Labor History* 19 (Fall 1978):510–31.

Donald, David H. *Lincoln Reconsidered: Essays on the Civil War Era*. New York: Vintage, 1956.

Duberman, Martin, ed. *Antislavery Vanguard, New Essays on the Abolitionists*. Princeton: Princeton Univ. Press, 1965.

DuBois, Ellen Carol. *Feminism and Suffrage: The Emergence of an Independent Women's Movement in America, 1848–1869*. Ithaca: Cornell Univ. Press, 1978.

DuBois, William Edward Burghardt. *Black Philadelphia: A Social Study*. Philadelphia: Univ. of Pennsylvania Press, 1899.

———. *The Philadelphia Negro*. Philadelphia: For the University of Pennsylvania, 1899; reprint ed., New York: Schocken Books, 1967.

Dumond, Dwight L. *Antislavery: The Crusade for Freedom*. Ann Arbor: Univ. of Michigan Press, 1961.

Durant, Thomas J., Jr., and Joyce S. Louden. "The Black Middle Class in America: Historical and Contemporary Perspectives." *Phylon* 47 (Winter 1986):253–63.

Eckhardt, Celia Morris. *Fanny Wright: Rebel in America*. Cambridge: Harvard Univ. Press, 1984.

Farrison, William Edward. *William Wells Brown: Author and Reformer*. Chicago: Univ. of Chicago Press, 1969.

Fladeland, Betty. *Men and Brothers: Anglo-American Antislavery Cooperation*. Urbana: Univ. of Illinois Press, 1972.

———. "Who Were the Abolitionists?" *Journal of Negro History* 49 (April 1964):99–115.

Foner, Philip. *History of Black Americans from the Emergence of the Cotton Kingdom to the Eve of the Compromise of 1850*. Westport, Conn.: Greenwood, 1983.

Frazier, E. Franklin. *The Negro Church in America*. New York: Schocken, 1964.

———. *The Negro Family in the United States*. Chicago: Univ. of Chicago Press, 1939.

Frey, Cecile. "The House of Refuge for Colored Children." *Journal of Negro History* 66 (Sept. 1981):10–25.

Gara, Larry. *The Liberty Line: The Legend of the Underground Railroad*. Lexington: Univ. of Kentucky Press, 1961.

Gates, Henry Louis, Jr., *Collected Black Women's Narratives*. New York: Oxford Univ. Press, 1988.

Genovese, Eugene. *Roll, Jordan, Roll: The World the Slaves Made*. New York: Vintage Books, 1974.

George, Carol V. R. *Segregated Sabbaths: Richard Allen and the Emergence of Independent Black Churches, 1760–1840*. New York: Oxford Univ. Press, 1973.

Giddings, Paula. *When and Where I Enter: The Impact of Black Women on Race and Sex in America*. New York: William Morrow, 1984.

Ginzberg, Lori D. "'Moral Suasion is Balderdash': Women, Politics, and Social Activism in the 1850s." *Journal of American History* 73 (December 1986):601–22.

Bibliography

Glassman-Hersh, Blanch. *Feminist-Abolitionists in Nineteenth Century America*. Urbana: Univ. of Illinois Press, 1978.

Gutman, Herbert G. *The Black Family in Slavery and Freedom, 1750–1925*. New York: Pantheon, 1976.

———. "Persistent Myths About the Afro-American Family." *Journal of Interdisciplinary History* 6 (Autumn 1975):181–210.

Hansen, Debra Gold. "Bluestockings and Bluenoses: Gender, Class, and Conflict in the Boston Female Anti-Slavery Society, 1833–1840." Diss., Univ. of Calif., Irvine, 1988.

Harley, Sharon, and Rosalyn Terborg-Penn, eds. *The Afro-American Woman: Struggles and Images*. Port Washington, N.Y.: Kennikat, 1978.

Hersh, Blanch Glassman. *Slavery of Sex: Feminist-Abolitionists in America*. Urbana: Univ. of Illinois Press, 1978.

Hershberg, Theodore. "Free Blacks in Antebellum Philadelphia: A Study of Ex-Slaves, Free-born, and Socioeconomic Decline." *Journal of Social History* 5 (Winter 1971–72):183–210.

Hewitt, Nancy A. *Women's Activism and Social Change: Rochester, New York, 1822–1872*. Ithaca: Cornell Univ. Press, 1984.

Hine, Darlene Clark. *Black Women in American History: From Colonial Times Through the Nineteenth Century*. 4 vols. New York: Carlson, 1990.

hooks, bell. *Feminist Theory: From Margin to Center*. Boston: South End Press, 1984.

Horton, James Oliver. "Black Activism in Boston, 1830–1860." Diss., Brandeis Univ., 1973.

———. "Generations of Protest: Black Families and Social Reform in Ante-Bellum Boston." *New England Quarterly* 49 (June 1976):242–56.

———. "Freedom's Yoke: Gender Conventions Among Antebellum Free Blacks." *Feminist Studies* 12 (Spring 1986):51–76.

Horton, James Oliver, and Lois E. Horton. *Black Bostonians: Family Life and Community in the Antebellum North*. New York: Holmes & Meier, 1979.

Horton, Lois E. "Community Organization and Social Activism: Black Boston and the Antislavery Movement." *Sociological Inquiry* 55 (Spring 1985):182–99.

Jackson, George F. *Black Women: Makers of History: A Portrait*. Sacramento: Fong & Fong, 1977.

James, Edward T., and Janet Wilson James, eds. *Notable American Women, 1607–1950: A Biographical Dictionary*. 3 vols. Cambridge: Harvard Univ. Press, 1971.

Jones, Jacqueline. *Labor of Love, Labor of Sorrow: Black Women, Work, and the Family from Slavery to the Present*. New York: Basic, 1985.

———. "'My Mother was Much of a Woman': Black Women, Work, and the Family under Slavery." *Feminist Studies* 8 (Summer 1982):235–69.

Jordan, Winthrop D. *White Man's Burden: Historical Origins of Racism in the United States*. New York: Oxford Univ. Press, 1974.

———. *White Over Black: American Attitudes Toward the Negro, 1550–1812*. Baltimore: Penguin, 1969.

Katz, William Loren. "Black/White Fight Against Slavery and for Women's Rights in America." *Freedom Ways* 16 (1976):230–36.

Katzman, David M. *Before the Ghetto: Black Detroit in the Nineteenth Century*. Urbana: Univ. of Illinois Press, 1973.

Kraditor, Aileen. *Ends and Means in American Abolitionism: Garrison and His Critics on Strategy and Tactics, 1834–1850*. New York: Pantheon, 1967.

Kraut, Alan, ed. *Crusaders and Compromisers: Essays on the Relationship of the Antislavery Struggle and the Antebellum Party System*. Westport, Conn.: Greenwood, 1983.

Kronus, Sidney. *The Black Middle Class*. Columbus, Ohio: Merrill, 1971.

Ladner, Joyce. "Racism and Tradition: Black Womanhood in Historical Perspective," in Berenice A. Carroll, ed. *Liberating Women's History*. Urbana: Univ. of Illinois Press, 1976.

Landon, Fred. "The Buxton Settlement in Canada." *Journal of Negro History* 3 (July 1918):360–67.

———. "Henry Bibb, A Colonizer." *Journal of Negro History* 5 (Oct. 1920): 437–47.

———. "The Negro Migration to Canada after the Passing of the Fugitive Slave Act." *Journal of Negro History* 5 (Oct. 1920):22–36.

Lapsansky, Emma Jones. "Feminism, Freedom, and Community: Charlotte Forten and Women Activists in Nineteenth-Century Philadelphia." *Pennsylvania Magazine of History & Biography* 113 (Jan. 1989):3–19.

———. "Friends, Wives, and Strivings: Networks and Community Values Among Nineteenth-Century Philadelphia Afroamerican Elites," *The Pennsylvania Magazine of History and Biography* 108 (Jan. 1984):3–24.

———. "'Since They Got Those Separate Churches': Afro-Americans and Racism in Jacksonian Philadelphia." *American Quarterly* (Spring 1980):54–78.

Lebsock, Suzanne. "Free Black Women and the Question of Matriarchy: Petersburg, Virginia, 1784–1820." *Feminist Studies* 8 (Summer 1982):270–92.

Lerner, Gerda. *The Grimké Sisters from South Carolina: Pioneers for Women's Rights and Abolitionism*. New York: Schocken, 1967.

———. *The Majority Finds Its Past*. New York: Oxford Univ. Press, 1979.

Levesque, George A. "Black Boston: Negro Life in Garrison's Boston, 1800–1860." Diss., State Univ. of New York, Binghamton, 1976.

———. "Inherent Reformers—Inherited Orthodoxy: Black Baptists in Boston, 1800–1873." *Journal of Negro History* 4 (1975):491–525.

Litwack, Leon. "The Abolitionist Dilemma: The Antislavery Movement and the Northern Negro." *New England Quarterly* 34 (March 1961):50–73.

———. *North of Slavery: The Negro in the Free States, 1790–1860*. Chicago: Univ. of Chicago Press, 1961.

Lutz, Alma. *Crusade For Freedom: Women of the Antislavery Movement*. Boston: Beacon, 1968.

Mabee, Carleton. *Black Education in New York State from Colonial Times to Modern Times*. New York: Syracuse Univ. Press, 1979.

———. "Sojourner Truth and President Lincoln." *New England Quarterly* 61 (December 1988):519–29.

Majors, Monroe A. *Noted Negro Women: Their Triumphs and Activities*. Chicago: Donohue & Henneberry, 1893.

Meier, August, and Elliott Rudwick. *Along the Color Line: Explorations in the Black Experience*. Urbana: Univ. of Illinois Press, 1976.

———. *From Plantation to Ghetto*. New York: Hill and Wang, 1970.

———. *The Making of Black America: Essays in Negro Life History*. 2 vols. New York: Atheneum, 1969.

Miller, Floyd J. *The Search for a Black Nationality: Black Emigration and Colonization, 1787–1863*. Urbana: Univ. of Illinois Press, 1975.

Moses, Wilson J. *The Golden Age of Black Nationalism, 1850–1925*. Hamden, Conn.: Archon Books, 1978.

Mossell, (Mrs.) N. F. (Gertrude Bustill). *The Work of the Afro-American Woman*. New York: Books for Libraries Press, 1984; reprint ed., 1971.

Moynihan, Daniel Patrick. *The Negro Family: The Case for National Action*. Office of Policy Planning and Research, United States Department of Labor, March 1965.

Nash, Gary B. *Forging Freedom: The Formation of Philadelphia's Black Community, 1720–1840*. Cambridge: Harvard Univ. Press, 1988.

Newton, Judith L., Mary P. Ryan, and Judith R. Walkowitz, eds. *Sex and Class in Women's History*. London: Routledge and Kegan, 1983.

Noble, Jeanne. *Beautiful, Also, Are the Souls of My Black Sisters: A History of Black Women in America*. Englewood Cliffs, N.J.: Prentice-Hall, 1978.

Painter, Nell Irvin. *The Exodusters: Black Migration to Kansas After Reconstruction*. New York: Knopf, 1977.

Palmer, Phyllis Marynick. "White Women/Black Women: The Dualism of Female Identity and Experience in the United States." *Feminist Studies* 9 (Spring 1983):151–70.

Pease, Jane H., and William H. Pease. *Black Utopia: Negro Communal Experiments in America*. Madison: State Historical Society of Wisconsin, 1963.

———. *Bound With Them in Chains: A Biographical History of the Antislavery Movement*. Westport, Conn.: Greenwood, 1974.

———. "Ends, Means, and Attitudes: Black-White Conflict in the Antislavery Movement." *Civil War History* 18 (June 1972):117–29.

———. *They Who Would Be Free: Blacks' Search For Freedom, 1830–61*. New York: Atheneum, 1974.

Perkins, Linda. "The Impact of the 'Cult of True Womanhood' on the Education of Black Women." *Journal of Social Issues* 39 (1983):17–28.

———. "Black Women and Racial 'Uplift' Prior to Emancipation," in Filomena Chioma Steady, ed., *The Black Woman Cross-Culturally*. Cambridge: Schenkman, 1981:317–34.

Perlman, Daniel. "Organizations of the Free Negro in New York City, 1800–1860." *Journal of Negro History* 56 (July 1971):181–97.

Perry, Lewis, and Michael Fellman, eds. *Antislavery Reconsidered: New Perspectives on Abolitionists*. Baton Rouge: Louisiana State Univ. Press, 1979.

Piersen, William D. *Black Yankees: The Development of an Afro-American Subculture in Eighteenth Century New England*. Amherst: Univ. of Massachusetts Press, 1988.

Pleck, Elizabeth H. "The Two-Parent Household: Black Family Structure in Late Nineteenth Century Boston." *Journal of Social History* 5 (Fall 1971):3–31.

Porter, Dorothy. "Sarah Remond: Abolitionist and Physician." *Journal of Negro History* (July 1935):287–93.

Prince, Nancy. *A Black Woman's Odyssey Through Russia and Jamaica: The Narrative of Nancy Prince*, with an Introduction by Ronald G. Walters. New York: Marcus Wiener Publishing, 1990.

Quarles, Benjamin. *Allies for Freedom: Blacks and John Brown*. New York: Oxford Univ. Press, 1974.

———. *Black Abolitionists*. New York: Oxford Univ. Press, 1969.

———. "Frederick Douglass and the Woman's Rights Movement." *Journal of Negro History* 25 (January 1940):35–44.

———. *The Negro in the American Revolution*. Chapel Hill: Univ. of North Carolina Press, 1961.

———. "Sources of Abolitionist Income." *Mississippi Valley Historical Review* 32 (June 1945):63–76.

Rabinowitz, Howard N. *Race Relations in the Urban South, 1865–1890*. New York: Oxford Univ. Press, 1978.

Render, Sylvia Lyons. "Afro-American Women: The Outstanding and the Obscure." *Quarterly Journal of the Library of Congress* 32 (October 1975):307–21.

Richards, Leonard L. *"Gentlemen of Property and Standing": Anti-Abolition Mobs in Jacksonian America*. London: Oxford Univ. Press, 1970.

Rigsby, Gregory U. *Alexander Crummell: Pioneer in Nineteenth Century Pan-African Thought*. New York: Greenwood, 1987.

Rorabaugh, W. J. *The Alcoholic Republic: An American Tradition*. New York: Oxford Univ. Press, 1979.

Ruchames, Louis. "Race, Marriage and Abolition in Massachusetts." *Journal of Negro History* 40 (July 1955):25–73.

Rury, John L. "The New York African Free School, 1827–1836: Conflict Over Community Control of Black Education." *Phylon* (Sept. 1983):187–97.

———. "Philanthropy, Self-Help, and Social Control: The New York Manumission Society and Free Blacks, 1785–1810." *Phylon* 46(1985):231–41.

———. "Vocationalism for Home and Work: Women's Education in the United States, 1880–1930." *History of Education Quarterly* (Spring 1984):21–44.

Scott, Anne Firor. *The Southern Lady: From Pedestal to Politics, 1830–1930*. Chicago: Univ. of Chicago Press, 1970.

Sernett, Milton C. *Black Religion and American Evangelicalism: White Protestants, Plantation Missions, and the Flowering of Negro Christianity, 1787–1865*. Metuchen, N.J.: Scarecrow Press and The American Theological Library Association, 1975.

Silcox, Harry C. "The Black 'Better Class' Political Dilemma: Philadelphia Prototype Isaiah C. Wears." *Pennsylvania Magazine of History and Biography* 113 (Jan. 1989):45–66.

———. "Philadelphia Negro Educator: Jacob C. White, Jr., 1837–1902." *Pennsylvania Magazine of History and Biography* 97 (Jan. 1973):75–98.

Smith, Anne Bustill. "The Bustill Family." *Journal of Negro History,* 10 (Oct. 1925):638–644.

Smith-Rosenberg, Carroll. "Beauty and the Beast and the Militant Woman: A Case Study of Sex Roles in Jacksonian America." *American Quarterly* 23 (October 1971):562–84.

Sobel, Mechal. *Trabelin' On: The Slave Journey to an Afro-Baptist Faith*. Westport, Conn.: Greenwood, 1979.

Soderlund, Jean R. "Black Women in Colonial Pennsylvania." *Pennsylvania Magazine of History and Biography* (Jan. 1983):49–84.

Sorin, Gerald. *The New York Abolitionists*. Westport, Conn.: Greenwood, 1971.

Staples, Robert. *Black Woman in America: Sex, Marriage, and the Family*. Chicago: Nelson-Hall, 1973.

Stewart, James Brewer. *Holy Warriors: The Abolitionists and American Slavery*. New York: Hill & Wang, 1976.

Sumler-Lewis, Janice. "The Forten-Purvis Women of Philadelphia and the American Anti-Slavery Crusade." *Journal of Negro History* 66 (Winter 1981–82):281–88.

Swerdlow, Amy. "Abolition's Conservative Sisters: The Ladies' New York City

Anti-Slavery Societies, 1834–1840." Paper presented at Third Berkshire Conference on the History of Women, Bryn Mawr College, June 9–11, 1976.

Takaki, Ronald. *A Pro-Slavery Crusade*. New York: Free Press, 1971.

Thernstrom, Stephan and Richard Sennett, eds. *Nineteenth Century Cities: Essays in the New Urban History.* New Haven: Yale Univ. Press, 1969.

Ullman, Victor. *Martin R. Delany: The Beginnings of Black Nationalism*. Boston: Beacon, 1971.

Walker, Juliet E. K. "Prejudices, Profits, and Privileges: Commentaries on 'Captive Capitalists,' Antebellum Black Entrepreneurs." *Essays in Economic and Business History* 8 (1990):399–422.

Wallace, Michelle. *Black Macho and the Myth of the Superwoman*. New York: Dial, 1979.

Walters, Ronald G. *Antislavery Appeal: American Abolitionism after 1830*. Baltimore: Johns Hopkins Univ. Press, 1976.

Warner, Sam Bass. *The Private City: Philadelphia in Three Periods of Its Growth*. Philadelphia: Univ. of Pennsylvania Press, 1968.

Welter, Barbara J. "The Cult of True Womanhood, 1820–1860." *American Quarterly* 18 (Summer 1966):151–74.

Wesley, Charles H. The Negro in the Organization of Abolition." *Phylon: The Atlanta University Review of Race and Culture* 2 (1941):223–235.

Wills, David. W., and Newman, Richard, eds. *Black Apostles at Home and Abroad*. Boston: Hall, 1982.

Winch, Julie. *Philadelphia's Black Elite: Activism, Accommodation, and the Struggle for Autonomy, 1787–1848*. Philadelphia: Temple Univ. Press, 1988.

Winks, Robin W. *The Blacks in Canada: A History.* Montreal: McGill-Queen's Univ. Press, 1971.

Wood, Ann Douglas. "'Scribbling Women' and Fanny Fern: Why Women Wrote." *American Quarterly* 23 (Spring 1971):3–24.

Woodson, Carter G. *History of the Negro Church*. Washington, D.C.: Associated Publishers, 1921.

Woody, Thomas. *A History of Women's Education in the United States*. 2 vols. New York: Octagon Books, 1929

Yacavone, Donald. "The Transformation of the Black Temperance Movement, 1827–1854: An Interpretation." *Journal of the Early Republic* 8 (Fall 1988):281–97.

Yellin, Jean Fagan. *Women and Sisters: Antislavery Feminists in American Culture*. New Haven: Yale Univ. Press, 1990.

Zorn, Roman, "The New England Anti-Slavery Society: Pioneer Abolitionist Organization." *Journal of Negro History* 52 (July 1957):157–76.

Index

Index

Index